You Are My Sunshine

JIMMIE DAVIS & THE BIOGRAPHY OF A SONG

You Are My Sunshine

ROBERT MANN

LOUISIANA STATE UNIVERSITY PRESS
BATON ROUGE

Published with the assistance of the V. Ray Cardozier Fund

Published by Louisiana State University Press
lsupress.org

Manufactured in the United States of America
First printing

DESIGNER: Michelle A. Neustrom | TYPEFACE: Vulpa
PRINTER & BINDER: Sheridan Books, Inc.

JACKET ILLUSTRATION: Davis and his campaign band, 1943–1944. Harry Pennington Jr. Photography Collection, Harry Ransom Center, The University of Texas at Austin.

LIBRARY OF CONGRESS CATALOGING-IN-PUBLICATION DATA

Names: Mann, Robert, 1958– author.
Title: You are my sunshine : Jimmie Davis and the biography of a song / Robert Mann.
Description: Baton Rouge : Louisiana State University Press, 2025. | Includes bibliographical references and index.
Identifiers: LCCN 2024033324 (print) | LCCN 2024033325 (ebook) | ISBN 978-0-8071-8350-2 (cloth) | ISBN 978-0-8071-8385-4 (pdf) | ISBN 978-0-8071-8384-7 (epub)
Subjects: LCSH: Davis, Jimmie, 1899–2000. | Singers—United States—Biography. | Country musicians—United States—Biography. | Hood, Oliver, 1897–1959. You are my sunshine. | Popular music—United States—History and criticism. | State songs—Louisiana—History and criticism. | LCGFT: Biographies.
Classification: LCC ML420.D315 M35 2025 (print) | LCC ML420.D315 (ebook) | DDC 782.42164092 [B]—dc23/eng/20241108
LC record available at https://lccn.loc.gov/2024033324
LC ebook record available at https://lccn.loc.gov/2024033325

for Sarah and Paul

CONTENTS

LIST OF ILLUSTRATIONS ix
PREFACE: A MUSICAL TAPESTRY xi
ACKNOWLEDGMENTS xv

1. Jimmie Davis Needed a Song 1
2. The Only Way I Ever Play Politics 15
3. Bull Market in Corn 30
4. I Belonged in Louisiana 38
5. Easier to Sing Than to Talk 51
6. How in the Devil Can You Fight a Song? 61
7. We Just Hung Around Jimmie 79
8. Come Home, Jimmie 90
9. A Brilliant Phantom 102
10. No "Sunshine" of Moderation 115
11. A Musical Act of Racial Trespassing 129
12. It's a Very Catchy Ditty 140
13. A Song beyond Politics 154

NOTES 163
BIBLIOGRAPHY 181
INDEX 189

ILLUSTRATIONS

The Pine Ridge Boys . . . 3
The Rice Brothers . . . 5
Oliver Hood, the probable composer of "You Are My Sunshine" . . . 12
Davis with his band in Shreveport in 1936 . . . 23
Western-movie singing cowboy Gene Autry . . . 43
Bing Crosby . . . 44
Davis campaigns for Louisiana governor in 1944 . . . 66
Davis and his band during the 1943–1944 Louisiana governor's race . . . 69
Moon Mullican performing a solo during a campaign rally in 1943 . . . 71
Poster for Davis's 1947 film, *Louisiana* . . . 86
Nat King Cole . . . 92
A Davis gospel album cover . . . 100
Davis sings with the Plainsmen Quartet in 1960 . . . 106
Davis's 1960 campaign band . . . 108
Campaign button from Davis's 1960 governor's race . . . 110
Campaign poster for state senator Willie Rainach's 1960 governor's campaign . . . 113
Davis and outgoing governor Earl Long . . . 114
Plaquemines Parish district attorney Leander Perez . . . 118
Davis and his horse, Sunshine, on the Louisiana Capitol steps, 1962 . . . 125
Ray Charles and producer Sid Feller . . . 134
Louisiana governor John McKeithen . . . 142
Davis's plaque in the Country Music Hall of Fame . . . 151
Johnny Cash . . . 156
Davis at his one-hundredth birthday celebration . . . 159

PREFACE

A Musical Tapestry

In a darkened museum in the heart of Bayeux, France, rests an ancient, vivid depiction of the 1066 Norman invasion of England: the 950-year-old Bayeux Tapestry. Crafted with colorful embroidery on linen backing, it is twenty inches wide, stretches 230 feet, and intertwines propaganda, history, and art. It has captivated scholars for centuries as they explored its origins, meaning, and messages—a scholarly Rorschach test for those interested in early Britain, textiles, propaganda, and art. I admire the tapestry and find its enigmatic nature as interesting as its artistry and historical significance. Everyone who examines it in a book or views it at the Musée de la Tapisserie in Bayeux discovers something different.

Like the Bayeux Tapestry, the beloved song "You Are My Sunshine" is a work of beauty, simplicity, and historical significance. It evokes different emotions in everyone who sings or hears it. For some, it's a classic country song celebrating wholesome love. Others know it as an R&B or rock ballad, exploring love's hardships and painful estrangement. "Sunshine" was the quasi-national anthem of the Solomon Islands during World War II. It has been a much-loved lullaby for generations of children. It was the theme song of singer and sometime governor Jimmie Davis of Louisiana from the 1940s through the early 1970s. In 1977, it became one of Louisiana's two state songs.

Yet, like the Bayeux Tapestry, the song's origins remain a mystery. No one can prove who wrote it or where it came from. And both are connected to places different from their likely origins. The tapestry is probably from England but resides in Normandy, while "Sunshine" was probably written in Georgia but is associated with Louisiana and Davis, its renowned "composer." The song can no more shake its association with Davis and the Bayou State than the tapestry can escape its relationship with Bayeux.

Like the Bayeux Tapestry, "You Are My Sunshine" is a transcendent work of art. Its emotional threads are woven into the fabric of our cultural memory, leaving an indelible mark on the hearts of generations. A seminal song of early country music, it was the foundation for a music career that would twice lead its purported creator to the Louisiana Governor's Mansion and then to the Country Music Hall of Fame. But it was—it is—far more than a sentimental song that Jimmie Davis rode to musical and electoral fame. It was also a potent political statement that helped deflect his critics' attacks. Not a hymn—it's not religious—"Sunshine" became a secular hymn of a state that it never mentions. "You Are My Sunshine" is a musical tapestry, almost mystical in weaving joy, sadness, longing, love, and state pride—all in three verses.

Although his name is in this book's subtitle, this is not a comprehensive biography of Davis. While I chronicle much of his 101-year life, I tell his story mostly through the lens of his famous song. Without what he often called his "meal ticket," Davis might never have been elected Louisiana governor. With it, he became a political and country music legend.

But this book is about far more than Davis. It's also about the life of his song. In the early 1960s, Davis surrendered some control of "Sunshine" when R&B artist Ray Charles introduced a new melody and made his reinvention a national pop hit. Though Davis still owned the composition and reaped lucrative royalties until he died in 2000, "Sunshine" became the public's song. That's not only because it became a state song. Its popularity and ubiquity also propelled it into the rare stratosphere of standards like "Happy Birthday," "White Christmas," and "Home on the Range"—recorded by hundreds of artists and known by most of the world's inhabitants.

The last time I finished viewing the Bayeux Tapestry, I emerged into the warm embrace of June sunlight. Adjusting to the glow, I wondered if I had just admired art, delved into history, or deciphered propaganda—or all three? A firm answer eludes me because my affection for the tapestry stems from its multilayered allure, just like my admiration for "You Are My Sunshine."

Maybe you never imagined a biography of a song. I call it that because this unusual, distinctive song was—*is*—alive. It's not an artifact. In the hands of new generations of singers, it remains a rich, living tapestry of history and emotion that touches souls and lifts hearts with each new rendition and interpretation.

A note for readers: In the early chapters, I sometimes use the term "country" music to describe what was then called "hillbilly" or "folk" music. The terms "country and western" and "country" were not widely used until the late 1940s and early 1950s.

ACKNOWLEDGMENTS

I appreciate the help and encouragement that friends, colleagues, and others offered during the research and writing of this book. Among those who read all or portions of the manuscript and made suggestions for improvements were Charlene Mann, Tim Landry, Dan Borné, Michael Wynne, Charlie French, and Ryan Pinkard. The anonymous reader who reviewed the manuscript for LSU Press offered many helpful suggestions, for which I am grateful. Two of my students, Taylor Ellis and Allie Held, helped with fact-checking and other revisions.

Librarians and archivists are the heroes behind most nonfiction works. I am thankful for the generosity and help of the following individuals and institutions: Kathleen Campbell, senior archivist at the Country Music Hall of Fame and Museum; Samuel C. Hyde of the Center for Southeast Louisiana Studies at Southeastern Louisiana University; Mikel LeDee of LSU's Music Library; the wonderful interlibrary loan staff at the LSU Library; the special collections staff at LSU's Hill Memorial Library; Barbara Johnson and Christie Weeks of the Jackson Parish Museum in Jonesboro, Louisiana; the staff of Special Collections and Archives at the Georgia State University Library; Laura McLemore and Fermand Garlington of the Northwest Louisiana Archives at the Noel Memorial Library at LSU-Shreveport; Elizabeth Garver at the Harry Ransom Center at the University of Texas at Austin; and the staff of the Louisiana State Archives.

Thanks to the extraordinary professionals at LSU Press who offered their support and encouragement. These include Alisa Plant, Jenny Keegan, and Catherine Kadair. I appreciate copy editor Susan Murray's exacting eye for detail.

Those who helped with aspects of my research were Michael Wynne, Randy and Rosemary Ewing, Sam Muffoletto, Jeff Gauger, Jim Brown, Tommy Hudson, Ryan Cross, and Richard Hood. Thanks to David Crook and Jessica Rose for helping me better understand Oliver Hood. Thanks to Louisa Bailey and Mary Pennington Cowmeadow for granting permission to use the photographs that Harry Pennington Jr. took of Jimmie Davis and his band during the 1943–44 governor's race.

I could not have completed this book without the financial support of the Manship family, which funded the endowed chair I held at LSU until 2024. I was honored to hold the chair for eighteen years and am grateful for how it made me a better teacher and scholar.

My wife, Cindy, has always been my biggest cheerleader, best friend, and the sunshine of my life. Thank you for all the ways life with you is such a joy and blessing.

Finally, I dedicate this book to my sister, Sarah, and brother, Paul. Thank you both for a lifetime of friendship, support, and love.

You Are My Sunshine

1

Jimmie Davis Needed a Song

Tuesday, August 22, 1939

In London and Paris, governments summoned reservists for a "peace front" to resist Nazi Germany's expected invasion of Poland. At the Bonneville Salt Flats in northwestern Utah, London fur dealer John Cobb clambered aboard his sleek 2,600-horsepower aluminum racecar—the "Railton Red Lion"—and rocketed north across the table-smooth desert floor faster than anyone on wheels before: 369.23 miles per hour.

At Brooklyn's Ebbets Field, three players carried away an unconscious Jimmy Brown, the St. Louis Cardinals' shortstop, after he crashed into a teammate while fielding a fly ball in short right field. In Lake Charles, Louisiana, a fifty-six-year-old Catholic priest from Cuba, traveling by bus from Mexico to New Orleans, suffered an attack of acute appendicitis. The Reverend Dr. Luis Sans Y Hortoneda died later that day.[1]

And, in Atlanta, Marvin Taylor and Doug Spivey—two close-harmony singers who called themselves the Pine Ridge Boys—arrived at a temporary recording studio for the Victor/Bluebird label in the Kimball House hotel at 30 Pryor Street. They would cut six songs for Bluebird, including "When Mother Prayed for Me" and a gospel standard, "Farther Along." It was the first of the duo's three sessions for the label between 1939 and 1941. On this day, Taylor and Spivey also covered a song credited to Jimmie Davis of Shreveport, Louisiana. The song, which Davis recorded for Victor Records in 1930, was "Where the Old Red River Flows." It remains among the most affectionate ever written about Louisiana.

Also, on that August day, the Pine Ridge Boys were the first artists to record a song that would become associated with Davis, who would claim for decades that it was his composition. But it wasn't. On August 22, 1939, it's unlikely Davis had ever heard of "You Are My Sunshine." The song was simple and appealing:

The other night, dear, as I lay sleeping,
I dreamed I held you in my arms.
But when I woke, dear, I was mistaken,
And I hung my head and cried.

(*Chorus*)
You are my sunshine, my only, only sunshine.
You make me happy when skies are gray.
You'll never know, dear, how much I love you.
Please don't take my sunshine away.

You told me once, dear, that you loved me,
That nothing else could come between.
But now you've left me for another.
And you've shattered all of my dreams.

I'll always love you and make you happy,
If you'll only say the same.
But if you leave me for another,
You'll regret it all someday.

Taylor and Spivey yodeled through the song's opening bars and sang in close harmony, accompanied by two guitars. Spivey later acknowledged that he and Taylor had not written it. "We first got it from a young lady that played guitar and sang from South Carolina that got it from some fellow there," he recalled. The woman suggested the song would be a good duet. "She said, 'Take the song. Do with it what you want to,' and we mentioned about recording it. She said, 'Take it. Get it copyrighted. It will be yours.'" Spivey couldn't remember her name but recalled meeting her at Atlanta radio station WGST. "She came from South Carolina

The Pine Ridge Boys (Doug Spivey and Marvin Taylor) were the first to record "You Are My Sunshine," on August 22, 1939, in Atlanta. (Georgia State University Archives)

there with a show," Spivey said, adding that the woman sang and played guitar in a band. The only other detail he could summon was that "she was slightly red-headed." Bluebird released the duo's record on October 6 with no author or copyright holder under the title. Spivey and Taylor never copyrighted it.[2]

But the Pine Ridge Boys weren't the only Atlanta musicians who knew about "Sunshine." On October 26 of that year, a local hillbilly band, the Blue Sky Boys (brothers Earl and Bill Bolick) sang it during their fifteen-minute program on WGST. The station's log recorded it as "You're My Sunshine."[3]

Was it a coincidence that this was the same station where the Pine Ridge Boys had met the red-haired singer from South Carolina? Maybe she had shared it with other Atlanta artists. Whatever the case, on September 13, three weeks after the Pine Ridge Boys recorded it, another

Georgia-born musical duo, the Rice Brothers, recorded an upbeat, hillbilly swing version of "Sunshine" in New York for Decca Records.

Hoke and Paul Rice's version differed from Pine Ridge Boys' recording: It had no yodeling, and the lyrics weren't exactly the same. But the significant differences in this rendition were in tempo, style, and accompaniment. The Pine Ridge Boys had sung slower, accompanied only by two guitars. The Rice Brothers arranged a livelier, jazzy foxtrot version with a multipiece swing band, including an electric steel guitar, harmonica, clarinet, and string bass. Paul Rice was the lone vocalist. His name under the title suggested that he was the composer or, at least, the copyright holder.[4]

The Rice Brothers had made music for most of their young lives. Natives of Chestnut Mountain, Georgia—near Gainesville, about fifty miles northeast of Atlanta—Hoke was older, born in 1909. Paul was four years younger. Their father was a part-time preacher and cobbler. Their mother—a talented musician who played the five-string banjo, fiddle, and piano—passed along her love of music to the boys. After the parents divorced around 1920, their mother remarried a respected old-time fiddler, Rufus "Uncle Bud" Silvey, who encouraged the musical careers of his two stepsons. By the late 1920s, Hoke was a popular guitarist, accomplished in jazz and pop styles, who recorded with Georgia artists and performed often on Atlanta radio stations. Paul grew into an accomplished musician who performed with prominent artists, including a pioneer of hillbilly music, Fiddlin' John Carson. Around 1934, the brothers formed a band. For years, they styled themselves the Rice Brothers and bounced around the country, performing on radio stations in Cincinnati; Roanoke, Virginia; Baltimore; Washington, DC; and Shreveport, Louisiana (in December 1935).

They returned to Atlanta in 1937 and formed a five-piece band that sometimes included an accordion and clarinet. They played not just hillbilly music but also pop and jazz. And their musical evolution came with a new name: the Rice Brothers' Gang. They performed on several Atlanta radio stations, including WGST, where the Pine Ridge Boys, the Blue Sky Boys, and the mysterious red-haired singer from South Carolina appeared that year.

The Rice Brothers (Hoke Rice and Paul Rice) were the second group to record "You Are My Sunshine." Paul Rice (*seated*) sold the song to Jimmie Davis in 1939 when the duo was based in Shreveport. (Georgia State University Archives)

In the fall of 1939, Hoke and Paul Rice left for Louisiana. In late September, about two weeks after they recorded their version of "Sunshine" in New York, the duo arrived in Shreveport to host a midday radio show (Monday through Saturday) on KWKH. Along with other KWKH hillbilly acts, the Rice Brothers' Gang also sang at the city's Municipal Auditorium on the station's *Saturday Night Roundup,* the precursor to the popular and influential *Louisiana Hayride,* originating from the same stage from 1948 through the 1960s.[5]

While there was only one mention of "You Are My Sunshine" in a local newspaper in 1939 (on December 20, over a picture of Paul Rice performing on the *Saturday Night Roundup*), it was a song the Rice Brothers brought to Shreveport's airwaves and the Municipal Auditorium's stage.

What's also undeniable is that Jimmie Davis lived in Shreveport, where he was the city's newly elected public service commissioner. An established blues and hillbilly singer with several hit records by the late 1930s, Davis hosted a KWKH show from the late 1920s through the fall of 1938. It's unknown if Davis met or heard Hoke and Paul Rice in 1935 when the duo performed briefly on Shreveport's KTBS radio. But, by late 1939, Davis and the Rice Brothers were in the same orbit. Also in that orbit was the song Paul Rice claimed to own and that he and Hoke had recorded a few weeks before arriving in Shreveport.

In December 1939, Paul Rice's wife became ill, and Rice couldn't pay her medical bills. Other than this, nothing more is known about why, on December 16, Rice signed a lopsided contract that transferred "Sunshine" to Davis and a band member, Charles Mitchell, for thirty-five dollars (about $650 in 2024 dollars). Maybe it was because, as music historian Ryan Bañagale asserted, "Paul Rice needed money and Jimmie Davis needed a song." Included in the deal was Rice's agreement to give Davis and Mitchell all royalties paid by Decca Records for the version the Rice Brothers' Gang had recorded in September: "Be it further agreed that Jimmie Davis and Charles Mitchell shall be listed as writers of the above musical composition and not include myself as co-writer. I, Paul Rice, do hereby state and declare that the above number is my own original composition and has not previously been assigned, transferred or sold to any person[,] firm or corporation." The following month, on January 30, 1940, Davis and Mitchell copyrighted the song.[6]

In 1956, a former Rice Brothers' Gang band member, Reggie Ward, maintained that the group had first recorded "Sunshine" for Decca Records in 1937. "Sales were very small," Ward told the *Shreveport Times,* adding, "But here's an oddity—when we played and sang it on the air, our mail response was heavy. We had hundreds of requests to play it." There's no evidence that the brothers recorded the song before September 1939, and there was no mention of it in Atlanta newspapers in 1937 or 1938. The comprehensive, authoritative *Country Music Records: A Discography, 1921–1939* lists no recording by the Rice Brothers' Gang before their first Decca session on June 13, 1938, in Charlotte, North Carolina. And "Sunshine" was not among the eight songs they recorded that day.[7]

Paul Rice later insisted he was the song's composer, claiming he got the idea "from a girl over in South Carolina [who] wrote me this long letter, about seventeen pages. And she was talking about I was her sunshine, and I got the idea for the song and put a tune to it." (Recall that Doug Spivey of the Pine Ridge Boys also credited the song to a young woman from South Carolina.) Another artist who released the song also mentioned a woman in Atlanta as the song's source. Country singer Bob Atcher and his wife and singing partner, Bonnie Blue Eyes (Loeta Applegate), would record "Sunshine" on January 17, 1940, in Chicago for Okeh Records. Atcher recalled that Art Satherley—a Columbia Records /Okeh executive and future Country Music Hall of Fame member—brought him "a manuscript copy" of the song for his consideration. Satherley told Atcher he got it from "a boy named [Marvin] Taylor" of the Pine Ridge Boys at a recording session. Atcher remembered hearing that Taylor "told Art that a little girl in Atlanta had written the song and had given it to them." Later, when Columbia Records sent Atcher the release for his signature, he was surprised to discover "the name of the composer had been put in to be Jimmie Davis."[8]

In a 1990 journal article, music historian Toru Mitsui reported the results of his extensive forensic investigation into the song's origins. He speculated that Rice might have been the composer, citing Ward's story about the band singing the song on Atlanta radio in 1937:

> It is possible the Rice Brothers' Gang began performing the song before the Pine Ridge Boys recorded it, and Paul Rice might have been right when he said he composed the song in 1937 or more probably learned it. If he really composed it himself, he must have shown it to the woman from South Carolina who unintentionally gave the idea for the song to Rice, or to some other person possibly in South Caro-

> lina. The Pine Ridge Boys learned the song from some other woman from South Carolina, who said she learned it back in the state, or who might be the same person as the one Rice was associated with. Did Rice learn the song from the woman who wrote him instead of composing it? Who was "some fellow" from whom the young woman told the Pine Ridge Boys that she got *You Are My Sunshine*?

Mitsui concludes that the "possibility of Paul Rice's authorship is lessened further by the fact that he must have copyrighted the song sometime after the recording of the song by the Pine Ridge Boys. One wonders why he did not have it copyrighted before if he composed it in 1937. Had it already been copyrighted, and the people who were involved in the recording of the song by the Pine Ridge Boys simply didn't know it?" But Rice never registered the song with the US Copyright Office. He sold a song to Davis that he hadn't copyrighted. Davis and Mitchell, not Rice, were the first to register "Sunshine."[9]

Davis and Mitchell now owned the song. But it was not their composition, nor does that distinction belong to Paul Rice, Doug Spivey, Marvin Taylor, or even the mysterious, young red-haired woman from South Carolina. In 1980, Paul Rice told music historian Wayne Daniel, "There's at least twenty people [who] 'wrote' 'You Are My Sunshine,'" adding, "I had a gal write me from California that she wrote it." Rice wasn't exaggerating. Perhaps the most unusual claim to authorship was by Minnie Hokanson of Cannon Falls, Minnesota, who died in 2013 at age 103. An amateur poet, Hokanson asserted until her death that she wrote the song as a poem and mailed it to Paul Rice in the 1930s.[10]

There were not only other musicians and poets who claimed to have composed "Sunshine" but several songs and poems in the early twentieth century with that title. "You are my sunshine" was a common refrain in poetry and music as early as 1900. In May 1900, the *Memphis Commercial Appeal* published a poem, "For My Alumnae Little Ones," by Clara Conway, with the first line, "You are my sunshine." In 1919 and 1920, the Aeolian Co. ran newspaper ads for its music rolls used in self-playing pianos. Among the "popular songs" it offered was "You Are My Sunshine."

The *Atlanta Constitution* published a story in March 1924 about a "little Armenian love song" that began, "I love you, I love you; you are my sunshine." In 1928, a legal dispute over the authorship of a song, "You Are My Sunshine on a Rainy Day," went to the New York Supreme Court. In 1932, the *Evening Star* of Franklin, Indiana, published a poem, "You Are My Sunshine," submitted by a reader. Three years later, the Missoula, Montana, *Missoulian* published a different poem with the same name. Before Davis and Mitchell registered "Sunshine" in 1940, copyrights for songs with that title were filed with the US Copyright Office in 1930, 1935, and 1936. None, however, appear to be the version that Davis and others recorded in 1939–40.[11]

But it wasn't simply the song's name that was familiar. The 1939–40 versions of "You Are My Sunshine" bear some resemblance to a popular song, "Little Darling, Pal of Mine," recorded by the pioneering hillbilly group the Carter Family in 1928 and again in 1935. While the tune and meter of "Sunshine" were reminiscent of the Carter Family standard (which later inspired the melody of 1944's "This Land Is Your Land" by Woody Guthrie), the earlier song may have influenced its lyrics, as well. While "Sunshine" began, "The other night, dear, as I lay sleeping, I dreamed I held you in my arms," the Carter Family song began, "Many a night, while you lay sleeping, Dreaming of your amber skies." And the chorus of "Little Darling'" was also like "Sunshine": "My little darlin', oh how I love you. How I love you, none can tell. In your heart you love another, Little darlin', pal of mine."

It's not clear where the tune of "Little Darling" came from, as the trio's male singer, A. P. Carter, acquired lyrics and melodies from musicians he met on song-gathering trips through the mountains of southwestern Virginia. In his analysis of "Sunshine's" provenance, Ryan Bañagale speculated that the tune was inspired by an African American spiritual, "O My Loving Brother, When the World's on Fire" (also known as the "Fire Song"). In 1928, gospel-blues singer Blind Willie Davis recorded it as "Rock of Ages" (not the traditional hymn sung in Christian churches). The Carter Family would record the song as "When the World's on Fire" in 1930. Bañagale observed:

> It is clear that rhythmic, melodic, and lyrical connections exist between these recordings. Along with such surface elements, these recordings also introduce individual *musical moments.* A number of these moments are present in Jimmie Davis's 1940 version of the song, each of which can be located on the branches of *You Are My Sunshine*'s family tree: The guitar based, country string band component comes out of the Carter Family recordings. A constant presence of a through improvised instrumental line is present as far back as Blind Willie Davis's record. The desire to preserve a sense of heritage while making a concerted effort to move musically beyond it, as heard in Jimmie Davis's attempt to sing in a more refined style, comes from the Rice Brother's [*sic*] Gang.[12]

As we will see, "You Are My Sunshine" has never remained frozen in time. In every succeeding decade, artists recorded dozens of versions. Some hewed to the tune and style of its earliest versions. Others differed. But before we explore that part of the story, there's another person worthy of attention—someone who claimed for years that "Sunshine" was his composition and has the most credible claim to its authorship.

Musician and singer Robert Oliver Hood was born in Rock Mills, Alabama, in 1897. Little is known about his early life except that he had only a seventh-grade education before he moved to Georgia. Hood was no longer married to his first wife when he arrived in LaGrange—a town of about seventeen thousand people on the Georgia-Alabama border, about sixty miles southwest of Atlanta—at around age twenty-three. Soon after that, he met and wed a local woman, Easter Mandy Nappier. The couple would raise eight children in a six-room house at 111 McGee Street in the town's Calumet Mill village. Described by family members as "a very big, rugged, good-looking man," Hood found occasional work in a cotton mill as a doffer (someone who removed, or "doffed," spindles that collected spun cotton fiber and replaced them with empty ones). To support his growing family, Hood often left for jobs in Atlanta and elsewhere in Georgia. He worked sometimes as a house painter and even entered bare-knuckle boxing matches, but mostly, he seemed to sing and make music.

A friendly, soft-spoken person, Hood was best known in LaGrange as "master of the mandolin, the most sought-after music teacher in town," according to grandson Theodore Pappas. Hood was also occasionally part of a comedy act—"Mr. Gallagos and Mr. Tibbs"—that performed in a minstrel show. He sang and played on a local radio station and in bands throughout western Georgia, Alabama, and South Carolina in the 1930s and 1940s.[13]

Family members recalled that despite having little formal education, Hood was also well-read and a wordsmith. "His command of the English language was nothing short of remarkable," Pappas wrote." Also remarkable was his mastery of the mandolin and his passion for teaching about it and other instruments to aspiring musicians in LaGrange. Another of Hood's grandsons, David Crook, observed, "McGee Street may not rival Beale or Bourbon Streets, but for years it was the center of music in LaGrange and an incubator for some figures who would have a profound impact on this artistic medium." Among the prominent artists from LaGrange who knew and played with Hood were acclaimed blind guitarist and banjo player Riley Puckett, who performed with the pioneering hillbilly band Gid Tanner and the Skillet Lickers, and LaGrange native Chips Moman, a prominent guitarist, songwriter, and record producer.[14]

Some family members and others who knew him during the 1930s insisted that Hood wrote "You Are My Sunshine" in the late 1920s or early 1930s. In 1990, Pappas maintained, "There are still people alive . . . who remember hearing the song before 1937." He claimed that Puckett performed it in the mid-1930s. Because Hood was prominent in music circles in rural east-central Georgia in the 1930s, and the Rice Brothers performed throughout Georgia during the same period, they may have encountered each other, perhaps often. Even if Hood and the Rice Brothers didn't cross paths, it's possible Hoke and Paul overheard someone like Puckett sing Hood's songs, as Puckett and the Rice Brothers both had radio shows in Atlanta in 1937.[15]

Oliver Hood (*center*), the probable composer of "You Are My Sunshine," and two music students in LaGrange, Georgia, in 1959. (Courtesy of David Crook)

Like the other songs his family said Hood wrote during this period, he neglected to copyright "Sunshine." And in the mid- to late 1930s, Hood lost control of his composition. This is where the mysterious red-haired woman, whom several artists insisted sang the song in the late 1930s, may have played a role in the story of "Sunshine." Some Hood family members recall that Oliver's relationship with a red-haired woman from South Carolina threatened his marriage to Easter. David Crook has speculated that the woman may have been Esther Mae Davis, known as "the Carolina Sunshine Girl," who sang with a hillbilly band, the Carolina Tarheels (not to be confused with a better-known band of the 1920s and early 1930s, the Original Carolina Tar Heels.) The Tarheels performed on WSB radio in Atlanta and toured around Georgia in the early 1930s. If Esther Mae—whose hair color is unknown—knew Hood and learned the song from him, she could have given it to musicians she knew, including Hoke Rice, who then played banjo for the Carolina Tarheels.[16]

Pappas, Crook, and other family weren't the only ones who attested to Oliver Hood's authorship of "Sunshine." Wayne Daniel—a Georgia State University professor who wrote the definitive history of country music in Atlanta, *Pickin' on Peachtree*—interviewed family members and "musical associates" of Hood who were "adamant in their assertion that Mr. Hood wrote the song." He added, "Those whom I interviewed consistently place the time of composition as the early 1930s." Chips Moman believed his musical mentor had written the song. Moman recalled visiting Hood one day in 1951 when an emotional Hood told him, "They stole my song." To the end of his life, Moman insisted that Hood wrote "Sunshine," saying, "I know who wrote that song."[17]

If Hood wrote "Sunshine," he did nothing in the 1930s to secure his rights to it or acknowledgment for it. In a biographical sketch of Hood, Crook correctly noted, "Not many people in those days, especially those from rural areas, knew how to protect their artistic rights or even knew they should." Pappas said registering the song didn't occur to his grandfather until it became a hit: "It was then that Oliver Hood began copyrighting his music—one song too late, as he so well knew." In the mid-1950s, Hood wrote a new song, "Somebody Stole My Sunshine Away," about what he considered the theft of his famous composition.

> Somewhere the sun is shining,
> But there's rain in my heart today.
> There's no denying, My heart keeps crying.
> Somebody stole my sunshine away.[18]

Hood copyrighted that song and arranged to record it in Los Angeles but backed out, family members recalled, because "Oliver was too distrustful [of the recording industry] to go through with it." Hood died in 1959 before he received credit for writing one of the world's most famous songs.[19]

The dispute over who wrote "Sunshine" or if anyone, including Hood, created it as an original idea (instead of taking lyrics or melodic pieces from another song or songs) may never be settled. Had Hood copyrighted it, the question of authorship—and original ownership—would be better established. That Paul Rice, a more astute and savvier musician than Hood, didn't copyright "Sunshine" suggests that he wasn't the song's author.

"The song has one of the most complex genealogies in the history of recorded music," Louisiana historian Kevin Fontenot has observed. Jessica Rose—a great-grandchild of Hood, who wrote her 2021 PhD dissertation at Georgia State University about the song—embraces the family's conviction that Hood wrote it. But she admits that nothing about it is clear-cut. "The song's history is a stew of fact, oral history, community practice, conjecture, and propaganda," she wrote, "requiring the aid of critical imagination to help recover a foundation that has remained obscured for nearly a century." While we may never know who wrote "You Are My Sunshine," we know who is responsible for its worldwide popularity and ubiquity. That, without question, was James Houston Davis.[20]

2

The Only Way I Ever Play Politics

As he approached ten decades of life, Jimmie Davis remained the tall, slim, and dignified presence he had been since his days as one of country music's first prominent performers. His blue eyes still sparkled beneath neatly combed gray hair. His north Louisiana drawl, thick as the Jackson Parish piney woods whence he came, had never faded. And when he sang, there were still hints of the once-strong, sweet tenor voice that had thrilled generations of devoted fans.

Davis sustained something else as he approached his centenary: he insisted he had written "You Are My Sunshine." Standing with him near a duck pond in Nashville's Centennial Park for an interview and photoshoot in the spring of 1999, photographer Maria von Matthiessen asked the country and gospel music legend when he'd composed the famous song. "'Bout 1928," Davis answered. "Then, went up to Chicago to record it with a bunch of good musicians. But I was a corn-fed person, you know. Didn't know what them musicians were doin', so it wasn't satisfactory. I carried it 'round then for 'bout eight years, tried to get someone else to record it. Carried it to all the community country bands and pop bands, and I couldn't get a deal makin' it." Left unasked: Why would someone as savvy as Davis—well known in the 1930s and 1940s for buying other musicians' songs—record and pitch to other artists a composition that he wouldn't register with the US Copyright Office until early 1940? That made no sense.[1]

Sometimes, Davis would change the subject or dodge the question when an interviewer asked how or when he wrote "Sunshine." In the mid-1940s, Davis confessed to a New Orleans journalist that he bought it from a down-and-out composer. Sometimes, he claimed he wrote it in graduate school at LSU. Other times, he suggested it was shortly after graduating LSU. "I started working on it right after I got out of LSU—in Shreveport—and that was in '29, working on it a little bit," he said in a 1990 interview. "Just time to time, just putting words together and writing it. Then, in '30, why, I finished it because I had two dozen verses." Once, asked whom he had in mind when he composed "Sunshine," Davis said, "I didn't write it about anybody special, although I might have been courtin' two or three at the time. I believe it was written after a rainy day in Louisiana like this. Sunshine is a welcome thing. It brings a lot of brightness. I still like to watch the sun go down in the afternoon."[2]

Davis often described failed attempts to record the song in the early 1930s. Asked by interviewer Bob Allen in 1987 if he wrote "Sunshine" in the late 1930s, Davis answered, "Well, I wrote it before that." Then, Davis recounted a story he shared with several interviewers over the years: The owner of KWKH, the Shreveport radio station for which he then performed, sent him to Chicago in 1932 to record songs for the station's Hello World label: "I recorded [Sunshine] on one side, and on the other side, it was 'My Blue Heaven.' It didn't sell." (One problem with this story is that Davis had made records for Victor since 1929.) The following year, Davis said, he tried to rerecord it, this time with disastrous results. A musician who accompanied him—a childhood friend who had never been in a recording studio—got nervous and "lost his mind," he claimed. Davis said he got the man drunk, trying to calm his nerves long enough to cut the song. But that plan failed when the musician cursed the producer and fled the studio, "and I didn't get to do it." Davis said he made another attempt in 1934 in Chicago, but drunkenness spoiled his plans again. "Two of the boys got drunk . . . they couldn't do anything." Davis said he gave up trying to record the song until 1940 but "carried it around," hoping to persuade others to record it.[3]

Regarding liquor in the studio, Wanna Coffman—who played bass with Milton Brown and His Musical Brownies, a groundbreaking Western swing group that backed Davis in a 1937 session—remembered that

Davis sometimes needed a sip of whiskey to make a decent record. "Jimmie used to carry a half-pint of whiskey with him all the time with rock candy in it," Coffman recalled. "And every time he sang, he'd take a teaspoon full of it." Coffman said Davis believed the whiskey "would open his voice up."[4]

In 1989, Davis told a different story about the first 1932 recording session in Chicago. In this telling, a troublesome piano player foiled him: "It sounded so terrible that when I got back, I told Mr. [W. K.] Henderson [KWKH's owner], 'We can't use that. If that comes out, whatever musical career I hope to have will end that day. . . . I think it's a good one, 'You Are My Sunshine,' and I don't want to ruin it." Why he would need to explain this to Henderson when Davis was making records for Victor in 1932 is unclear.[5]

Davis spoke at length about "Sunshine" in 1990 with Japanese historian Toru Mitsui. In this exchange, he said he first tried to record the song in Dallas (apparently on December 4, 1928, when Davis made several records). And Davis claimed this was the session with the musician he got drunk. After the man cursed studio employees, Davis said, "They ran us home, took us off, wouldn't let us record." But Davis's recollection of that session doesn't match the historical record. Davis recorded two songs that day: "Nobody's Business" and "Out of Town Blues." Perhaps he confused the session with another in Chicago the previous summer—his first studio session. But he and the musicians present recorded four numbers for KWKH's Hello World label. It wasn't a failed session. Davis told Mitsui, "I went back later on, and in about '32 or ['3]3, to record 'Sunshine.' . . . And I made it, but two musicians—I had four boys—two of them got sour and liquored up." So, Davis said, he couldn't record the song that day. In 1939, he said, "I made my third stab at 'You Are My Sunshine.'"

In this interview, Davis also told Mitsui that in the late 1920s, he pitched "Sunshine" to Ralph Peer, the record producer responsible for discovering and recording many of hillbilly music's early stars, including Jimmie Rodgers and the Carter Family. "He [Peer] didn't care for 'Sunshine' too much. I tried to get some other people to record 'Sunshine' . . .

maybe '33 or '34, somewhere there. But nobody was interested in it." Davis implied he sang "Sunshine" on Shreveport radio in the 1930s and that it had many more verses. "We had, I guess we had twenty verses, you know, all kinds of verses," Davis said, adding, "And everybody was singin' at the time, but I sang it on the air." In another 1990 interview, he made the same claim. "I was singing it a long time before I recorded it," he said. "And I was on KWKH there every Friday night and I think everyone knew it better than I did."[6]

Davis also claimed he permitted the Rice Brothers' Gang to record the song. "I told them to record it if they wanted to," he replied when asked how the duo had recorded "Sunshine" before him. "But, I mean, I was singin' it all the time, you know." Mitsui didn't ask Davis why, if he owned the song, he had to buy it from Paul Rice in December 1939. Mitsui speculated, "Was Davis generous enough to give them permission to copyright the song when he 'told them to record it if you wanted to'? Or, did Paul Rice copyright it simply because it was a song which had no copyright holder and which had nothing to do with Davis or, less plausibly, because it was his own composition? In other words, has Davis just been making up an imaginative story about his allegedly long association with the song prior to his first recording of *You Are My Sunshine* released in 1940?"[7]

Few of Davis's stories about his most famous song bear scrutiny. Some speculated that he wrote it in the late 1920s and never copyrighted it. Maybe the song got away from him and drifted around the South until the red-haired woman from South Carolina heard it and shared it with Paul and Hoke Rice. Perhaps, then, Davis was repurchasing his song. But Davis never told that story, and it would have been a straightforward story to tell had it been true. But if he had repurchased his song, why would he sign a contract with Paul Rice in which Rice is identified as the song's author? Why not state that he was *reacquiring* his song? And why did Davis identify Charles Mitchell as the cowriter if he were the song's sole author? After all, he hadn't known Mitchell during his LSU days or in the late 1920s, so they couldn't have collaborated on a song then. Maybe Mitchell composed the tune? If so, Davis never credited his partner with it.

And soon, Davis would pay Mitchell for his portion of the song, making Davis the sole owner. When Davis recorded the song in 1940, he didn't list his or Mitchell's name in parentheses under the title, a rare instance of missing attribution on one of his early recordings. Unlike almost every other recording by Davis in the 1930s and early 1940s, this record lists him only as the performer along with "Charles Mitchell's Orchestra." (In the sheet music distributed by Southern Music Publishing in 1941, Davis and Mitchell were listed as creators of the "words and music.")

If Jimmie Davis wrote "You Are My Sunshine," the historical record and his contradictory and changing stories about how and when he recorded (or tried to record) the song undermine his case. And that's before addressing the undeniable fact that he bought the song from Paul Rice in 1939, almost two months before he recorded it and after two other acts had released their versions.

One more critical piece of evidence supports the conclusion that Davis didn't write the song: his own words. On June 13, 1999, about three months before Davis's one-hundredth birthday, independent historian Michael Wynne of Alexandria visited the aged singer at his Baton Rouge home. Wynne had befriended Davis in the mid-1990s and saw him at least once a month. Wynne had organized a symposium on Davis's life and music at Pineville's Louisiana College in May 1999. During his June visit, Wynne asked the former governor to tell him the "truth" about "Sunshine." According to notes Wynne made immediately afterward, Davis hesitated, then said, "In writing the song, you have important rights. But *owning* the song is more important. I bought the song and own the song. That is all that is important. I don't like the song, but it is my bread and butter; it pays for my gas and my Cadillacs."[8]

Jimmie Davis may not have been the biological parent of "You Are My Sunshine," but he became its adoptive father in 1939. In the early 1940s, he was responsible for the song's early popularity and eventual place among seminal country music songs. Davis's promotion and stewardship of "Sunshine" also made it one of the early country songs to cross over to the popular charts, securing "his" song's importance to the genre's acceptance and development as an established musical category.

Davis wanted journalists, historians, and fans to believe that he made "Sunshine" when, in a way, it was the other way around. "Sunshine" would propel Davis to musical stardom. And it would help secure his place in the pantheon of country music pioneers who widened the genre's appeal and earned it greater respectability within the recording industry. To understand "You Are My Sunshine," we must learn about Oliver Hood, the Pine Ridge Boys, and Paul and Hoke Rice. But for social, musical, and political reasons, it's just as important to know about Davis.

Throughout Davis's long life, he claimed he never knew when he was born. He was sure of the date but not the year. In his 1927 master's thesis for Louisiana State University, Davis reported it as 1901. For a 1959 questionnaire for the *Country, Western, and Gospel Music Encyclopedia*—completed in his hand—Davis wrote that he was born on September 11, 1902. But in an undated biography released by Capitol Records (his label from 1949 to 1951) and edited by Davis, he listed his birth year as 1904. Later in life, he said he was born in 1899. Other times, he said he did not know what year he was born, as no official record existed. But such a record had existed. For the 1910 US Census, his parents reported in May 1910 that he turned ten on his previous birthday. If accurate, that would make his birth year 1899.[9]

If the year was sometimes in doubt, it was always certain that James Houston Davis was born to Sam Jones Davis and Sarah (Works) Davis near Beech Springs, Louisiana, a remote Jackson Parish village about a hundred miles southeast of Shreveport. The oldest son of eleven children, the Davises—including Jimmie's paternal grandparents—lived in a primitive, four-room log cabin owned by a local merchant whose land they sharecropped. "I thought everybody was supposed to be poor and ragged," Davis said late in life. "I didn't know anybody who was rich." Like his siblings, Jimmie hoed and picked cotton from an early age. The landowner provided the seed, fertilizer, mule, and plow, and the Davises provided the labor. The two sides split the profits. The family's finances improved by the time Jimmie was six or seven. They moved into Beech Springs, where his father—who had only a third-grade education—worked as a section hand for the Rock Island Railroad. Davis recalled his father earned a dollar a day, adding, "Two or three years later, he had worked himself up to a dollar and a dime." Over the years, Davis said, his family would alternate between village and farm, depending on their fortunes.

Music was a way of life on the farm and around the small community. Davis's father played the fiddle, and his mother sang and played the harmonica. From an early age, Davis said, he loved singing—in church and at all-day singings with dinner on the church grounds. "My father was a right good singer, and he used to lead in the singing [here] about," Davis later recalled. Before long, Jimmie began performing at his Beech Springs school every Friday as part of the musical "Friday Afternoon Society." Davis recalled many years later that a local farmer whose tenor voice he admired said "my singing wasn't all that bad and maybe I ought to sing some more."[10]

After graduating from Beech Springs High School—his graduating class was three people—Davis enrolled at Louisiana College (a Baptist institution in the central Louisiana town of Pineville) and supported himself by washing dishes and doing yard work. "I had to start from scratch," he recalled. "Because we didn't have a library back home, I simply had no idea of how to use one or, for that matter, what one was." During the first year, he struggled through every course. "I wasn't trying to do well; I just wanted to get caught up," he said. He seldom went home to Jackson Parish. "I knew that if I had any future at all, it wasn't in Beech Springs."

Davis sang when he wasn't working, studying, or in class. First, he joined the college Glee Club, then graduated to the college quartet, for which he sang lead. This is when Davis's understanding of showmanship and how to read an audience emerged. The professor who directed the quartet insisted the young men sing classical songs, but Davis said, "I couldn't feel our audiences responding to them. We didn't understand [the songs], and neither did most of our listeners." Davis suggested the group sing popular songs and spirituals. With that change, he said, the group was a hit and began accepting invitations to perform at area churches and schools.

When a brother-in-law gave him a beat-up guitar, Davis learned enough chords to accompany himself while he sang. He was soon singing on street corners in nearby Alexandria to pay his bills. When a police officer chased him off, Davis moved to another corner. “I was desperate,” he said. “If I didn’t make some change, I knew I wouldn’t eat.” Some days, he collected six or seven dollars from passersby. Before his fourth year of college, the money ran out, and Davis returned to Jackson Parish and farming. Between selling cotton, traveling to Alexandria to sing on the street, and borrowing the rest, he saved enough to finish his studies. He graduated from Louisiana College in 1924 with a bachelor’s degree in history, moved back into the family home outside Beech Springs, and became a teacher and assistant principal at his former high school. After school, he helped with the farming.[11]

In the fall of 1926, with the money he saved from teaching, Davis left Beech Springs for good. He enrolled at Louisiana State University in Baton Rouge to pursue a master’s degree in education. At LSU, his smooth singing voice earned him a spot in the Glee Club, and he became first tenor in the school’s popular Tiger Quartet. As he had in Alexandria, he sometimes sang for money on city streets. He graduated in the spring of 1927. His thesis topic: “Comparative Intelligence of Whites, Blacks, and Mulattoes.” By the fall, he had a job teaching history and social sciences as one of nine faculty members at the newly established Dodd College, a Baptist junior college for women named after a well-known radio preacher and senior pastor of First Baptist Church of Shreveport, Monroe E. Dodd.[12]

It’s unclear how Davis got his musical break on Shreveport radio, but his guitar playing and singing around town caught the ear of W. K. Henderson, the owner of KWKH radio, who was looking for local talent to fill airtime on his station. By one account, the station invited Davis to make a guest appearance, and after his performance generated dozens of favorable letters, telegrams, and phone calls, KWKH gave him a show. In early 1928, Davis began appearing on the station at eight o’clock each Friday night, accompanied on piano by James Enloe, a Centenary College student from Mansfield. His program was called *The Jimmie Show.*

Davis with his band in Shreveport in 1936, where he hosted a popular radio show on KWKH. *Left to right:* Bill Harper, Claudette Mitchell, Charles Mitchell, Davis, Buddy Jones, Ernest Hatley, A. B. Rische. Tex Swaim is seated. (Courtesy *Shreveport Times*)

Henderson admired Davis's singing so much that he invited the young man to record four songs for the station's Hello World record label in the summer of 1928. His first was "Ramona," the title song from a 1928 film of the same name. In this first session, Davis also sang "Think of Me Thinking of You" and "You'd Rather Forget Than Forgive," accompanied only by Enloe. While he sang most of the songs in a formal, stilted tenor, Davis revealed hints of a future style with his final recording. It was a carefree and emotional song, a cover of Jimmie Rodgers's 1927 recording "Away Out on the Mountain," featuring Davis yodeling in Rodgers's style. In this recording, Davis joined a handful of artists in the late 1920s and early 1930s (including Gene Autry, Cliff Carlisle, Hank Snow, and Ernest Tubb) who revered and imitated the popular "Singing Brakeman" from Meridian, Mississippi, the first true national hillbilly and folk music star. "Most of us were influenced by him," Davis once said.[13]

In December 1928, Davis went to Dallas for an audition with Columbia Records. He recorded two songs, "Nobody's Business" and "Out of Town Blues." The label released neither of the songs. (This may have been the troubled session at which Davis would later claim he failed to record "Sunshine.")[14]

In the fall of 1928, a Shreveport city court judge, David B. Samuel, gave the young man his first opportunity to meld music with politics. Samuel hired Davis not only to sing at campaign events but also to make speeches on his behalf—and not only speeches but attacks on his opponents. Davis, who left his teaching job at Dodd College for the campaign, later said he hated being a "hatchet man" but explained, "I was with the judge, sink or swim. It's the only way I ever play politics." After the campaign, Samuel gave Davis a full-time job with the court and, in the spring of 1929, made him clerk of the criminal section. The job paid better than teaching, giving the twenty-six-year-old Davis more time for his budding music career. In 1929, the pioneering hillbilly and "race" record producer for RCA's Victor label, Ralph Peer, reportedly heard Davis perform on KWKH and signed him to a contract.[15]

Combining a radio show with the opportunity to make and sell records was an enormous career boost. "From the mid-1920s through the end of the Depression," country music historian Diane Pecknold observed, "radio remained the cornerstone of the hillbilly economy: a means of advertising the upcoming local performances that was the mainstay of every hillbilly musician's livelihood, and a vehicle for the direct sale of photographs and self-published song folios." Though performers and groups moved from town to town, station to station, searching for a bigger payday, many never made records. This was because some record companies, including Victor and Decca, discouraged radio stations from broadcasting their records. So, most hillbilly singers performed live on the air and earned money from local appearances that they plugged during broadcasts. Many worked side jobs to support their families while they dreamed of musical stardom. Before he became a country music star in the early 1940s, Ernest Tubb combined music with his job selling beer for several Texas beverage distributors. Reflecting on his lean early years in country music, band leader and musician Pee Wee King recalled that his first radio show in Racine, Wisconsin, in 1933 "didn't pay us one red cent. But we got something better than money. We got publicity. We could announce where we'd be playing and everybody would know our name." Unusual among early country artists, Davis did not become a musical vagabond. He had a steady government job, made records for an established label, hosted a popular radio show, and was in demand for personal appearances.[16]

On September 19, 1929, Davis went to Memphis for the first of seven recording sessions with Victor and Peer over the next four years. He would release more than sixty songs with the label. On his first recordings for Decca—including "The Barroom Message," "The Baby's Lullaby," "Out of Town Blues," and "Home Town Blues"—he emulated Jimmie Rodgers. But he was experimenting, searching for a unique style. In doing so, he migrated into the world of blues. The following spring, Davis made music history. On May 20, 1930, in a studio at the Municipal Auditorium in Memphis, Davis likely became the first country singer to record with a Black musician. According to the most authoritative research of early country records—Tony Russell's *Country Music Records*—Davis recorded "She's a Hum Dum Dinger from Dingersville." Russell's research suggests that Black Shreveport guitarists Oscar "Buddy" Woods and Ed "Dizzy Head" Schaffer accompanied him. (In July that year, Rodgers would become the second country artist to record with Black musicians when he went into a Hollywood studio to record "Blue Yodel No. 9" with Louis Armstrong and his wife, Lillian Hardin Armstrong.)

A bluesman from Natchitoches, Louisiana, Woods was a master of the Hawaiian-style slide guitar—sometimes known as a resonator guitar or Dobro—whose style would influence many blues musicians. The *Encyclopedia of Music in the 20th Century* would call Woods "one of the most impressive prewar slide guitar Blues stylists." Of Schaffer, little is known except that he was a gifted guitarist who also played slide guitar. Together, Woods and Schaffer often performed as the Shreveport Home Wreckers at a local after-hours speakeasy, the Blue Goose. The two Black musicians and Davis may have played together in shows in and around northwest Louisiana in the early 1930s. From May 1930 to February 1932, Woods and Schaffer—or sometimes only Schaffer—would accompany Davis on twenty-two recordings in field sessions for Victor in Memphis, Dallas, and Charlotte. In a makeshift studio at Dallas's Jefferson Hotel on Monday, February 8, 1932, Davis and Woods made more music history when they became country music's first mixed-race duet on a record, "Saturday Night Stroll." (Also present in the studio that day to record two songs were Western swing artists Bob Wills and the Light Crust Doughboys.)[17]

These early Davis records were interesting in ways that would later threaten Davis's political career and his standing as an upright, God-fearing singer of gospel tunes: many of them explored sexual themes that would not comport with the image he would portray. In later years, Davis would dismiss or deemphasize those records, despite their historical significance. But they were noteworthy for several reasons, not least because they showed how much the music and lyrics of Black musicians influenced Davis and other white musicians of this era. While racial segregation was the law, it didn't mean that white musicians couldn't, or wouldn't, associate with, learn from, and borrow from Black musicians. A cursory review of Davis's music in the early 1930s would persuade even the casual listener that he was borrowing from the Black musicians he heard and played with. "Black blood flows in the music of Jimmie Rodgers and Cliff Carlisle; it was in Gene Autry's and Jimmie Davis's, too, before they went pop in the late 1930s," music historian Nick Tosches wrote in *Country: The Twisted Roots of Rock 'n' Roll.* As two other prominent historians of country music, Bill C. Malone and Tracey E. W. Laird, have observed of early artists like Davis and Jimmie Rodgers, "Much of the feel for the blues style came directly from black singers (either in the flesh or on records)."[18]

In 1931, Davis told a newspaper reporter that the ideas for some of his songs came from criminal cases at Shreveport City Court, where he worked as a clerk. Tony Russell claimed that later in the 1930s, when Davis became Shreveport's commissioner for public safety, he exploited his position to buy songs from down-and-out musicians. "If a musician was hauled in on a charge," Russell wrote in *Country Music Originals,* "Davis would quietly bury the case in exchange for the rights to some songs. Even without a charge sheet to their name, hard-up writers would often sign away a half-share in a song for a timely cash offer. Consequently, the catalog of songs solely or jointly credited to Davis includes many to which his claim is more legal than authorial." While Davis is listed as the writer of most of his early music, some suspected that he bought the songs from Black musicians and composers, something he denied.

Whatever the case, Black music—especially the blues—was so much a part of Davis's early repertoire that he could be classified as a white blues singer until the mid-1930s. "Though he was fond of pieces in the [Jimmie Rodgers] blue yodel vein," Russell wrote, "[Davis] made a distinct, if less influential, contribution to white blues, by exploring the world of sexual symbolism with a wit and metaphorical command that were typically black." Among Davis's songs with sexually suggestive lyrics were "She's a Hum Dum Dinger (from Dingersville)," "Bed Bug Blues," "Bear Cat Mama from Horner's Corners," "Yo Yo Mama," "Tom Cat and Pussy Blues," "Organ-Grinder Blues," and "The Shotgun Wedding."[19]

One song, "High Behind Blues," pushed the boundaries of race and sex further by suggesting a sexual relationship between a Black woman and a white man:

When I get to Mexico,
Gonna get me a big, big brown,
No matter how big she is,
I'm the man who can hold her down.[20]

In "Bed Bug Blues," Davis's lyrics relied on symbolism and sexual innuendo to describe illicit nocturnal visits to "The Bottoms," a Black section of Shreveport:

These bed bugs were long and skinny,
Long ways from the floor.
Let's go down to The Bottoms,
Where the bed bugs come and go.
Bed bugs 'bout to make a wreck out of me.[21]

Davis wasn't the only singer of his era to record songs with risqué and suggestive lyrics. Other early country artists, including Roy Acuff and Gene Autry, performed acts or recorded songs that didn't conform with their respectable images. But, by the early 1940s and beyond, Davis would regret these songs. Opponents would use them against him in political campaigns, making his 1940 recording of "You Are My Sunshine" even more important to his image as a singer and writer of wholesome American music. "I used to sing some that were a little suggestive," Davis acknowledged in a 1976 interview. A decade later, in another interview, he dismissed those early recordings as "not anything very good." A few years later, however, he was more philosophical about the political attacks the recordings drew—"I have to live with it," he said—perhaps because the racy songs did not cost him enough votes to lose any of his early elections.[22]

Davis's views of the recordings' quality notwithstanding, many of his early-1930s records were hits. "Almost everything he recorded for Victor was issued, and then usually reissued a few years later on the 35-cent Bluebird line, and frequently on the Montgomery Ward mail order stores label too," Tony Russell wrote, adding that two songs—"She's a Hum Dum Dinger" and "Bear Cat Mama from Horner's Corners"—were featured by retailer Montgomery Ward & Co. on a half-dozen occasions. "Selections came out on Canadian labels, Australian labels, African labels . . . and no fewer than 16 went through the [His Master's Voice] presses at Dum Dum [India] to appear on the Indian market."[23]

In the fall of 1934, Davis's musical style grew into a more polished country sound when he left Victor for the nascent Decca Records. In September, he became one of the first country singers to make a record for the new label. Although he would continue to record risqué songs like "Good Time Papa Blues" and "Shirt Tail Blues," he also made more traditional hillbilly records, like "It's Been Years (Since I've Seen My Mother)." In the words of one historian, his style in this period was "a combination of the sentimental and the suggestive."[24]

One of Davis's early recordings for Decca was a hit and a turning point in his career. In April 1935, he released "Nobody's Darlin' But

Mine," for which he registered the copyright as the composer. Although Davis would brand the song as his own, he did not write it. It was probably penned by Bill Nettles, a Natchitoches, Louisiana, native and disabled World War I US Navy veteran who played on KWKH in the 1930s and 1940s with his brother, Norman, as the Nettles Brothers. In June 1937, Davis would buy eleven more songs from Bill and Norman Nettles. Bill would later write a song—"The Story of Nobody's Darlin'"—about having written Davis's hit. Over the decades, dozens of artists would record the mournful country song, including Bing Crosby, Tex Ritter, Gene Autry, Merle Haggard, Eddy Arnold, and Patti Page. The song's popularity put Davis on the map as a notable recording artist and musician. "That was my first big one," he recalled. He recorded and rereleased the song in October 1937, and it would spend one week in nineteenth place on the national pop chart in December. Davis would release his second national hit the following year, a cover of the waltz standard "Meet Me Tonight in Dreamland." It spent one week on the pop chart, in thirteenth place, in December 1938.

The songs "pushed Davis to the forefront of regional stardom at a time when Southwesterners had begun to dominate the hillbilly field and left him on the verge of national popularity," historian Stephen R. Tucker observed. Davis was now one of Decca's most promising new artists. He had the potential to become a national star.[25]

3

Bull Market in Corn

All his musical success didn't mean Davis was wealthy. In the mid-1930s, earnings from record and sheet music sales and in-person performances couldn't support many hillbilly artists. Before country music became a nationwide phenomenon, a hillbilly "hit" might generate a few hundred dollars for the artist and songwriter. That wasn't enough for someone like Davis to quit a dependable government position during the Great Depression. Davis seemed to believe he could manage his day job as Shreveport's court clerk while singing on the radio, recording songs, and making personal appearances around north Louisiana on nights and weekends.[1]

In 1987, a Davis contemporary, country artist Bob Atcher, reflected on the pitiful royalties singers earned during country music's infancy (assuming they received royalties at all): a half-penny for the writer and half-penny for the artist on each side of a record. "If [a singer] wrote all the songs on [both sides of] the record," Atcher said, "you'd get two cents for the record." (By law, artists were entitled to two cents per record, but some negotiated deals with their record or management companies that shared those royalties. Atcher probably had such an arrangement with Okeh Records.) Songwriters could also sell songbooks, which Davis, Atcher, the Rice Brothers' Gang, the Carter Family, Roy Acuff, Jimmie Rodgers, and others did. Some, like Acuff, made good money from them, but such sales didn't generate significant income for most. Many artists had no royalty agreement, particularly if they recorded no original compositions. In that case, they earned a set fee, often twenty-five to fifty dollars per song.[2]

What growing musical success Davis achieved in the mid to late 1930s was likely because he added elements of Western swing to his performances and recordings. Popularized in the late 1920s and 1930s by groups including the Light Crust Doughboys, Milton Brown and His Musical Brownies, and Bob Wills and His Texas Playboys, Western swing resembled hillbilly music but had a bigger sound and tempos conducive for dancing. (Wills once said that Davis's music influenced him as he searched for his style in the early 1930s.) Besides the horns and drums seldom found in hillbilly bands, groups like Wills's enhanced their distinctive sounds with an electric steel guitar. The Playboys featured a groundbreaking electric steel guitar virtuoso, Leon McAuliffe, a Houston native who began playing with the Light Crust Doughboys at age sixteen before leaving to join Wills's band.

Adopting aspects of the Western swing sound that Wills and others popularized, Davis brought a slender, unassuming steel guitar player into his band. Charles Mitchell was one of seven children born to a tenant farming couple from Woodland, Texas. After his father died in 1911, Mitchell's family moved to Blue, Oklahoma, where the young man worked as a section hand for a railway company. Mitchell loved music and learned to play the piano, drums, mandolin, and electric steel guitar. His professional performing began at seventeen when he played piano in several small Oklahoma movie theaters. He became a telegraph operator for a local railroad and took his skills to an oil company in Smackover, Oklahoma, before the company transferred him to Shreveport in 1928.

Mitchell grew interested in country music and played the steel guitar with a Shreveport Hawaiian-style band. It was a new genre, popular throughout the country, especially in the South, including New Orleans. Beginning in the late 1800s, Hawaiian musicians migrated to Southern California, where their style—particularly the unusual, exotic sounds of the acoustic slide or steel guitar—beguiled listeners. "Louisiana residents were hardly passive recipients of these new sounds," music historian John Troutman wrote in his history of the Hawaiian steel guitar. "Perhaps lured by the novelty or exoticism, they succumbed to the Hawaiian guitar craze like the rest of the country." In 1918, the LSU Men's Glee Club, which Davis joined a few years later, included a Hawaiian guitar in its performances. Mitchell and his band began performing on KWKH radio, where Davis also appeared. He recalled meeting Davis in a Shreveport record store in 1930. By 1934, Davis and Mitchell began their musical collaboration, appearing on the radio and at events in and around Shreveport. In 1936, Mitchell joined Davis's band. He accompanied Davis on an electric steel guitar in their first joint recording session in New Orleans at the Roosevelt Hotel on March 19, 1936.[3]

The partnership with Mitchell—who had a gift not only for playing the steel guitar but also for arranging and writing songs—rejuvenated Davis's sound. Besides "Nobody's Darlin'," Davis had recorded other hits in the mid-1930s, including "When It's Round-Up Time in Heaven" (released in 1934), inspired by a 1932 Cliff Carlisle song, "When It's Roundup Time in Texas." While Mitchell's steel guitar was heard during his first recording session with Davis, the style sounded like the Davis of the previous two years: a series of straightforward sentimental ballads with limited musical accompaniment. However, Davis's music changed when he and Mitchell recorded in Los Angeles in June 1936. The steel guitar was more prominent. And his songs, including "My Blue Bonnet Girl" and "Ridin' Down the Arizona Trail," had a more robust Western flavor.

By 1936, many of Davis's records included elements of Western swing and jazz. The location of his recording sessions may have influenced his musical migration. He recorded more in Dallas, San Antonio, Houston, and Los Angeles. Among the songs he and Mitchell recorded in their first California session in June 1936 was a jazz-and-swing version of "Come on Around to My House," written by bluesman "Blind Willie" McTell, who had recorded it in 1929. In 1936, Davis acquired the copyright and, in 1938, published its words and music in *The Songs of Jimmie Davis* songbook, listing it as his composition.[4]

When not taking Mitchell into the studio, Davis made recordings with various Western swing musicians, including former members of Milton Brown's Musical Brownies in Dallas in February 1937. And in another departure from his earlier style, he recorded four songs in New York in October 1937, including a remake of "Nobody's Darlin' But Mine" with Lani McIntyre's Hawaiians. This popular group had backed Bing Crosby on several records that year. By the time he went to Dallas for the first of five recording sessions in Texas from February 1937 to September 1939, he was almost always accompanied by Charles Mitchell's Texans, featuring Mitchell on steel guitar, Tex Swaim on guitar, Ova Mitchell (Charles Mitchell's wife) on ukulele, and Hershel Woodal on string bass.

Writing about Davis on the cusp of national stardom, music journalist and historian Nick Tosches noticed a transformation in the singer's voice and style. "Even Jimmie's voice changed," he observed. "It got warmer, lighter, and less churlish." Within a few years, Tosches noted, the risqué songs would cease. "Jimmy Davis was a crooner."[5]

Davis made another stride toward country music stardom in 1938 when he recorded "It Makes No Difference Now," written by Floyd Tillman, a twenty-four-year-old singer, musician, and songwriter from West Texas. A prolific writer of country hits who would enter the Country Music Hall of Fame in 1984 (twelve years after Davis), Tillman hoped to record the song, but his producer rejected it. So, he pitched it to a friend and colleague (and future Davis band member), Cliff Bruner, who first cut it for Decca with his Texas Wanderers in September 1938. Bruner's version was so ubiquitous in Texas, Tillman recalled, that "one guy in Baytown . . . shot the jukebox out with a shotgun because he was so sick of it."[6]

In San Antonio for a recording session just nine days after Bruner had recorded the song there, Davis took notice. "He came by and wanted to buy it," Tillman remembered. "He offered me two hundred dollars for it. I held out for three hundred." Tillman would reacquire his song in 1966. "And my first royalty check was ten times bigger than what I sold it for originally," he said. (In 1941, Davis would approach another struggling singer in Fort Worth, Ernest Tubb, and offer the future Country Music Hall of Fame member a hundred dollars for the rights to a song he had just composed but not yet recorded: "Walking the Floor over You." Tubb's version of the song would rocket the singer to national stardom. Tubb needed the money, but a friend of Tubb's recalled that he suspected Davis's intense desire to buy his song meant that he had a hit on his hands. Tubb declined the offer.)[7]

Davis made his version of "It Makes No Difference Now" in Los Angeles in November 1938 with Rudy Sooter's Ranchmen, a California Western swing band. The song was a hit for Bruner and Davis. (Tom Dickey's Show Boys, with Adolph Hofner on vocals, would record it, too.) But when Davis released it, the platter listed him as coauthor with Tillman. By August 1939, *Billboard* magazine would list Davis's and Bruner's versions as the nation's most popular hillbilly song. Years later, in an interview with country music historian Tony Russell, Tillman expressed annoyance at how Davis profited from his composition. And he would cast aspersions on Davis's purported songwriting prowess. "Jimmie Davis never wrote a song in his life," he insisted.[8]

But as he would with "You Are My Sunshine" in 1940, Davis would propel another artist's composition into the national musical consciousness and give the burgeoning field of hillbilly music greater stature and respectability. As *Time* would note in a 1943 article on the new genre's growing popularity, "Bull Market in Corn," Davis's recording of "It Makes No Difference Now" caught the ear of Decca Records executive David Kapp. "Within a few months record buyers were clamoring for Decca's later Bing Crosby version," the magazine noted. "Shrewd David Kapp barged wholesale into the hillbilly field, boomed local hits into national smashes by giving them successive recordings by bigger & bigger names." Before long, *Time* declared, Crosby was "the most popular singer of hillbilly as well as other popular music."[9]

Buying a song from the writer and pretending the new owner composed it might seem unethical. But then as now "the music business sees a song as a property," country music journalist and historian Barry Mazor observed, comparing the practice to leasing property. Whether it was dishonest to credit himself as the writer of the lyrics and music (as opposed to listing himself as the song's owner, which was a different matter), Davis did what performers and others in the music recording industry had done for years: they not only recorded songs they liked, but they bought them—or purchased the rights to them—to maximize their revenue if they became hits. Davis, who collaborated with producer Ralph Peer in the late 1920s and early 1930s, probably also noticed that Peer only signed artists who recorded original work. A recording artist, Peer said, had to "write his own music, or you've got to get it for him, and *then* you take him to a record company." Davis almost certainly understood Peer's approach, once noting that Peer "knew how to write a contract."[10]

Buying songs or their mechanical (i.e., recording) rights was how recording artists made better money in the industry in the 1920s and 1930s. Recording a song owned by someone else would not generate much revenue in an era when most singers—especially hillbilly performers—did not pack large auditoriums or concert halls. Even when artists drew a sizeable crowd, the admission price was negligible, meaning the earnings from proceeds might be less than fifty dollars—and that was before paying the band. Owning your music was a straightforward way to make a little more money. A successful hillbilly record in the Great Depression's early years might only sell ten thousand copies, which wouldn't generate more than two hundred dollars in royalties (from $3,600 to $4,700 in 2024 dollars) for the writer at one or two pennies per disc. But most hillbilly artists had no royalty agreements. The record companies kept the profits from sales of their records.[11]

In the late 1920s, Peer set the stage for his ultimate wealth when he began negotiating personal management and publishing contracts with artists like Jimmie Rodgers and the Carter Family. The artists kept their songs' copyrights in these arrangements but assigned them to Peer, who paid them a portion of royalties. Such deals gave the artists what they wanted—earnings from a recording contract and broader distribution and sales—without ceding ownership of songs. "I never, never bought a copyright," Peer once said. Despite helping his artists earn much-needed income during the Depression, Peer profited far more than the artists he managed. For example, in the first quarter of 1934, the Carter Family reported earning $209 in royalties on sales of 76,027 records. Years later, one of Carters remarked: "Mr. Peer made us famous, and we made him rich."[12]

Davis, however, employed a less complicated approach to acquiring rights to the songs he recorded, which was often even less profitable for the writers: he bought their songs, or half of them, outright. In a lucrative deal with Peer's Southern Music Publishing Company, Davis would record these songs, sell them in song folios and sheet music, and present them as his compositions. Ernest Tubb biographer Ronnie Pugh believed Davis may have bought compositions from Elsie McWilliams—Jimmie Rodgers's sister-in-law and the author/coauthor of thirty-nine of his recordings—in the years after Rodgers's death in 1933. Davis sometimes paid artists a pittance for their songs and agreed to split the royalties from any records he or another artist might make. In 1937, for example, when he purchased eleven songs from singers Bill and Norman Nettles, he paid them one dollar and promised the duo 50 percent of royalties resulting from any recordings of the songs. Songwriters like the Nettles Brothers sometimes negotiated these lopsided deals because they believed the best way to get their songs recorded was to sell them at discounted prices to someone like Davis, hoping he might record them and split royalties. Nashville songwriter Mel Foree recalled meeting his future boss, music publisher Fred Rose, in 1942 and discussing with Rose if Davis would record one of his songs. "Well," Rose said, "he will if you give him half of it." Peer wouldn't condemn Davis's aggressive song-buying methods. However, two authorities on business methods of the era did. Music historians Brian Ward and Patrick Huber regarded the practice as "less-than-scrupulous."[13]

For song-buyers like Davis, the earnings from a hit grew when he persuaded other artists to record it. And that's one reason Davis would have been delighted that Bing Crosby recorded "It Makes No Difference Now" in 1941. Not only did Crosby's performance become a national hit, resulting in increased royalties for Davis from record and sheet music sales, but having a star like Crosby record songs labeled as "hillbilly" gave Davis additional respectability and stature within his embryonic genre. It also signaled to music fans and industry leaders that hillbilly songs were worthy of attention and could cross over to the pop charts. After Crosby covered one of Bob Wills's compositions, "New San Antonio Rose," the Western swing bandleader remarked that the crooner had lifted him "from hamburger to steak." Crosby not only conferred legitimacy on hillbilly music, but, as music historian Don Cusic noted, he also recorded the songs "with integrity instead of as 'hokum' and looking down his nose on this music."[14]

Even as Davis was buying and pitching songs, he did little to discourage journalists and fans from believing he was their composer. "Jimmie Davis has written the music and lyrics to nearly 100 songs," the author of a rhapsodic profile in the *Hammond Progress* wrote in June 1939. "The remarkable thing about his achievement is not that he has composed so many melodies of exceptional quality and has popularized a great many of them through his own talents as a vocalizer . . . but that he has done those things as an avocation, in his spare time."[15]

Despite his crucial role in nurturing the emerging genre of country music and introducing its songs to artists like Crosby, Davis still saw music as his sideline. Fans would soon learn, however, that politics not only paid his bills but paved the way to one of the most unusual dual careers in politics and entertainment in American political history.

4

I Belonged in Louisiana

In April 1938, *Collier's* magazine wrote about "hillbilly" and "race" music in a piece headlined, "Thar's GOLD in Them Hillbillies." The writer didn't make it clear where hillbilly music ended and the music of Black performers began. But it was apparent that something exciting was afoot in American music, which, before now, had only two official major categories: classical and popular. (Hillbilly records had been selling well for years, but major publications like *Collier's* were only now taking notice). But in the years since Ralph Peer and others had ventured south to record artists like Jimmie Rodgers, Bessie Smith, Fiddlin' John Carson, Sleepy John Estes, and Georgia White, Americans had learned new musical languages. These included jazz, blues, and folk/hillbilly, already spawning its subgenre of Western swing.

While *Collier's* cautioned that "the cult of the hillbillies may be a passing fancy," the magazine suggested that record companies like Victor and Decca may have capitalized on something more popular and permanent. "If there needs to be another picture at this point," the journalist observed, "the camera can leap agilely to such distant parts of South Africa and Australia where the native bushmen are busy humming a little number written by Jimmie Davis of Shreveport, Louisiana, entitled Nobody's Darling but Mine." The song's real author, Floyd Tillman, earned no mention. First among artists the writer identified as hillbilly's "big stars" was Davis, followed by singing movie cowboy Gene Autry and the Carter Family.[1]

Davis might have been a star, but music was still his sideline. He had married a local teacher, Alvern Adams, in 1936. He and his bride lived with her mother. "I walked to and from work every day unless somebody gave me a ride," he said. "It took me seven years to pay off all my debts and to be able to buy a car." The problem was, he said, "I needed a better job." In mid-July 1938, two months before he went to San Antonio to record "It Makes No Difference Now," Davis announced his candidacy for Shreveport's public safety commissioner. The position supervised the city's police and fire departments. His opponents were the incumbent commissioner and a state senator supported by the political organization of the late governor and US senator Huey P. Long.[2]

His announcement in the *Shreveport Times* didn't mention his musical success. But the city's afternoon paper, the *Shreveport Journal,* cited Davis's near-decade as clerk of court while noting he "is a widely known singer and composer" of hillbilly songs. "I tried one speech without the band," Davis recalled of that campaign, adding, "After it was all over, the people wanted to know why there wasn't some singing. They wanted entertainment—a show. I decided if that's what they wanted, I'd give it to them."[3]

Davis knew he couldn't pretend his musical career didn't exist, so why not use the band to attract an audience? "We drew huge crowds as we'd set up, sing some, and speak some," he remembered. "After a while, other candidates [for other offices] asked us if they could appear with us." He gave them each three minutes to speak. Davis sang his way into the job in rallies and events around town and on the radio. He beat the incumbent with ease.[4]

Despite the new, better-paying position, Davis continued recording and performing. Even amid the campaign, in September 1938, he spent two days in a San Antonio studio, making his hit version of "Meet Me Tonight in Dreamland." And, the Sunday before his November 8 election, he was in Los Angeles for another session, where he recorded another version of "It Makes No Difference Now." In 1939, he went to Houston for sessions in March and early September and to New York for a session in late September. During his first year in the commissioner's job, *Billboard* credited Davis with four hillbilly hits, including "Two More Years (and I'll Be Free)" and "It Makes No Difference Now." The following year, in 1940, he recorded sixteen songs in three sessions in New York and Houston.[5]

In performances later in his life, Davis would often introduce "You Are My Sunshine" to audiences with a story about his life as a struggling singer without a hit before he recorded his signature song: "It was with three other country musicians quite a few years ago. We were barnstorming the country, trying to make a little dough. We made all the chili joints, eating hot dogs and steamers. And at nighttime, three deep in a four-bit bed—all singin' the hard-time blues—hoping that someday we'd record a hit and things would be sweet. Then, we'd settle down on that place called Easy Street. It so happened that one July the sixth, we recorded a little ditty. It went something like this."[6]

Actually, it was at a session in New York on Monday, February 5, 1940, that Davis—with a Decca contract, several hits to his name, and in his second year as Shreveport's commissioner of public safety—recorded the song that he and Charles Mitchell bought from Paul Rice the previous December. Accompanying Davis was "Charles Mitchell's Orchestra" (previously "Charles Mitchell's Texans"), a group featuring at least six instruments, including trumpet, clarinet, electric steel guitar, piano, string bass, and rhythm guitar. It wasn't the ragtag, chili-chomping hillbilly troupe Davis would later portray. Tony Russell's authoritative and comprehensive *Country Music Records: A Discography, 1921–1942* doesn't contain the names of every musician on this session. Only Leon Chappelear on guitar and Mitchell on steel guitar are identified. Evidence points to the trumpet player as T. E. "Sleepy" Brown, a twenty-year-old Texas-born musician who moved to Vivian (north of Shreveport) as a teenager. In 1939, Brown toured Arkansas with Smokey and Bunny's Medicine Show, an ensemble that pitched an awful-tasting laxative called Satanic Medicine. When Davis and Mitchell asked him to join this session, Brown was playing for a Hot Springs, Arkansas, Western swing band, the Skyliners. In the late 1940s, Brown would join Davis's band after a stint in the military during World War II.[7]

The other musicians' names are lost to history, but not the energetic sounds they created that day. Davis recorded two songs—"Baby Your Mother" and "Roll Along, Kentucky Moon"—reminiscent of his earlier, sentimental style. In a cowboy-themed song, "Old Timer," Davis displayed his ability as a crooner. But his rendition of "I'd Love to Call You Sweetheart" allowed the musicians the most leeway. They produced an upbeat, Dixieland jazz song that rivaled "Sunshine" for its energy, virtuosity, and lightheartedness.

"Sunshine" was the first of the five-song session. And his buoyant rendition of it bore little resemblance to a traditional hillbilly song. It was more swing and Dixieland jazz than hillbilly, not unlike the foxtrot version the Rice Brothers recorded the year before. The musicians backing Davis in this session were among the best who had ever accompanied him. One journalist observed in 2013, "The clarinet, piano and trumpet sound like they're about to burst right out of the song, and Mitchell's stately guitar solo can't escape the instrument's Hawaiian associations or its relative newness in country music." Musicologist Ryan Raul Bañagale wrote of the recording: "The diversity of sound present in the 1940 recording rings through immediately. This is not a standard 'hillbilly' record." Even "the twang heard in Davis's voice is mild compared to contemporaries like [the late] Jimmie Rodgers and Gene Autry."[8]

The upbeat tempo, the Dixieland style, and Davis's smooth tones masked the mournful lyrics about lost love, regret, betrayal, and, maybe, retribution. Sung by another artist, at a slower tempo, and with less musical accompaniment, listeners might have perceived the song as something other than the cheerful song it pretended to be. Like the less-prominent Rice Brothers, Davis had pulled off some musical sleight of hand. Distracted by the joyous arrangement, many overlooked the melancholy words and concluded this was a sunny number about love and devotion. Only the chorus—which still defines it—fits that definition.

The evidence that Davis's rendition of "Sunshine" was the monster hit he and others suggested in the decades since is anecdotal and confusing. One scholar declared in a 2004 academic journal article that Davis's version "sold over a million copies in the United States." (A journalist attributed the same sales to Bob Atcher's December 1942 recording.) In an April 1942 article, syndicated Hollywood journalist Paul Harrison claimed the song had produced $22,000 in sheet music royalties for Davis and had sold 1.25 million records. He didn't state if those were sales of Davis's recording or a combination of all recordings by other artists. According to *Variety,* the song was a national sheet music bestseller in 1941, reaching eighth place in June.[9]

Decades later, *Billboard* listed Davis's version as the thirtieth-most-popular record of 1940 and big-band leader Wayne King's recording as the forty-first most popular of the following year. The music chart aggregation website Tsort.com ranked Davis's version as the seventh most popular in 1940. But, according to Music ID, an academic database of popular music chart information, Davis's record was ninth. The evidence for these varied rankings isn't clear. As Music ID's editors noted, "Between 1920 and 1940 there are few available charts (at least that we can find). These results should be treated with some caution."[10]

It's possible that Davis's record, while not a million-seller, performed well with the record-buying and jukebox-playing public. *Billboard*'s *1944 Music Year Book* implied that the song "sold into the millions of copies" and had "plopped at the Hit Parade heap," although it did not specify Davis's version. That's probably because the popular NBC radio show *Your Hit Parade* ignored songs by hillbilly artists during this period.[11]

Despite stories about the song's success, it's not clear that, in 1940 at least, most country music fans would have regarded Davis's song as a blockbuster. If they had, it would be difficult to prove because of how *Billboard* and other publications defined a "hit" record. Before the late 1940s, radio stations rarely made records the focal point of their on-air programming. A "hit" didn't suggest radio airplay. And in each *Billboard* edition in the early 1940s, the categories weren't so much about musical styles as distribution modes and publicity: "Songs with Most Radio Plugs" (on national radio shows originating from New York), "National and Regional Best Selling Retail Records," "National and Regional Sheet Music Best Sellers," and "Leading Music Machine Records." The publication wouldn't rank "folk" records until January 1944, and even then, it listed "most played" on jukeboxes, not record sales. Before then, the magazine published a list of recordings and artists, but it wasn't apparent how—or if—they were ranked. If Davis's version of "Sunshine" was the hit that some contend, it didn't appear in *Billboard* in 1940. The first mention of the song among the magazine's "Hillbilly and Foreign Record Hits of the Month" came in the July 27, 1940, edition about a version released by Bob Atcher and Bonnie Blue Eyes. In late September, Atcher's record earned another *Billboard* mention for "Sunshine," this time next to Davis's release of "You're Welcome as the Flowers in May." "Sunshine" appeared again in *Billboard* in late October, but it was the Pine Ridge Boys' version. In May 1941, more than a year after Davis released his recording, the song showed up once more in *Billboard,* identified as a hit by the Airport Boys, who recorded it in September 1940. In January 1942, the magazine listed Gene Autry's recording as one of the top hillbilly songs.[12]

Western-movie singing cowboy Gene Autry recorded a popular version of "Sunshine" in 1941. (National Portrait Gallery, Smithsonian Institution)

In 1941, Bing Crosby had a national hit with "Sunshine." (Wikimedia Commons)

In his impressive aggregation of song popularity information from 1900 through 1949, musicologist Edward Foote Gardner did not rank "Sunshine" as a 1940 pop hit. He lists the song (but no artist) as reaching tenth place in July 1941. Gardner shows the song charting from June through September and then again in November. But this was long after Davis released his version and a time when other artists—including Wilf "Montana Slim" Carter (1940), Lawrence Welk (April 1941), Bing Crosby (July 1941), and Gene Autry (July 1941)—had also released their versions.[13]

Country music historians Bill C. Malone and Tracey E. W. Laird didn't refer to "You Are My Sunshine" when commenting on Davis's popularity in the early 1940s in *Country Music USA.* But they noted that his music, along with that of Ernest Tubb and others, was popular on jukeboxes in bars and taverns in Baltimore, Detroit, Cincinnati, Chicago, and Washington, DC. This was especially so among migrants from Kentucky, West Virginia, Virginia, and Tennessee, who "poured into the areas and demanded music for their own tastes." Davis's version of the song may have been a hit on jukeboxes (which, by some estimates, accounted for about 40 percent of all record sales in those years) that didn't earn attention in the pages of music industry publications.[14]

When bandleader Wayne King released his version of "Sunshine" in 1940, and Crosby and Autry released theirs in 1941, they were recognized as hits. But, despite the legend about the song that grew in later years, there's little evidence that Davis's rendition took the country by storm. Davis's name didn't appear in *Billboard* associated with the song until March 7, 1941, when the magazine identified him as the "writer of *You Are My Sunshine.*" *Billboard* mentioned his recording in April 1942, noting, "Gene Autry and Jimmie Davis seem to be matching each other almost song for song in the report these weeks. Both boys' versions of *You Are My Sunshine* are showing high in the lists from the Midwest and the South."[15]

Davis may have sold a million copies of "Sunshine," but no contemporaneous evidence exists. Perhaps his singing the song in two movies in the early 1940s contributed to the notion that his version was a colossal hit. But those movies were not released until late 1942, almost three years after Davis made his first recording of the song. Some may have assumed Davis's recording was *the* hit version because people believed he was the song's creator. Crosby, and maybe Autry, had bigger success with "Sunshine," but neither owned the song or claimed to be its writer. Davis did and would until he died.

Davis wasn't even the first artist to bring "You Are My Sunshine" to the silver screen. Tex Ritter beat him by almost two years, singing it in *Take Me Back to Oklahoma,* released by Monogram Pictures in November 1940. Autry beat Davis by over a year, singing the song in *Back in the Saddle,* released by Republic Pictures in March 1941. He also sang it in his film released by Republic in May 1942, *Stardust on the Sage.*[16]

But Crosby's version of "Sunshine" in July 1941 attracted the most national attention. It was the most lavishly produced to date, including a creative lilting guitar intro by Perry Botkin and the lush sounds of Victor Young's Orchestra. (Botkin would play guitar on three of Davis's 1944 hits, "There's a New Moon over My Shoulder," "Is It Too Late Now," and "There's a Chill on the Hill Tonight.") By then the nation's most popular recording artist, Crosby sang in a tempo slower than Davis's, crooning in his familiar syncopated, casual style. "Unquestionably," *Billboard* declared in a review of Crosby's new single, "'You Are My Sunshine' is fast becoming the taproom and tavern classic of the year." Crosby's record peaked at nineteen on the national pop chart in August 1941.

Many in the music industry viewed Crosby's recording of "Sunshine" as proof that hillbilly songs were becoming genuine works of art that could be sung with orchestras and swing bands, as well as with guitars, fiddles, and banjos. As *Billboard* noted on August 23, 1941, "This hillbilly song is already an established phonograph seller. And now that Bing Crosby comes around with a record of it, the song will probably have an even longer life." Music historian Don Cusic argued that the "importance of Bing Crosby to country music has often been overlooked," explaining that by recording country songs, the crooner "helped establish country music as a legitimate source of material." In fact, Crosby's disc featured two "hillbilly" songs. The B-side of "Sunshine" was "Ridin' Down the Canyon (When the Desert Sun Goes Down)," a song Autry had performed in a 1935 movie, *Tumbling Tumbleweeds.*[17]

Davis said that he persuaded Crosby to record "Sunshine," insisting the singer hadn't known about the song until Davis showed him the sheet music. That's almost certainly not the case. The idea probably came from Decca Records founder Jack Kapp, who managed Davis's recording career and often recommended songs from other genres, especially country, to Decca pop artists like Crosby. Crosby trusted Kapp's judgment. "All the song pluggers that used to annoy the artists asked [Crosby] to record their song or sing them on the radio," Kapp's wife, Frieda, recalled. "But [Crosby] wouldn't. He would say, 'If Jack says I should do it, I'll do it.'" Crosby later said, "With Jack, I felt that I was in the hands of a friend and that whatever he told me to do was right."

Including "Sunshine," Crosby recorded at least a dozen country songs from 1940 to 1944. These included Floyd Tillman's "It Makes No Difference Now" in 1940, Ernest Tubb's "Walking the Floor over You" in 1942, Bill Nettles's "Nobody's Darlin' but Mine" in 1942, and a major hit in 1943 with the Andrews Sisters, "Pistol Packin' Mama" (a country hit first recorded by Al Dexter the same year). In 1946, Decca reissued the dozen songs in a six-disc compilation album, *Don't Fence Me In: Songs of the Wide Open Spaces.*[18]

Davis's day job in Shreveport city government didn't keep him off the stage and out of the recording studios and his local radio station. He continued hosting a half-hour music show on KWKH, now every Wednesday night at eight. He performed "every weekend and [made records] during my vacation period. I had a few fellows working as a band, and I'd book them easily. We didn't make much, but we made more than if we weren't working. It helped me pay out of debt." (Left unspoken was that Davis gave jobs on the Shreveport police force to members of his band.)[19]

In 1941, Davis recorded another twenty-five songs in four sessions in New York and Dallas, with "I'm Sorry Now" becoming a hit. Late March 1942 found him in Los Angeles on vacation, where he stumbled into even greater renown: a series of roles in Western movies. When Jack Kapp invited him to lunch in the Universal Studios commissary, Davis said he was surprised to learn that Universal Pictures executive Cliff Work and actress Deanna Durbin would join them. When Work asked Davis if he would like to sing in a movie, Davis stayed over the weekend for the Monday filming. The film was *Strictly in the Groove,* a musical starring Shemp Howard of the Three Stooges and Ozzie Nelson. Davis had no speaking part. His appearance came in the movie's last five minutes, and his role was to introduce the grand finale, a swing version of "Sunshine."

Dressed in a light-colored suit and holding a large Stetson hat, Davis led with a solemn, traditional version of his song that transitioned into a rip-roaring, upbeat swing interpretation led by the Dinning Sisters.

Sensing an opportunity for greater fame, Davis signed with an agent who found him a singing role in *Riding Through Nevada,* a Columbia Pictures Western starring Charles Starrett. This time, Davis sang "Sunshine" with a band that the producers called the Rainbow Ramblers. Between 1942 and 1950, Davis would have roles in seven movies, including his starring role in a 1947 biopic, *Louisiana.* His roles singing "Sunshine" in two films released in November 1942 solidified his association with the song. Having his song featured in the movies may not have earned him much money, even after Tex Ritter and Gene Autry sang it in their films. For example, when singer Ernest Tubb went to Hollywood in 1942 to sing several of his compositions—including "Walking the Floor over You"—in a Columbia Studios film the studio paid him only fifty dollars a song (in addition to one thousand dollars for his acting role). Regardless of what the studio paid Davis for the rights to his song and singing role, the prominence of "Sunshine" in the movies undoubtedly boosted his record and sheet music sales and jukebox plays.[20]

Movies were another vital outlet for songs, giving performers like Davis another opportunity for greater national publicity. "If you look at any list of the hit songs of the 1930s," longtime music industry executive Russell Sanjek observed in 1979, "virtually all of them . . . are songs from either Broadway or Tin Pan Alley or from Hollywood. Almost all of them had exposure in a movie." Appearing in movies, especially Westerns, also appealed to hillbilly artists for another reason: it broadened the genre's appeal by helping change the image of country singers from that of uncultured hillbillies to the more romantic cowboys.[21]

Autry had been the first hillbilly singer to become a singing movie cowboy, starring in his first Western, *In Old Santa Fe,* in 1934. By singing Western and hillbilly songs in his movies, the former telegraph operator from Oklahoma helped introduce country music to a broader audience. And he opened the studio doors to a generation of country performers to sing—and sometimes star—in movies. Those included Davis, Tex Ritter, Roy Rogers, Bob Wills, Red Foley, Eddy Arnold, and Ernest Tubb. *Grand Ole Opry* star Roy Acuff made a few movies but refused to wear cowboy costumes. "I *am* a hillbilly fiddler and singer," he insisted, "and if that's a crime, I'll have to plead guilty to it." Davis, however, didn't mind playing a cowboy, believing he fit the part. He was also proud that he could ride a horse without instruction.[22]

If the prospect of a full-time Hollywood career like Autry's beguiled Davis, the temptation to stay in California didn't last. "I always knew I belonged in Louisiana," he would say later. Within a few weeks of returning to Shreveport, he decided he wanted a different job. It was the one Huey Long used as a stepping stone to the Louisiana governor's office almost fifteen years earlier: one of three positions on Louisiana's Public Service Commission. Davis announced his candidacy for the north Louisiana seat in July, challenging the Long organization's incumbent, John S. Patton of Homer. As he had the year before, he took his band to rallies and other events. "It wasn't long before I found out that people just don't want to hear some long-winded speech," he explained after the campaign. "They have a much better time hearing a few words and then listening to some band music and a song or two." He beat Patton handily.[23]

The demands of campaigning for an office representing a third of the state hadn't stopped Davis from expanding his musical and theatrical sidelines. On August 15, 1942, he appeared on the *Grand Ole Opry,* the popular country music radio program broadcast from Nashville's WSM, where he sang "Sunshine" and "Sweethearts or Strangers." The same month, *Billboard* reported Davis was under contract with Columbia Pictures to sing more "prairie lullabies." In late November, he and his band went to Memphis to join Roy Acuff and other country singers at the fourth-annual Hillbilly Jamboree, attended by more than sixteen thousand country music fans. The event's sponsor billed Davis as the "nation's number one song writer." At the event, a local reporter asked Davis about rumors that he had higher political ambitions. "Do you intend running for governor to accompaniment of your hillbilly band?" Davis was cagey.

"I'm just going into my new office of public service commissioner in a few days, and I'd rather not forecast any further political plans now," he replied with what the reporter described as "a sly smile." But Davis was already considering the race. Indeed, by the following September, he and the band would launch a historic musical campaign for Louisiana governor.[24]

5

Easier to Sing Than to Talk

On the afternoon of September 15, 1942, about two hundred miles south of the eastern Solomon Islands, Japanese submarines prowling the South Pacific waters attacked a US Navy aircraft carrier group. Three kerosene-and-oxygen-fed Type 95 torpedoes fired from a Type B1 submarine struck the starboard side of the carrier USS *Wasp.* After about an hour, the crew evacuated the crippled ship, and later that night, US submarines shot torpedoes to sink the listing vessel. While the *Wasp* was under attack, sailors on a nearby destroyer, the USS *O'Brien*—nicknamed *Obie* by its crew—saw the explosions. Soon, they were also under attack. The destroyer sustained a strike from a single torpedo that, in the words of one journalist, "tossed her men about like chaff in a gale." No one died in the assault on the *O'Brien,* although there was a broken arm and some cracked ribs. The *O'Brien*'s crew determined their vessel wasn't sinking and could limp back to San Francisco for repairs. But the torpedo damaged the ship more than was first apparent. Soon, large cracks appeared in the hull. The ship's bottom opened and closed in the swells as if on hinges. On October 19, thirty-four days after the attack, the crew abandoned the *Obie.* Under clear skies, as the men hoisted life rafts over the side, someone began singing a song familiar to everyone onboard. The water vibrated with the sounds of "You Are My Sunshine."[1]

It was a song that American servicemen had sung for several years. Looking for ways to relate to the friendly people of the Pacific islands where they were stationed in the war's early months, soldiers and sailors there often shared their favorite songs. Among the most popular was "Sunshine." American Samoans embraced it almost immediately. It wasn't long before the servicemen considered it the islands' unofficial anthem.

Years later, some sailors claimed that their most vivid wartime memories from the islands included hearing the song sung by the Samoan people. "They really got into ["Sunshine"] and never tired of singing it," one American stationed at Pago Pago recalled. An American soldier who attended a local church service reported being surprised to hear congregants sing hymns to the tunes "Sunshine" and "I've Been Working on the Railroad."[2]

It wasn't only the people of American Samoa who loved it. America's fighting men and women took it to places like Hawaii, the Philippines, and England. "On the Allied side," the editors of *The Garland Encyclopedia of World Music* declared, "the most popular song may have been 'You Are My Sunshine.'" After a German U-boat torpedoed their ship en route to North Africa in February 1943, dozens of British nurses clambered into lifeboats. As they waited to be fished from the sea by nearby destroyers, some sang "Sunshine" to buoy their spirits. (Among them, eager to join the commander in chief of Allied Forces in North Africa, General Dwight D. Eisenhower, was a young Irish woman and the general's driver, Kay Summersby.)[3]

In 1943, as his US Navy patrol torpedo boat, *PT-244*, pulled onto a sandy beach on one of the Solomon Islands in the New Georgia Sound, crewman Bill Centro recalled, "We came upon quite an intriguing sight." It was a canoe with "eight muscular, sweaty, tall, dark natives, rowing in unison and singing at the top of their voices, 'You Are My Sunshine!'" Centro claimed it was the only "formal" entertainment he experienced during his twenty months at sea. "What a fine entertainment that was! Short but memorable."[4]

In 1944, stationed at a US Army base on Saipan in the Northern Mariana Islands in the western Pacific, folk singer Pete Seeger was eager to meet "the people who lived on this island before the Americans came." On Sundays, he and a friend visited the civilian enclosure. Strumming his trademark banjo, Seeger would "swap songs" with the children. He was not surprised to hear them sing "Sunshine." "Of course," he wrote at the time, "they have all learned [it] from the American soldiers."[5]

As a child on Saipan, Marie S. C. Castro rejoiced when US Marines expelled the Japanese invaders from her island in the summer of 1944. A Catholic nun and an educator in Kansas City for many years, Castro wrote in her 2014 memoir, *Without a Penny in My Pocket,* that she rejoiced at the sight and sound of a Marine Corps band that played for refugees living at Camp Susupe, calling it "a haven of our newfound freedom." And she remembered "the image of the handsome khaki-clad musicians beckoning us to join in the singing of *You Are My Sunshine*" and how "its catchy rhythm never failed to bring us to our feet, clapping hands and humming loudly as the band played on. Even today, because the Americans did in truth bring back the sunshine into our lives."[6]

Perhaps it was the uncomplicated lyrics that appealed to so many. Or was it the cheery chorus about fervent love? Maybe, for lonely servicemen and women, the words, "I dreamed I held you in my arms," resonated. Or, "If you leave me and love another," might have reassured them they weren't alone in fretting that relationships might not survive years of separation. (This was the theme of other popular country songs during the war, including Gene Autry's "I'll Be True When You're Gone," Ernest Tubb's "Rainbow at Midnight," and Patsy Montana's "Goodbye, Soldier.") Whatever the reason, "Sunshine" was easy to remember—a simple melody (only four lines with few variations) in a major key that required only three chords (C, F, and G). A soldier or sailor with rudimentary guitar or ukulele skills could play and teach it to others. And many did. As Canadian-born dance band leader Guy Lombardo once explained when asked about the popularity of his tunes: "Simple arrangements, simple beat, everything goes so easy." That's a perfect description of "Sunshine."[7]

Maybe that's why British prime minister Winston Churchill enjoyed the song so much. In January 1943, the British leader was in Casablanca for ten days of meetings with President Franklin D. Roosevelt. One morning, as Roosevelt trailed in a car, Churchill walked on a French Morocco beach. Marching along the shore with hands behind his back and chomping a cigar, he came upon a group of American soldiers singing to the sounds of a guitar. When the soldiers recognized the prime minister, they fell silent. "Don't stop, boys," Churchill insisted. "Sing something else for me." For a moment, the men seemed embarrassed until Churchill made his request: "You Are My Sunshine."[8]

Churchill knew the song because it was popular with US soldiers, sailors, and airmen in England and the British public. In Hull, in December 1942, members of the city's police dance orchestra hosted American soldiers at an evening concert in a local school auditorium. When the musicians played "Sunshine," the local newspaper reported, "the audience almost brought the rafters down as they joined in the choruses." On a train to London in October 1943, American journalist Raymond A. McConnell Jr. sat in a dark, crowded train car as it crept into the city during a German air raid. The car was full of soldiers, most of them American. Out of the darkness, McConnell recalled, "Some English service women in the car started singing 'You Are My Sunshine,' and the [American] soldiers took up the tune." As the soldiers sang, McConnell stole a glance through the train's blackout curtain. "You could see now and then the flash of gunfire in the distance."[9]

The British government had long used music to relieve the monotony of wartime factory work. Factory owners often piped radio broadcasts of choir and band concerts and other music onto factory floors. A recruit to the Women's Auxiliary Air Force in 1943 recalled her early days in training: "As we were herded from hut to hut, we were encouraged by our officers and NCOs to sing 'You Are My Sunshine.' Hundreds of very young, very homesick, very cold and miserable girls sang this song lustily."[10]

And it wasn't only soldiers, American or otherwise, who delighted in the song. In Manchester in March 1944, British authorities tried four people on witchcraft charges for holding an illegal séance. One defendant testified in court that the spirit of a woman named "Peggy" had asked those attending the ritual to sing "Sunshine." The self-professed medium, a dockworker from Southsea, reported that the group belted out the song. Among those also bellowing "Sunshine" were three young men arrested for disturbing the peace by singing it in the streets of Whitstable, Kent, at 8:20 p.m. on March 11, 1945. "All three were dismissed, under the Probation of Offenders Act," the local newspaper reported, "with a warning not to be rowdy again." A few days later, after midnight in Chesham, Buckinghamshire, police arrested four young men for wailing the song in the town's streets. The judge released the boys with a stern warning.[11]

England wasn't the only place where drunks and night owls shattered the peace with the now-famous song. In 1943, writing about the neighbors of a narrow street in Washington's Georgetown neighborhood, journalist Harriet Hughes Crowley described some boisterous, drunken residents who she said enjoyed singing "Sunshine" throughout the night. The street—then Bell's Court and now known as Pomander Walk—was an alley of ten tiny, dilapidated row houses. Several prominent journalists and US government officials lived around the corner. Crowley wrote:

> Nobody sleeps in Bell's Court. So nobody in the neighborhood does either. When it comes to physical endurance there isn't a man on the outskirts of the alley who can match the men and women of the court who start singing and playing before sundown and are still going strong when the sun comes up. . . . If [journalist] Walter Lippmann were to write a column on the engrossing subject "You Are My Sunshine," his neighbors, including myself, would not be surprised, but would understand and sympathize. Archibald MacLeish's house overlooks Bell's Court, and if his next volume of poems does not reflect the music of Georgetown and the relentless rhythm of the strumming of a washboard, it will be a great surprise to all of us who live near him.
>
> It is an accident of fate that has made "You Are My Sunshine" the symbol of riotous, sleepless nights in our section of Georgetown. One of the singers, a young girl with a high, plaintive voice, exists for the sole purpose of singing it. She is known to many of the picked brains of the country, assembled in Washington to plan the war, simply as "Sunshine" and her nightly renditions of her favorite song have brought many of them to the verge of nervous crackups.
>
> It was "Sunshine" who caused a naval commander and his wife to move out of their house, and, in spite of the fantastic overcrowding, embark on a weary search for a quieter diggings.

> It is "Sunshine" who made a back porch orator out of my husband. His personal appearances on the porch off our bedroom at 4 a.m. clad in pajamas to ask for peace and quiet are being resumed now that spring and bedlam are here. These unrehearsed outpourings occurred with such frequency last summer that by the end of July his drawing capacity was equal to that of a fifth rate travelogue.[12]

It sometimes seemed the song was on everyone's mind—the classic case of what we now call an "earworm," a catchy tune that bores into one's consciousness and plays constantly. The renowned war correspondent Ernie Pyle recalled a flight from North Africa to England in May 1944 on a converted British bomber with blacked-out windows. While most of his fellow passengers slept, Pyle sat in the darkened cabin and imagined he heard music playing. "Most everybody has some little quirk about traveling, and mine takes the form of airplane motors playing tunes," he wrote. "It's just as clear as though there were an orchestra in the cabin. And to me they always play 'You Are My Sunshine, My Only Sunshine.'" Pyle couldn't get the song out of his head. "And so out there over the ocean the motors of our big plane droned on and on with 'You Are My Sunshine,' and I couldn't go to sleep."[13]

In the early morning of June 6, 1944, Frederick Wright of the Royal Navy watched from a ship off Normandy as Allied battleships began bombarding the French coast to prepare for the Allied invasion of France. He heard singing as he and the Royal Engineers waited to launch their assault. "Our lads are singing 'You are my sunshine,'" he wrote in his diary. "Full of good spirits." More than a year later, a piano-playing US Army staff sergeant from Oklahoma, Herschel D. Root, reported to his local paper that "Sunshine" had become the most popular song in the Czechoslovakian village of Líšťany, where he was stationed with the US Army's Sixteenth Tank Battalion. Root reported playing the song often for fellow soldiers and townspeople who memorized it. "Now if the song is not forthcoming the children will soon begin to beg for it," his local newspaper reported, "and in the interest of friendly relations Root had to play it. Although few of them know what the words mean, they sing it in passable English and they seem fascinated by the tune and rhythm."[14]

While not weapons, songs like "Sunshine" were important tools in the Allied struggle during World War II—at home and abroad. Seeing entertainers from home, and hearing them sing popular songs, bolstered morale. In 1941, the United Service Organizations (USO) began sponsoring USO Camp Shows at hospitals and large and small military installations, including in the field in Europe and the Pacific, sometimes close to the front lines. More than seven thousand performers—including Bing Crosby, Bob Hope, Dinah Shore, Fred Astaire, Bob Wills, Minnie Pearl, and Pee Wee King—signed up to entertain the troops. Among the shows broadcast to soldiers by the Armed Forces Radio Service were recordings of the *Grand Ole Opry* and the *National Barn Dance.*[15]

More than eight million records by Crosby, Frank Sinatra, Glenn Miller, and dozens of others were shipped overseas by the US military on larger twelve-inch V-Disc label records (the *V* was for "victory"). Because of a strike by the American Federation of Musicians, many American record labels didn't make new records using instrumental music from August 1942 through 1944. (Decca, Davis's label, would reach an agreement with the union in September 1943.) V-Disc records—circulated only to the troops—were produced and distributed because they were transcriptions of live performances of previously recorded music. Country music records were in the minority of those shipped abroad, but the V-Disc catalogue included recordings by Gene Autry, Bob Wills and His Texas Playboys, Roy Acuff, Al Dexter, Ted Daffan, the Light Crust Doughboys, and the Hoosier Hot Shots. (Jimmie Davis never made a V-Disc record.)[16]

There were many country songs by noncountry artists, primarily Crosby, who recorded V-Disc versions of "The Last Roundup," "Empty Saddles," "Sioux City Sue," and "On the Sunny Side of the Street." In 1943, the US military released Crosby's swing version of "You Are My Sunshine," a transcription disc of an April 1, 1943, performance on his weekly NBC radio show, *Kraft Music Hall.* It would be the only version of the song released by V-Disc.[17]

In wartime, music is always far more than entertainment. It draws people closer, transcends cultural barriers, and gives average citizens and those on the battlefield a break from the monotony of war work or the horrors of battle.

Since the early days of the American republic, music has also been an integral part of political campaigns. Even before his first campaign for president, admirers of George Washington sang "God Save Great Washington" to the tune of "God Save the King." The 1840 presidential election featured a book of patriotic songs entitled *Tippecanoe Song Book,* supporting the eventual winner, William Henry Harrison. "No candidate for the office of the presidency was ever elected or defeated on the strength of a song," historian William Miles wrote in his comprehensive 1990 bibliography of American campaign songs, *Songs, Odes, Glees and Ballots.* "Few, however, have been without one to assist in their efforts. Indeed, since at least 1800, the campaign song has reappeared every four years to sing the praise of the candidate, excoriate the opposition, simplify the issues, and arouse the enthusiasm of the faithful for party and ticket." As Revolutionary-era Connecticut diplomat and poet Joel Barlow observed, "One good song is worth a dozen speeches or proclamations."[18]

Robert P. Letcher, a Kentucky congressman and friend to President John Quincy Adams, was known for his wry wit and fiddle-playing. "Often in the heat of angry and fierce debate," Adams observed, "he throws in a joke, which turns it all to good humor." Letcher used music when he ran for Kentucky governor in 1840 by entertaining crowds with his fiddle and taking song requests from audience members at gatherings. He won the election. Another accomplished fiddler, George M. Bibb, served as a US senator from Kentucky and, later, as US treasury secretary from 1844 to 1845. When serving as chief justice of the Kentucky Court of Appeals in the late 1820s, Bibb solidified political alliances by playing for legislative dances. "He kept the lawmakers in a giddier whirl with his fiddle bow than he ever did with decisions from the high bench," one historian noted. Fiddler Tom Watson played songs like "Mississippi Sawyer" and "Buffalo Gals" on the stump in his successful 1882 Georgia US House race.[19]

Huey Long campaigned for Louisiana governor in 1928 with the Leake County Revelers, a popular string band imported from Mississippi to entertain crowds at rallies in rural areas. Gene Austin, a popular singer from Yellow Pine, Louisiana, also performed at some Long rallies. Across the Sabine River, folksy Wilbert Lee "Pappy" O'Daniel of Fort Worth won the governorship of Texas in 1938 on the popularity of his Western swing band, Pat O'Daniel and His Hillbilly Boys. His statewide radio show and the band had first been vehicles to promote his company's Hillbilly Flour. The company's bags featured a lone billy goat over the words to a poem that O'Daniel said he had composed: "Hillbilly music on the air, Hillbilly Flour everywhere. It tickles your feet, it tickles your tongue. Wherever you go, its praises are sung." The band's popularity (the original unit included Western swing pioneers Bob Wills and Milton Brown) soon lured O'Daniel into politics. "O'Daniel was known in thousands of Texas homes," Bill Malone and Tracey Laird wrote, "where he was perceived as an almost fatherly presence and a quasi-populist champion of common people." He won the race.[20]

In Shreveport, a shrewd entertainer and emerging politician like Jimmie Davis surely noticed how O'Daniel exploited the fame his band and statewide radio show generated, as well as how he first used music to promote flour and then his candidacy. In quick succession, O'Daniel had won landslide victories for governor in 1938 and 1940 and a special election for US senator in 1941, beating then-congressman Lyndon Johnson. He won a full term in the Senate the following year.

In Baton Rouge in January 1943, Davis took his seat on the state's Public Service Commission, explaining to reporters that his method of stumping was preferable to the traditional mode of waging a campaign. "I'll tell you something about my campaigning," he told a reporter. "It wasn't long before I found out that people just don't want to hear some long-winded speech. They have a much better time hearing a few words and then listening to some band music and a song or two. And I don't mind saying I find it a whole lot easier to sing than to talk." It was also the case that Davis was uninterested in the finer details of public policy. He once admitted that after leaving LSU, he rarely read a book, and he got much of his information by flipping through newspapers and magazines. Like many successful politicians in every era, he was far more interested in the performance part of the business and less attracted to governing and policy formulation.[21]

What Davis had done—singing his way into two public offices—was fine for one of the more rural regions of the state. But could a quick speech, followed by some spirited hillbilly music, work in a governor's race in Louisiana as it had in Kentucky, Georgia, and Texas? By September 1943, when Davis announced his candidacy for Louisiana governor, he was ready to find out.

6

How in the Devil Can You Fight a Song?

The two movies Davis made in 1942—*Strictly in the Groove* and *Riding Through Nevada*—began appearing in theaters around the time of his election to the state's Public Service Commission in the spring of 1943. While boosting his renown, they were also reminders that the new commissioner's devotion to his elected position was questionable. And as his name appeared in newspaper stories about the coming governor's election, he surely understood that he might be ill-advised to run for another office so soon—especially when it seemed that his new job was a sideline to a recording and movie career.

For Davis, a politically helpful result of the nationwide American Federation of Musicians' strike that began August 1, 1942, was that he could not make new records until Decca reached an agreement with the union. His most recent recording session had been on July 27, 1942, four days before the strike. He wouldn't enter a studio again until March 1944.[1]

In early 1943, opportunities to make new records were behind him (for now), while the enticing opportunity of a governor's race lay ahead. The election to replace Governor Sam Jones—a term-limited self-styled "reformer" who beat Earl Long in a close race in 1940—wouldn't be held until January 1944. However, by the spring and summer of 1943, potential candidates were jockeying for positions. Jones wanted a successor who would preserve his policies, which included creating a civil service system for state workers and repealing many of the authoritarian measures enacted by Huey Long and his successors in the 1930s. But he was reluctant to expose himself to the charge that, like Long, he had created a political machine. That did not mean he was without ideas about a suitable replacement. And that was Jimmie Davis.

Davis had ample government experience and had won two campaigns in a region of Louisiana that often provided the winning margin in statewide races. He was a bona fide celebrity who could charm audiences with his songs. Neither an ally of the Long organization nor an established member of the anti-Longs, Davis was ideally situated in the state's political spectrum. He could argue that he was a candidate who, because he belonged to no faction, might unify the state after almost fifteen years of tumult. Voters' desire for less drama in Baton Rouge was especially acute after 1939–40, when dozens of state officials, including Governor Richard Leche, went to prison in a wide-ranging scandal that enveloped the Long organization and prominent Louisiana State University officials. Writing about the race, historian Mark T. Carleton observed that Jones's organization searching outside their circle was evidence that "they themselves and what they really represented were dangerously unpopular in Louisiana," and they needed someone with charisma to save them from the Long organization.[2]

While some have framed the era as a struggle between the Longs and the "reformers," journalist A. J. Liebling correctly observed in 1960 that Louisiana political contests were between Longs and anti-Longs. The Long faction, he wrote, favored "a welfare state, soaking the oil companies and sharing the spoils." Meanwhile, the anti-Longs "fought chiefly to lick the Longs and get a share of the gravy." The "reformers" didn't favor reform as much as they opposed the Longs. "Neither side espoused rigid philosophies of government," historians Michael L. Kurtz and Morgan D. Peoples maintained, "the main distinction being their desire to win elections." As a Baton Rouge attorney quipped, "Reform in Louisiana consists of turning the fat hogs out and letting the lean hogs in."[3]

As early as February 1943, Davis's name surfaced as a potential candidate for governor. "Davis isn't talking out loud but he has a glint in his eyes and an ambition in his mind that reveals that he would like to be the state's chief executive," columnist Rupert Peyton wrote in the *Shreveport Journal* on February 25, adding that "it's no deep dark secret that Jimmie has the boys [the other possible candidates] worried." Davis claimed he was, at first, reluctant. "I didn't want to run for governor," he said in 1985, "because I was working in a few Western pictures, and I was recording and playing dates and making money. I had money in the bank for the first time, and I knew I couldn't do that by being governor if I played the game straight." When Jones sent emissaries to Shreveport to assess the new public service commissioner's ambitions, Davis rebuffed them. Jones persisted, and Davis agreed to meet the governor at a camp on Lake Bruin in Tensas Parish. Davis told Jones he worried that he knew little about the oil and gas business and would expose himself to scandal when setting industry policies. He also hesitated to lead a state government that might overrule local law enforcement officials in prosecuting illegal gambling. Jones responded that the State Mineral Board would set energy policies and added, "I guess the best thing on [gambling] is just to let [locals] handle their own business."[4]

Davis said he told Jones he didn't want the governor's public support because "I don't believe the people will go for the show of a lot of power." And he said he promised to quit the race if Jones ever publicly endorsed him. Jones claimed he remained neutral because of his aversion to political machines. Regardless, running without Jones's endorsement would prove wise, allowing Davis to attract votes from Long organization supporters who disdained Jones.[5]

While he pondered Jones's entreaties, Davis went to Hollywood to sing in another film, *Frontier Fury,* a Western starring Charles Starrett, released in June 1943. And he made personal appearances on weekends, including headlining the so-called *World's Championship Hillbilly Jamboree* at Galveston's City Auditorium on May 8 and two shows the next day in Houston's Sam Houston Coliseum. He visited the city's Stage Canteen between performances to entertain armed services personnel.[6]

By September, whatever concerns he had about the governor's race vanished. He announced his campaign in a prepared statement on September 11, his forty-fourth birthday. He wanted to work for "unity and harmony among all groups and factions in this state." And he stressed his independence. "Not having been aligned in the past with any faction and seeking this office as an independent candidate," Davis said, "I feel that I can, to a great extent, reconcile the views and coordinate the efforts of all political groups to the end that we may better meet the great problems which are out far from our threshold." In a nod to the song that had earned worldwide renown and that he encouraged people to believe he had written, Davis added, "I shall do all in my power to bury the hates and distrusts of the past and raise the curtain that will let in the sunshine of Louisiana's future greatness."

Davis promised "adequate" old-age pensions and "social welfare," free schoolbooks, preserving the civil service system, and continued highway construction and maintenance. Except for civil service, the Long organization instituted and supported these policies. By the time of Davis's candidacy, they were also programs no astute politician would oppose. Beyond supporting the status quo and advancing unity, he pledged not to make many promises. "I do not believe our citizens desire that any candidate make promises impossible of fulfillment, and I do not intend to make any such promises," he said. "On the contrary, I do intend to advocate and support a sound, sensible and businesslike program for the development of what was once the richest state in the union and which can be made so again." When describing Davis's announcement, most Louisiana newspapers identified him as the state's new public service commissioner and the "composer" or "author" of "You Are My Sunshine."[7]

It would be a crowded field. At first, Earl Long had announced he would run again. As lieutenant governor, Long became governor in June 1939 when Richard Leche resigned in disgrace. Long failed to win a full term in 1940. When his organization couldn't unify around him in 1943, he ran for lieutenant governor on a pro-Long ticket headed by sixty-seven-year-old Lewis Morgan of St. Tammany Parish, a former district attorney and a US congressman of questionable health and uncertain stamina. Davis and Morgan would emerge as the two leading candidates. But the race would also include flamboyant US representative James H. "Jimmy" Morrison of Hammond, who ran a campaign for governor in 1940 that included staging a thirty-five-float "convict parade" in New Orleans that featured dozens of friends behind bars and dressed in stripes depicting convicted Long organization officials. Morrison also campaigned with a monkey he named "Earl Long." There would be no monkey or convict parades this time, but, ever the showman, Morrison would try matching Davis by hiring a band to attract crowds.[8]

Also running were anti-Long candidates Shreveport mayor Sam S. Caldwell, who pledged to free local governments "from domination from Baton Rouge," state senator Dudley J. LeBlanc of Abbeville, and Opelousas lawyer Vincent Moseley. Another pro-Long candidate was state senator Ernest S. Clements of Oberlin.[9]

Decades later, Davis would recall his first rally of the race in the fall of 1943. "My first speaking engagement was in [Allen] Park in Shreveport," he said. "There was about two thousand people in the park that night to see what was happening. I spoke a long, long time. I just jacked the world up and put blocks under it. I just fixed it up like everybody would want it." Davis said that when he finished, some in the crowd asked him to sing. "Women came with their children unfed, dishes unwashed, cow unmilked," he said. "They had come to hear me sing. I said this wasn't a singing matter. They said, 'Well, he's a big shot; he's gone high hat on us.'" Davis claimed he went home and told his wife, "I'm getting my band together."[10]

There's no evidence of such a rally in Shreveport in 1943. Davis's first campaign event after his announcement was a radio address on October 14, carried over stations in Shreveport, Baton Rouge, Lake Charles, Alexandria, Lafayette, New Orleans, Monroe, and Natchez, Mississippi. And his first rally came on October 23 in Jonesboro, near his birthplace. Later that day, he held events in Ruston and Arcadia. At all three, Davis spoke before he and his seven-piece band entertained the crowds with music and song.[11]

Davis told this story in 1984, forty years after the race, so he may have conflated the response he claimed he received at his first rally for Shreveport's public safety commissioner at Allen Park in the Allendale section of the city, where he held several rallies during the 1938 race. Davis had addressed a gathering there on August 4, 1938, less than three weeks after he announced his candidacy for the citywide office. But, as it wasn't an event sponsored by his campaign and six of his opponents also spoke at the same forum, it may have been inappropriate for Davis and his band to provide entertainment. And it's unlikely anyone in attendance expected him to sing at a gathering of this kind. A week later, however, Davis spoke to the Friends of Huey Long at the Municipal Hall in the Cedar Grove neighborhood. At this meeting, he and his band performed for a sizable crowd.[12]

It's not likely he held an event in 1938 or 1943 where audience members begged a reluctant Davis to sing. In fact, from the beginning, Davis was eager to use his band at rallies. After all, his initial foray into politics in 1928 had included singing at campaign events for a Shreveport city judge. Perhaps, in later years, Davis hoped reporters, historians, and

Davis speaks to a crowd in DeQuincy from a flatbed trailer as he campaigns for Louisiana governor in 1944. (Louisiana Digital Library)

others would believe he exploited his fame for political purposes reluctantly and only after his supporters demanded it. But Davis always knew his musical renown would help him on the stump. No one had to persuade him of this.

His first rally in Jonesboro established a familiar pattern that Davis followed throughout the campaign. The seven-piece band would arrive in a truck outfitted with loudspeakers that announced the rally. Once a crowd gathered, band members quickly unfolded the sides of a trailer that became a stage. They set up speakers, fired up a portable generator, tuned their instruments, and began playing lively songs. After a few minutes of music to draw a bigger crowd at most rallies, the guitar player and master of ceremonies, Joe Shelton (his real last name was Attlesey), kicked off the speaking part of the rally. Shelton was an attraction in his own right. He and his brother, Bob, were a well-known duo, the Shelton Brothers, who also performed in a band known as the Sunshine Boys. The Sheltons were among the most prolific country acts on the Decca label in the late 1930s and early 1940s. After Shelton introduced Davis, the candidate would deliver brief remarks, rarely lasting more than fifteen minutes. Davis was almost always light on policy specifics and heavy on broad themes of unity and civility. "I could stand here tonight and promise you the world with a fence around it," he often said. "But I won't make promises I can't keep." In almost every speech, he included some variation of:

> I am accused of being a backwoods hillbilly country yodeling singer. I'll admit that I love music and always will, and I am not going to let a political campaign stop me. If I can bring a little sunshine to anyone in their way down through the pathway of life, then I am happy. I think we need more singing in this old world. One thing is that when people are singing, they are not fighting. I think that if the dictators of the world would lay down their guns for three minutes and start to sing some good old song, they would not pick them up again. Honestly, friends, if I could after this meeting, I would like to join with you and go back down to the old country home and gather around

the old organ with the uncles, aunts, cousins, and friends and sing some good old songs like, "Blessed Be the Tie That Binds."

Then, he often asked audience members to join hands while he led them in singing the well-known Christian hymn:

Blest be the tie that binds
our hearts in Christian love;
the fellowship of kindred minds
is like to that above.

Before our Father's throne
we pour our ardent prayers;
our fears, our hopes, our aims are one,
our comforts and our cares.

We share our mutual woes,
our mutual burdens bear,
and often for each other flows
the sympathizing tear.

When we are called to part,
it gives us inward pain;
but we shall still be joined in heart,
and hope to meet again.[13]

Often, he would punctuate his sentiment about unity with the assertion that people should "live and let live." And that would cue the band to strike up again, and Davis would sing one of his hit songs, "Live and Let Live." The song was about lost love, but few in the audience noticed the dissonance. Sometimes, Davis would talk about ensuring adequate benefits for returning soldiers after the war. To that, he would deliver a tear-jerker like "Soldier's Last Letter." The song signaled a profound concern for the well-being of the men in uniform without the need to provide spe-

Davis and his campaign band perform somewhere in Louisiana during the 1943–1944 governor's race. The band was one of the best in country music. *Left to right:* Charles Mitchell, Jimmy Thomason, Joe Attlesey (stage name Joe Shelton), Moon Mullican, Davis, Zeke Clemons, William "Curly" Perrin, and Johnny Gimble. (Harry Pennington Jr. Photography Collection, Harry Ransom Center, The University of Texas at Austin)

cifics about what he proposed or how he would pay for it. When touting his support for old-age pensions, Davis crooned another song guaranteed to prompt a tear or two, "The Boy Who Never Grew Too Old to Comb His Mother's Hair." Davis and the band often played Cajun numbers, including "Big Mamou" and "Jole Blon," at rallies in south Louisiana.[14]

After his brief speech and several songs, Davis turned the program over to his band, each member dressed in Western garb, including large white cowboy hats. The band was an impressive, accomplished unit, arguably one of the best groups in country music at the time: Charles Mitchell (steel guitar), Joe Shelton (guitar and mandolin), Moon Mullican (piano), Jimmy Thomason (fiddle), William "Curly" Perrin (guitar and vocals), Zeke Clemons (bass), and Johnny Gimble (banjo and fiddle). The band sometimes included Bob Shelton, Cajun string-band musicians

Oran "Doc" Guidry and Leroy "Happy Fats" LeBlanc, and brothers Leo and Randall "Red" Raley, on leave from Cliff Bruner's Texas Wanderers. Davis later said he sought to hire not only good musicians but also men who "were good at shaking hands and meeting people."[15]

Shelton wasn't the only band member popular with audiences. Davis's band featured a seventeen-year-old banjo player, Johnny Gimble, from Tyler, Texas. Also an accomplished fiddle and electric mandolin player, Gimble would join Bob Wills's Texas Playboys in the late 1940s and play fiddle with him off and on through the early 1960s. Gimble's mournful fiddle would be heard at the beginning of one of Wills's biggest hits, "Faded Love," released in 1950. In the late 1960s, Gimble settled in Nashville and became one of his generation's most honored and influential country fiddle players, touring with Willie Nelson and winning two Grammy awards with the Western swing group Asleep at the Wheel. In 1999, he would be installed, along with Wills and the Texas Playboys, into the Rock and Roll Hall of Fame. In 2018, he would be elected posthumously to the Country Music Hall of Fame.

Thomason, a Shelton Brothers' band member, had also recorded with Ernest Tubb, including playing rhythm guitar on Tubb's April 1941 recording session that produced several hits, including "Walking the Floor over You" and "I Wonder Why You Said Goodbye." Perrin was a veteran of prominent Western swing bands, including the Light Crust Doughboys and Bill Boyd and His Cowboy Ramblers.[16]

But no band member earned more applause than Aubrey Wilson "Moon" Mullican, a well-known, high-energy, thirty-four-year-old honky-tonk "piano-pounding wild man" from Corrigan, Texas, who began performing in East Texas saloons and bordellos at age sixteen. He had already played with several popular groups, including the Blue Ridge Playboys and Cliff Bruner's Texas Wanderers. Mullican and Bruner, a gifted fiddle player, had performed and recorded with Davis in the early 1940s before decamping to Port Arthur, Texas, where they and their band, the Showboys, performed at the Lighthouse Club and on a daily program on KPAC radio. Mullican was also a talented songwriter and vocalist whose dynamic barrelhouse piano style, he once boasted, could

Moon Mullican was an energetic piano and accordion player and a gifted songwriter who later joined the *Grand Ole Opry*. Mullican was a popular member of Davis's band during the 1944 gubernatorial campaign. Here, to Davis's delight, Mullican performs a solo during a campaign rally in 1943. (Harry Pennington Jr. Photography Collection, Harry Ransom Center, The University of Texas at Austin)

"make them goddam beer bottles bounce on the table." His patented three-finger playing style involved dancing along the treble keys with his right hand while his left hand pounded out a bluesy, syncopated boogie-woogie bass line.

Later known as the King of the Hillbilly Piano Players—and an artist singer Jerry Lee Lewis would cite as a significant influence on his frenetic musical style—Mullican would score seven top-ten country hits from 1947 to 1951. He would join the cast of the *Grand Ole Opry* in 1951. In early 1952, Mullican and his *Opry* costar Hank Williams wrote Williams's most-recorded song, "Jambalaya (On the Bayou)," a composition whose tune was almost certainly inspired by a popular Cajun song, "Big Texas," recorded in 1948 by Chuck Guillory and His Rhythm Boys of Mamou, Louisiana. (Variations of the tune had floated around south Louisiana since the late 1920s.) That and other country hits Mullican wrote in the

1940s and 1950s would merit his election to the Nashville Songwriters Hall of Fame in 1976.

Davis recalled that when he resolved to use his band for campaign events, his first decision was to invite Mullican back into the fold. He chartered a plane to Port Arthur to plead with the piano player to rejoin the unit. Mullican, who some recalled worshipped Davis, jumped at the opportunity. It also helped that Davis offered Mullican ten thousand dollars. Bruner said he rejected a similar offer from Davis. (After the campaign, Mullican reportedly invested his earnings in ten slot machines he placed in dance halls around south Louisiana. He went broke when the machines disappeared, apparently targeted by a gambling syndicate that had not approved Mullican's venture.)

Mullican's presence in the band was an electrifying experience. Especially admired in southwestern Louisiana, he improvised lyrics to popular songs, adapting them to campaign themes. He also played the accordion and, during some songs, would dance into the crowd while singing—to the tune of "That's What I Like about the South"—a retooled song he called "That's What I Like about Jimmie."[17]

That was the positive side of Mullican's presence in the troupe. The flip side was his propensity for heavy drinking. (Some believe he earned his nickname because of a taste for moonshine whiskey.) Davis made the early mistake of giving Mullican a partial payment up front. But after a rally in Monroe, the piano player vanished for two days. The campaign found him staggering down a dirt road, absent his money, his shirt, and one of his boots. He had been binge drinking with a woman he met in town. "I never paid Moon in advance again," Davis said.[18]

At a Ruston rally in October, Mullican astonished the audience with his riotous rendition of a novelty song, "The Baptizing of Sister Lucy Lee," which a *New Orleans Times-Picayune* reporter wrote, "literally stopped the show." What really ended every show was Davis's version of "You Are My Sunshine." As he sang, many in the audience would join him. They knew every word. From beginning to end, a rally lasted about forty-five minutes. "Davis used songs as tools to emphasize his political stances in lieu of long or detailed speeches," Davis biographer Kevin S.

Fontenot wrote. "There was no overt political message in any of the songs Davis sang at his rallies, but when combined with a brief speech, they were political dynamite." Davis's campaign style would later prompt Governor Sam Jones to comment that Davis was "not a good candidate, but he was a good campaigner."[19]

Davis and his band scoured the state for votes. In one five-day stretch in early November, he held events in seventeen towns. A typical day in southeastern Louisiana was 10:30 a.m. in Gonzales, 1:00 p.m. in White Castle, 4:00 p.m. in Donaldsonville, and 8:00 p.m. in St. Francisville. It was a sometimes-brutal schedule, made even more challenging by government-mandated gasoline and tire rationing because of the war. "You could hardly get tires or gas or anything," Davis recalled. "People would give me their gas tickets. And give me a car to use and, sometimes, tires. Otherwise, I couldn't have bought them myself to make the trip."[20]

While those who attended his rallies might have loved Davis's singing, his opponents ridiculed the practice as evidence that he was a lightweight. "Jimmie is a nice boy and a nice singer," Earl Long, who did most of the public campaigning for his organization's ticket, scoffed in early October, "but it takes more than that to be governor." Sam Caldwell, the Shreveport mayor, was particularly contemptuous. "One of the candidates in this race served on a commission council with me in Shreveport," he said at Bogalusa in late November, "and I have not and will not . . . say anything against this man's character, but I can honestly say that his best accomplishments are singing and playing a guitar." A few weeks later, Caldwell asked a gathering in Lake Providence, "Do the people of Louisiana want to become the laughingstock of other states? If so, all they must do is to elect a crooner of sweet nothings to the highest and most dignified office within their gift."[21]

The *Shreveport Times* supported Caldwell's attacks on Davis and ran a scathing editorial on November 28, attacking him as lacking the executive experience to serve as governor. The paper said that while he served as the city's public service commissioner, Davis was absent from 20 percent of all the city's council meetings. The editors also ridiculed Davis's claim that he had written, or cowritten, "You Are My Sunshine."

> As a result of reports that he did not write this song but bought it and then feasted on the glory of supposedly having written it, we asked Mr. Davis by long-distance telephone to New Orleans for the facts. He replied, "Some of us worked together on it" and identified "some of us" as a man named Charley [*sic*] Mitchell and then added that "a fellow named Rice also worked on it—Paul Rice." In printed copies of the song there is no mention of Paul Rice—nor of his brother, Hoke Rice, who has been credited in some quarters with having been a part author of the song. . . . It may simply be unfortunate for Jimmy [*sic*] Davis that he never has had any experience for the high post of governor for which the [Sam Jones organization has] picked him, but the facts seem unalterably clear that his chief claim to fame has been that he sang his way to glory on the song credited to him in the public mind but which actually was the work of "a couple of other fellows" also!
>
> Whether "You Are My Sunshine" is 33 1/3 per cent Jimmy [*sic*] Davis's or whether some greater or lesser percentage would be correct, what Louisiana will need in the governor's chair in the coming war or post-war years will not be 33 1/3 per cent sunshine or 20 per cent absenteeism, but 100 per cent capable, independent, administrative and executive ability. There is nothing in Jimmie Davis's record to show any percentage as to those essential qualifications.[22]

Davis did not respond to these attacks on his record or character. "If lambasting my opponents, their families or mudslinging is necessary to win," he said on November 29 in Covington, "then I don't want the job."[23]

His opponents kept up the pressure. Hoping to turn Davis's most famous song into an object of scorn, Morrison had his band play the tune of "You Are My Sunshine" and added new lyrics, which began, "Oh, Jimmie Davis, you'll be defeated." The number attracted scant attention but generated a response from the players in Cajun artist Leo Soileau's Rhythm Band, whom Morrison hired to entertain crowds at rallies in Acadiana. The band's drummer, Crawford Vincent, confessed later that the musicians only helped Morrison for the money. Everyone in the band voted for Davis "because he was one of us." A Decca recording artist and pioneer of Cajun music, Soileau made clear his and the band's loyalties. In Cajun French, he sometimes announced, "Folks, I'm gonna play a song by my friend Jimmie Davis. You all know who he is, and you all vote for him on election day." Then, the group would play a Davis song that Soileau had also recorded, "Columbus Stockade Blues" or "Nobody's Darling." As Vincent explained, "The crowd knew what was going on. Leo was pluggin' Morrison's opponent. But [Morrison] couldn't speak French, so he never knew."[24]

Davis's music threatened to cause him other, more severe problems. His opponents would uncover and try to exploit the series of risqué blues songs he had recorded in the early 1930s. No one was better equipped for such ridicule than Morrison, whose showmanship was exceeded only by that of Davis and, perhaps, Earl Long. In December, Morrison held a rally at Shreveport's Caddo Parish Courthouse, to which he invited the public to hear examples of Davis's scandalous, bawdy songs. When Morrison played Davis's "Red Nightgown Blues"—about a promiscuous woman who molests her fiancé—he expected the crowd to be repulsed. He didn't count on Davis's campaign seeding the audience with supporters who were told to dance. Soon, most in the audience were swaying to the song. An angry Morrison tossed the record player off the stage and mocked the gathering, "Well, go ahead and elect the son of a bitch, then."[25]

Morrison wasn't the only opponent to attack Davis for suggestive lyrics. In late December, Lewis Morgan's campaign published a broadsheet called the *Monroe Times,* which resembled a legitimate newspaper. The front-page banner headline screamed, "JUKE-BOX JIM PLANS JIVE JOB AS GOVERNOR." One story claimed, "Juke Box Jimmie Davis . . . has made arrangements to take care of his Hollywood moving picture contracts in the event he is elected governor. Juke Box Jimmie has agreed . . . to name a committee of five to run the governor's office while he is out of the state making movies and juke box records."[26]

In January 1944, Morgan supporters placed an ad in the *Baton Rouge Advocate* attacking Davis for recording songs like "High Geared Mama" and "Bed Bug Blues," the words "to which songs cannot be repeated over the air." Morgan's campaign was probably the source of a similar broadsheet flier attaching Davis that circulated around the state. Headlined "FOR MEN ONLY," it contained the lyrics of both songs with the admonition, "Do not allow this circular to be read by women and children." Later in January, Morgan ran a large ad in the same paper with the headline, "Indisputable Proof That Jimmie Davis Composed, Recorded and Sung the Salacious Song 'Bed Bug Blues.'" The ad featured a photograph of the Decca Records disc. "The good citizens of this parish," the ad stated, "will not place their stamp of approval on Jimmie Davis or any other Candidate for Governor whose utter disregard for public morals and decency permits him to compose and sing suggestive songs that materially contribute to juvenile delinquency and the destruction of public morals." That month, another opponent, Ernest Clements, attacked Davis in New Orleans as a "fine singer" but added that "any man who would compose 'The Bed Bug Blues' and songs of that type is not fit to be governor of the state."[27]

Running for lieutenant governor, Long hoped to help his running mate, Lewis Morgan, by convening a group of ministers at a New Orleans hotel to play "Bed Bug Blues." He expected righteous outrage. Instead, one pastor reportedly cried, "Praise the Lord; Jimmie Davis is a man who used to be on the wrong side of the fence, and now he's seen the light! Thank the Lord!" In a 1970 speech to a Louisiana Bandmasters convention, Davis lamented, "This one, I wish I had never recorded because this is the only song certain people mentioned when I was running for governor."[28]

In their attacks on his music, Davis's opponents were limited. They couldn't print the lyrics in the newspaper or recite them on the radio or at rallies. Most voters had to take their word about how much they might offend. Davis, meanwhile, had his impressive, professional band with whom he sang hymns and other wholesome songs, including the climax of every rally, "You Are My Sunshine." Long had summed up the other candidates' frustration well. In February 1943, months before Davis announced his candidacy, Long made it clear how hard it would be for opponents to puncture Davis's righteous persona. "You can't fight Jimmie," he said. "How in the devil can you fight a song?"[29]

Shortly before the election, Roy Acuff, Davis's friend and the top star of the *Grand Ole Opry,* paid homage to the candidate. "This is for Jimmie Davis down in Louisiana," Acuff said one night on the *Opry* to his national audience, including thousands tuning in from Louisiana. Then, he sang "Sunshine." It wasn't, technically, an endorsement, but the message was unmistakable to even the most casual Louisiana listener.[30]

Davis's opponents didn't know about another aspect of his recording career that might have been more damaging than risqué lyrics: the records he'd made with Black musicians. Had they known, it's difficult to imagine they wouldn't have made race-mixing an issue. At least one detractor learned about Davis's early collaborations. In Shreveport, someone defaced a Davis billboard with graffiti and wrote in the names of Black artists Louis Armstrong and Lena Horne as supposed running mates.[31]

None of it made a difference. In late January 1944, Davis won a plurality of Democratic votes in the party primary. He led Morgan 167,000 votes to 131,000, carrying forty-four of the state's sixty-four parishes. During the runoff for the nomination—tantamount to victory in the general election—LeBlanc was the only former opponent to endorse Davis. Morgan and his supporters didn't go down without a fight. A former state judge allied with Morgan claimed that Long and Davis had agreed that Davis would resign if elected governor. Long would become governor, and Davis would return to Hollywood to continue his movie career. There's no evidence that the two men ever discussed such an arrangement, and both denied it.

Davis won the nomination with 54 percent of the vote. All the other anti-Long, so-called "reform" candidates also won their campaigns. Sam Jones called it a "great victory for clean government."[32] Davis's election made most newspapers nationwide, if for no other reason than his association with "Sunshine." Not all the coverage was positive. "Jimmie H. Davis, known as the author of the song, 'You Are My Sunshine,' will be Louisiana's next governor," the *St. Louis Post-Dispatch* sneered in an editorial. "We predict that after Mr. Davis has served his term, he will still be known as the author of 'You Are My Sunshine.'" In Michigan, the *Grand Rapids Press* noted that while musicians in politics weren't new, it wasn't ideal. "It would seem, nevertheless, that a state should so live that it never would have to choose a hillbilly musician as the lesser of two evils in a race for high office."[33]

Not all the press commentary was disparaging. Celebrating Davis's election, the *Bunkie Record* noted that friends and admirers from across the country congratulated him. "Lots of the people," the paper concluded, "now are glad to look him in the face and say 'You Are My Sunshine.'"[34]

7

We Just Hung Around Jimmie

Davis became governor on May 9, 1944, before a crowd of ten thousand at the Louisiana Capitol. His band attended the inauguration in Western garb but did not play for these ceremonies. No one was surprised, however, that the new chief executive assigned them places of honor near his box. Upon arrival, Davis greeted the musicians before he acknowledged the dignitaries. "They must be here," he explained. "I wouldn't be myself without them."[1]

Though no one sang "You Are My Sunshine" at the swearing-in, Istrouma High School Band members played the song for Davis as they marched in that morning's parade. And at a dance that night in LSU's Huey P. Long Field House, the crowd begged Davis to sing "Sunshine." He obliged after attendees agreed to join him in the chorus. "Campus walls vibrated with the governor's most famous hillbilly song," the *Baton Rouge State-Times* reported. Davis's band provided entertainment across town at the Governor's Mansion. "The boys didn't play in the parade," the paper noted, "but they cut loose at the mansion reception, swinging out with old-time favorites, including the inevitable 'You Are My Sunshine.'"[2]

Soon, Davis would find state jobs for band members in the governor's office and the state Office of Civilian Defense (OCD). He gave fiddler Jimmy Thomason an "equipment inspector" position at OCD. By December, Thomason's supervisor would report that he hadn't seen him at work for four months. At first, Davis placed guitar player and vocalist Joe Shelton (his legal name was Joseph Attlesey) in his office but moved him to the OCD payroll in September. J. C. Compton, who managed the band's sound equipment, got an OCD job. Davis made Charles Mitchell, the band's leader and erstwhile "coauthor" of "Sunshine," his executive assistant. He paid him five hundred dollars a month. Davis would later make Mitchell the director of the Division of Health and Hospitals. Except for Mitchell's, the jobs were temporary. By year's end, most of the band had left state employment.[3]

To those who wondered if Davis would divide time between making music and movies and running Louisiana government, he promised his priority was the governor's job. "Making the Westerns was fun," he said two months before taking office, "but my state, like others, is faced with problems I'm afraid won't leave me much time for even fishing." Despite what he said about pausing his entertainment career, he wouldn't pass up an opportunity for a recording session or a good excuse for a performance. In early June, he and the band appeared at the LSU Agricultural Center Coliseum (now the John M. Parker Agricultural Coliseum) to perform at the Quiz Kids war bond show. Davis and First Lady Alvern Davis hosted a reception for lawmakers at the Governor's Mansion during his first legislative session, where he and his band were the featured entertainment. "He can bear down on 'You Are My Sunshine' without sacrificing gubernatorial dignity," the *Baton Rouge State-Times* reported. At the session's end, House members demanded an appearance by the governor. Davis and the band served up "Sunshine" and "It Makes No Difference Now" in the House chamber. Then, they crossed the Capitol and serenaded senators, too.[4]

In July 1944, he took the band to the Democratic National Convention in Chicago, where he and the group performed for a gathering of the Louisiana, Texas, and Mississippi delegations. "Now, I have been succeeded by a man whose golden voice and kindly deportment has inspired our people to drop their haggling," former governor Sam Jones said, introducing Davis and his band. "Life is sweeter and better for Jimmie Davis. He's sounding a new note in our political carryings on." Davis led an enthusiastic crowd in a series of songs, including "Home on the Range," "It Makes No Difference Now," "Dixie," "America the Beautiful," and "Sunshine." So effusive was the reaction to his performance, the *New Orleans*

States reported, that Davis "had to be smuggled out to bring an end to the singing and rocking." In Chicago, Davis met with Missouri senator Harry Truman, whom President Franklin Roosevelt would nominate to be his running mate that year. The future president asked Davis for his help, explaining that he needed support from some southern leaders. "I don't particularly want this job," a Davis aide recalled Truman telling the Louisiana governor, "but if I don't take it, Henry Wallace will be vice president again." Davis not only seconded Truman's nomination; he was the only prominent southern politician to publicly back Truman.[5]

Davis added more national hits to his credit after Decca released two recordings in September. Both approached the top of *Billboard*'s folk chart. "Is It Too Late Now?" peaked at number three, and "There's a Chill on the Hill Tonight" reached fourth place. He had recorded both songs and eight more in Los Angeles on March 23 and 24, just three weeks after his election. By November, he and the musicians hit the road again—to Biloxi, Mississippi, for the Southern Governors' Conference (now the Southern Governors' Association) annual meeting. At the Buena Vista Hotel nightclub, Davis charmed fellow chief executives with songs about their states, including "Alabamy Bound" and "My Old Kentucky Home." And he sang "Sunshine," the song that thirty-three years later would become a state song of Louisiana. Also that month, Columbia Pictures released another movie featuring Davis, *Cyclone Prairie Rangers,* with Charles Starrett. He had made the film in July of the previous year.[6]

The following January in New Orleans, after speaking to members of the Orleans Club to whom he pledged the state's support to preserve the historic buildings of the city's French Quarter, Davis and the band entertained the crowd with four songs. "I'm really in a whirl," he told his audience before singing. "I don't know any long-haired music, only the kind they call 'corn fed.' But if you can stand it, you're fixin' to get it." He ended the set, as usual, with "Sunshine."[7]

When the British ambassador to the United States, Lord Halifax (Edward Frederick Lindley Wood), visited Baton Rouge with his wife, Dorothy, in February 1945 for lunch with LSU president William B. Hatcher, the former British foreign secretary and House of Lords leader requested a visit to the Governor's Mansion. He wanted to hear Davis and his band sing "Sunshine." Davis welcomed them and sang for so long that the couple were late for their plane flight to Mississippi. Leaving the mansion, Halifax gushed that he "never more enjoyed music."[8]

In May, Davis took the band on tour across several midwestern and southern states—Mississippi, Alabama, Indiana, Illinois, Missouri, and Kentucky—ostensibly to discuss their and Louisiana's postwar plans and to promote Louisiana as a business location. He also played at war bond rallies. In Chicago, he and the band played on the network broadcast of the *National Barn Dance* radio show to support the Seventh War Loan drive. Back home, Davis lent his voice to the postwar effort in late June, performing with his band at the Baton Rouge Woman's Clubhouse in the War Service Musicale. "There's no telling how many war bonds 'You Are My Sunshine' sold," he later boasted. In January 1946, he and band members flew to Yucatán, Mexico, to perform at the inauguration of Governor José González Beytia. He called it a "good neighbor" gesture. They went farther south to Guatemala to sing at President Juan José Arévalo Bermejo's invitation.[9]

Until then, Davis and his band had only performed at events related to his official duties as governor. In February 1946, however, he traveled to Los Angeles for his first recording session as governor. He hadn't made a record in almost two years. Over two days, February 18 and 19, he recorded eight new songs, including "Bang Bang" and "I'm Gonna Write Myself a Letter." Davis also found time to appear on Frank Sinatra's CBS radio network show—on location in Palm Springs—where he sang "Sunshine" with Sinatra and then gave a solo performance of "There's a New Moon over My Shoulder." During his banter with Sinatra, Davis bragged about the size of Louisiana's oranges. They were so big, he joked, "that one man is assigned to every orange." To reporters curious about why he was visiting California, Davis mused about making another movie. "I might be able to do a picture during a summer vacation," he said. By August, it was official: Davis would star in a musical about his life.[10]

Despite Davis once suggesting he would be too busy to make records or movies, his performing days were not behind him. According to one accounting of his travels, he was absent from Louisiana for 44 days during fiscal year 1944–45 (July 1944 through June 1945), 68 days during fiscal 1945–46, and 108 days in fiscal 1946–47. When Davis left the state, the state constitution made Lieutenant Governor J. Emile Verret the acting governor, and he received the governor's salary—an extra nineteen dollars a day—until Davis returned. By the spring of 1947, the $2,000 state account that funded this extra pay for the state's second-ranking official was exhausted and running a deficit. In September, with Davis resting for two weeks in West Texas on his doctor's advice, Verret became acting governor and managed the state's response to a strong hurricane that hit south Louisiana.[11]

Davis later defended his absences as weekend and vacation excursions. "Most of the time, no one knew the difference, except, of course, the lieutenant governor, who has to be informed when the governor leaves the state," he said. "I had become established in the recording business . . . and I didn't intend to give it up as long as I could do this without taking any time from my official duties. And I did it without taking one hour of the state's time." It wasn't only Davis's absences that would prompt criticism. Near the end of 1947, about six months before his term ended, one prominent detractor claimed that Davis's band cost the state fifty thousand dollars annually. "You can get a sight better music just by turning on your radio, and you get it free," Rufus J. Fontenot, a former federal internal revenue official and candidate for secretary of state, declared.[12]

During Davis's term as governor, his new and old songs continued getting wide play across the country, especially on jukeboxes. By February 1945, less than a year into his term, he released his recording of "There's a New Moon over My Shoulder." It would be a number-one *Billboard* folk hit. It spent eighteen weeks on the magazine's list of "Most-Played Juke Box Folk Records" in the spring and summer. It was the country's third-most-popular jukebox folk song that March and would be the year's second-most-popular country recording. Davis scored another hit that summer with "I'm Beginning to Forget You." The following March, his version of "Grievin' My Heart out for You" climbed to fourth place on *Billboard*'s jukebox folk list. In the spring of 1947, Davis released a collection of previous recordings titled the *Jimmie Davis Souvenir Album.* It featured "Sunshine."[13]

Between all his performances and recording sessions, Davis found time to govern the state, presiding over more funding to drainage, health, and education programs—including a pay raise for teachers. He created a state employees' retirement system, passed (by one vote) the first state driver's license law, and increased old-age benefits. Amid a postwar backlash against organized labor in the South, Davis rejected an antilabor right-to-work bill in 1946. To accusations that he vetoed the legislation under pressure from the head of the powerful American Federation of Musicians (AFM) union, Davis explained he was only an honorary member of Shreveport's AFM branch. "A singer, playing no instrument, is not required to join," he said, adding, "I make my own decisions." He preserved the civil service changes his predecessor instituted and would leave his successor, Earl Long, a $45 million surplus ($600 million in 2024 dollars). Yet, perhaps because he often exhibited a light touch over legislative affairs and was absent from Louisiana for more than two hundred days, critics and some voters considered him a "do-nothing governor."[14]

In retrospect, his tenure may have had its best success in instituting the "peace and harmony" promised by his sunshine-infused campaign. For almost twenty years, disputes between the pro- and anti-Long factions had riven Louisiana's politics. Davis did not eliminate the state's bifactional politics. It would return in full force during the 1948 governor's election. But it was, in the words of one Louisiana historian, "considerably subdued" during Davis's four years because his detached, often-absentee leadership allowed for fluctuating, interchangeable coalitions of pro- and anti-Long lawmakers to guide much of state policy. "Entering office with few specific pledges," Allan P. Sindler wrote in his authoritative political history of Louisiana from 1920 to 1952, "Davis refused to stake his prestige on any subsequent policies. Most important, state revenues were so plentiful as to blunt bifactional alignments and, since no new taxes were enacted, to arouse few special-interest groups to opposition."[15]

Writing about Davis's first term, another historian, Mark T. Carleton, suggested Davis may have been successful because he "was everyone's second choice, but for entirely different reasons. For 'reform' leaders and voters, he was always an acceptable alternative—singing, spending and all—to any Longite administration. For Longite voters and some Longite leaders . . . Davis was the next best governor if Earl [Long] was unavailable." Carleton regarded Davis as "a Longite in 'reformer's' clothing, and voters knew it. If Davis was in fact the only 'reformer' [of his era] to serve two terms, it was because he was the only one of the three [Davis, Sam Jones, and Robert Kennon] who was never burdened with either a reputation for advocating reform legislation or a record of having enacted any."[16]

In February 1947, with about fifteen months left in office, Davis and his band (now billed as the Sunshine Serenaders) took a three-week "vacation" to film the movie about his life. Early in his term, he had scoffed at the notion of a musical biopic called *The Singing Governor.* By late 1946, however, the idea of starring in a film about his rise to the governor's office became too tempting to resist. The movie *Louisiana*—based loosely on his early life and political career—was shot in Hollywood and Louisiana. Davis played himself and sang several of his hit songs, including "You Are My Sunshine," "Bang Bang," "Nobody's Darling," and "There's a New Moon over My Shoulder." In October 1947, Shreveport's government and business leaders hosted a lavish "world premiere" of the Monogram Pictures movie, attended by his costars and Governors Jim Folsom of Alabama, Fielding Wright of Mississippi, Strom Thurmond of South Carolina, and Phil Donnelly of Missouri. Thirty thousand people lined the streets to see Davis and a host of Hollywood stars and movie executives pass by in a parade. The next day at a theater in New Orleans, Davis appeared before a crowd of locals with several Hollywood personalities, including Jackie Cooper, Gale Storm, Smiley Burnette, and nineteen-year-old Roddy McDowell. Davis sang "Sunshine" to the gathering.[17]

"If Abraham Lincoln had been alive, Monogram Studios would have snagged him for the part," reviewer Ollie E. Bissmeyer Jr. wrote of the

Poster for Davis's 1947 film about his musical and political careers, *Louisiana*. (Everett Collection)

film in Louisville, Kentucky's *Courier-Journal,* adding that it "patterns itself after the life of Honest Abe." Bissmeyer wrote that despite featuring "every pat formula," the movie "has a great deal of entertainment value." More than anything, the reviewer concluded, "There's no doubt the film will be a terrific political weapon."[18]

If Davis hoped his increased stardom would help him anoint a successor, it wasn't apparent that voters were yearning for his thoughts on whom to support in the 1948 election. Nonetheless, he worked to return the office to his predecessor. After four years in the political wilderness, former governor Sam Jones returned to run against three opponents for the Democratic Party nomination: the Long organization's candidate, Earl K. Long; Robert F. Kennon—a state appeals court judge and former Webster Parish district attorney—running on an anti-Long platform; and Congressman Jimmy Morrison of Hammond, who was backed by former New Orleans mayor Robert Maestri and his Old Regulars machine.

When Davis ran four years earlier, he and Jones had agreed that Jones's endorsement would be implicit. But, in this race, Jones did not hesitate to accept Davis's active support, and Davis appeared to have no qualms about giving it. Davis helped in several ways, including making a statewide radio address on Thanksgiving night in 1947, praising Jones as a reformer. "I am convinced that time and experience have tempered his attitude and make him more tolerant of all people—his foes as well as his friends," Davis said, adding, "I am convinced that the era of political bitterness is ended and that Sam Jones can work with all the elements who have cooperated with me in the last four years." Davis also sent his band—rebranded as the Sunshine Band—on the road with the former governor. Unlike Davis, Jones didn't sing, but he hoped the entertainment and the constant reminder of Davis's backing would help.[19]

In January 1948, Davis and his band appeared with Jones at a New Orleans rally. "I think he has an opportunity to be the finest governor we have ever had in our lifetime," Davis said of his predecessor before singing "Sunshine." The crowd responded with riotous applause and a demand for an encore, which Davis obliged.[20]

Unwilling to concede the reformer mantle to Jones, Kennon fought back. "Oh, yeah, this machine in charge of the state government is honest," a sarcastic Kennon said in December. "That band quit working for Jimmie Davis. But now they are on the Sam Jones payroll. But they were on the people's payroll when they went to Hollywood. This goes on while we need roads. Why should you carry a band on the state payroll and spend enough money on it to blacktop hundreds of miles in our state?" Jones mocked the bandleader-cum–state health director, Charles Mitchell, as "the musical secretary of Louisiana." In truth, Jones said, "Mitchell is what you call a musical dead-head." The comment of one band member did not diminish the lasting image of Davis's band members as a group holding do-nothing state jobs. In 1948, a newspaper reporter asked one of them what they had done during Davis's term. "Aw, we just hung around Jimmie," the unnamed musician replied.[21]

A feisty, fifty-two-year-old Earl Long barnstormed Louisiana, trying to reclaim the job he had held for eleven months from 1939 to 1940. Long blanketed the state, holding raucous rallies and attacking his opponents with gusto and creative invective. Ridiculing Kennon as a pampered elite, he said of the World War II veteran, "The Army tested Kennon's blood and found it contained 65 percent champagne and 35 percent talcum powder." Long also criticized Davis for devoting so much time to music. The governor, Long said, "has made thousands in addition to his $12,000-a-year salary while letting the roads go to rot and ruin."[22]

Campaigning with Huey Long's elder son, Russell, Earl promised a restoration of Long-era largesse. "Practically every benefit you enjoy today you got under the regimes of Huey Long and O.K. Allen," Long said, promising new state benefits. "The people are for Long because they want the $50 old-age pension, and I am going to give it. You people who have had been eating dust and getting your windshields knocked out with rocks want some good roads, and I am going to give you good roads." In return, Jones attacked Long for having presided over the 1939 "Louisiana scandals," a theme that had worked in 1940 but lost much of its punch after eight years of self-styled "reform" administrations led by Jones and Davis.

Long and Jones led in January's election and headed into a February runoff. One month later, Long beat Jones for the Democratic nomination with 66 percent of the vote. Whether it was a repudiation of Davis's tenure or weariness with anti-Long rule, Long's victory was decisive. In his 1977 authorized biography, Davis ignored the election.[23]

On May 11, his last day in office, Davis rode with Long in the pre-swearing-in inaugural parade. The outgoing governor blew kisses to LSU coeds who lined the route. That evening, now a private citizen, Davis left for Shreveport. By the weekend, he and his band hit the road for a concert tour.[24]

8

Come Home, Jimmie

Davis's notoriety as a governor, movie star, and chart-topping singer made his theme song more famous. By the time he left office in early 1948, more than a dozen artists—some experimenting with new styles and interpretations of the song—had released versions of "You Are My Sunshine." In 1941, big-band leader Lawrence Welk became the first to turn it into swing music, with vocals by Parnell Grina, Jayne Walton, and Shirlie Grundy. The following year, a British swing group—Harry Roy and His Band, featuring Marjorie Kingsley and Renee Lister—recorded the song. Roy made the sensible decision to revise the first stanza. In previous versions, the line, "I held you in my arms," did not rhyme with, "So I hung my head and I cried." Roy reworded it to, "I dreamed that you were by my side." That rhymed with the stanza's last verse, which was changed to, "When I awoke dear, you were gone, and then I cried."[1]

Also recording the song in 1942 was Big Bill Campbell and His Rocky Mountain Rhythm. Campbell was a Canadian-born entertainer who performed on the BBC and throughout England and helped popularize country music on that side of the Atlantic. His version (including the vocal chorus by Jack Curtis and the Mounties) was a creative interpretation that kept the song's country flair and featured innovative fiddle and accordion solos. Other artists who recorded versions in the 1940s included the Vagabonds (1946), New York City radio cowboy Denver Darling (1946), Mutual radio network star Kate Smith (1948), and singing movie cowboy Tex Ritter and the Dinning Sisters (1948). Popular boogie-woogie pianist Albert Ammons and His Rhythm Kings released a joyous, up-tempo instrumental version in 1948.[2]

The 1950s were a decade of discovery and reinterpretation for the many singers and musicians who recorded "Sunshine" and kept it alive and fresh, showcasing its suitability for any genre. During the 1950s, more than twenty-five artists and groups covered it; most weren't country performers. As more rhythm-and-blues, rockabilly, and mainstream pop artists experimented with "Sunshine," it took on new life. The first group to record it in this decade was the Ames Brothers, the popular quartet that scored a hit in 1950 with "Rag Mop" and performed on national radio shows, including *Arthur Godfrey and His Friends.* The group's 1952 recording of "Sunshine" for Decca's Coral label wasn't a hit, but it was an original, jazzy, upbeat two-minute version that featured a lively steel guitar solo. It was also the second recording to use the revised line, "by my side," to rhyme with "hung my head and cried."[3]

Much like Bing Crosby did in 1941, crooner Nat King Cole gave the song greater mainstream pop respectability in early 1956 with what one biographer described as "a raucously jazzy reinterpretation." The arrangement for Capitol Records featured Cole's signature velvety tones backed by the lush symphonic accompaniment of arranger Nelson Riddle's orchestra. Cole's understated, smooth baritone glides over the melody, giving the song a romantic, intimate feeling. It may have been the most luxurious version of the song to date. Cole was also the first Black vocalist to record "Sunshine."[4]

In August 1956, country star Faron Young, who had toured recently with Elvis Presley in the *Hank Snow All-Star Jamboree,* recorded his debut album for Capitol Records at Nashville's Columbia Studios. The Shreveport native had notched a number-one country hit in 1955 with "Live Fast, Love Hard, Die Young." Young's song "If You Ain't Lovin' (You Ain't Livin')" reached number two on *Billboard*'s country chart earlier that year. He named his album *Sweethearts or Strangers* after the title cut, a Jimmie Davis song. And he recorded another Davis song for the album, "You Are My Sunshine." A stripped-down country arrangement featuring steel guitar and a touch of fiddle, Young's smooth, plaintive delivery didn't produce a hit. (He wouldn't release it as a single.) However, it was the first and one of the song's better modern country versions.[5]

In 1956, Nat King Cole was the first Black solo entertainer to record "You Are My Sunshine." (Library of Congress)

The following year saw the most inventive interpretation of the song yet. Doo-wop singer Richard Berry—born in Extension, Louisiana (about fifty miles southeast of Monroe), and raised in Los Angeles—had performed with several rhythm-and-blues groups, including the Flairs and the Robins, before forming the Pharaohs in 1954. In 1957, the twenty-one-year-old singer became the second Black performer to record "Sunshine" and the first to cover it with a different tune. With the Pharaohs singing close-harmony backup, Berry's version for Flip Records was a thorough departure from the traditional rendition. Besides introducing a new tune, Berry added this bridge between stanzas: "You are, because I love you so, And I will never, never let you go."[6]

Berry later described his approach to reinterpreting the standard: "I dissected it and put it together with the harmony and stuff, and even added my own little bridge. . . . I just made that up, you know, 'cause you always had to have a bridge in a song in those days." Berry acknowledged he should have requested Davis's permission to change the song, but "nobody ever bothered us about it." Berry said he recorded it because it was a childhood favorite: "We used to sit up in the living room quite a few nights with the red light on, and we'd be singing 'You Are My Sunshine.' I thought that if I was ever gonna have a hit record, it was going to be off of 'You Are My Sunshine.'"[7]

Davis may not have noticed this version because the B-side of Berry's 45-rpm record attracted more attention. The song was "Louie Louie," Berry's composition from 1954 and a minor regional success that became a national sensation in 1963 when the Kingsmen released it. In April 1957, *Billboard* commented on "Louie Louie," declaring it an "okay reading of sprightly calypso, but flip side ["Sunshine"] is [the] side to watch." But "Sunshine" wasn't the side to watch. "Louie Louie" would become the "Sunshine" of the R&B genre after being recorded more than 150 times since the 1950s. And, like the original author of "Sunshine," Berry lost control of his song. Needing money for his wedding, he sold the copyright in 1959 for $750. (In the 1980s, living on welfare in Los Angeles, Berry reacquired part of his lucrative composition—25 percent of the publishing rights—which earned him $2 million during the last ten years of his life.)[8]

R&B artist Andre Williams recorded his upbeat interpretation of "Sunshine" for Fortune Records in 1957. Like Berry, Williams altered the lyrics—"But when I awoke, dear, your love, your love, your love, was gone"—but he left more evidence of the original tune. Williams's version featured a spirited tenor sax solo. The record company reported a "strong response" to the single.[9]

The fourth noteworthy release of the song in 1957 was another exciting interpretation. Handsome twenty-six-year-old construction worker Carl McVoy—an Epps, Louisiana, native—was a gifted piano player like his first cousins Jerry Lee Lewis and Jimmy Swaggart. Almost five years older than Jerry Lee, McVoy had lived briefly in New York City with his father, a traveling evangelical preacher. There, he heard his first strains of "boogie-woogie," a high-energy style of piano pioneered by, among others, Davis band alumni Moon Mullican and distinguished by its driving rhythm, syncopated patterns, and repetitive bass lines. McVoy soon mastered the style and shared it with his cousin during a visit to Ferriday. "He was a genius," Jerry Lee later said of McVoy, adding that he thought, "Boy, if I could do what he's doin', that'd be something else." In Memphis, McVoy met Ray Harris, a former singer for Sun Records who recognized the young man's vocal and piano talents and encouraged him to make a record. The two men paid a local studio $3.50 so that McVoy could produce a demo. McVoy arranged a rockabilly/boogie-woogie interpretation of "Sunshine." His version impressed a local record store owner, Joe Cuoghi, so much that he and a few partners pooled their money to create a label, Hi Records. And, in the fall of 1957, they sent McVoy to Nashville to make a more professional recording. With guitarist and producer Chet Atkins's help, McVoy recorded two songs, including "Sunshine."

It was the first release by the new Memphis-based label that would become known as a dependable producer of rock and R&B instrumental hits, mainly by Elvis Presley's former bass player, Bill Black, and a former jazz band leader, Willie Mitchell. By late 1957, McVoy's "Sunshine" caught on. A Memphis radio disc jockey loved it so much that he played the song on air twenty-six straight times. "I don't know whether this signifies extravagant music appreciation," a local reporter wrote, "or a way to take an extra long coffee break."

As McVoy's record grew popular, Cuoghi struggled to finance record pressings. One East Coast distributor ordered eight hundred copies and, later that day, eight hundred more. "His hit," music historian Colin Escott observed, "was bankrupting him." In April 1958, McVoy sang his song on a new ABC television program, *The Dick Clark Show.* (His cousin Jerry Lee had been a guest on the show's first episode on February 15, singing "Breathless" and "Great Balls of Fire.") Word of McVoy's appearance increased demand for the record so much that Cuoghi saw no option but to sell the master. Sam Phillips of Sun Records bought the recording and McVoy's contract for $2,600. (He released "Sunshine" on his Phillips International label.) McVoy made a few records for Phillips's label but never had another hit. He returned to construction work and performed occasionally with Jerry Lee.[10]

The eagerness of artists to reinterpret a song was nothing new. But the growing diversity in American music, including the exploding popularity of rock and roll and R&B, altered how artists approached their covers of "Sunshine" and other songs. "The central reality of the pop mainstream's evolution was that it was changing from a market dominated by Tin Pan Alley principles and practices to one where musics of differing provenance shared the same stage, and audiences' preferences followed no set patterns," music historian Albin J. Zak wrote of the "crossover" phenomenon of the era. Zak distinguished between songs that cross over and are recorded by an artist from a different genre, as opposed to a recording that crosses over from one genre's chart to another. The latter was rare in the 1940s and 1950s, but, as "Sunshine" proved, the former was becoming more common. "Because so many of the same small labels that had taken over the R&B market were also dabbling in country & western music, and vice versa, these musics had been drawing closer together," journalist Robert Palmer wrote in *Rolling Stone* in 1990. "The younger generation of C&W fans were also listening and dancing to black music, and as a result, white country musicians were encouraged to record R&B songs and play with a heavier, emphatically rocking beat."[11]

By the end of the 1950s, rock-and-roll and R&B versions of "Sunshine" were common. This didn't mean people had forgotten about the country versions by Davis and Gene Autry or the pop versions by Bing Crosby and the Ames Brothers but, rather, that the song had a simple, timeless quality that made it easy for younger music fans to embrace. A fresh breed of singers and musicians found the song fun to adapt and interpret. Tamer recordings still appeared. Country duo Johnnie and Jack Anglin recorded a traditional version in early 1958, while Mitch Miller and the Gang made a conventional pop recording later that year. But as the 1950s gave way to the 1960s, there would be more versions like the one Johnny and the Thunderbirds recorded in 1959—upbeat, with a rock-and-roll feel and rhythm, and made for dancing. Jimmie Davis might have still owned the copyright to his famous song—and pocketed the royalties that poured into his bank account—but a new generation of artists and musicians were remaking and adapting it for a younger audience. In doing so, they kept "Sunshine" fresh, engaging, and alive.[12]

As the rock-and-roll generation embraced and reimagined his song, Davis spent the 1950s reinventing himself. When he left the governor's office, he and his band embarked on a vaudeville tour (seven musicians, a female vocalist, and a comedian). Davis said he was done with politics, although he confessed to "leaving the door open." His first engagement after departing Baton Rouge was at Loew's Capitol Theatre in Washington, DC, where he and the band performed to a packed house. While there, he went to the White House for a visit with President Harry Truman. "It was just a social visit—no politics," he told reporters. Davis also played shows in Chicago; Grand Rapids, Michigan; and Louisville, Kentucky.[13]

That winter, he and the band decamped to Palm Springs, California, where he leased a popular nightclub, the Stables. Billed as "America's Greatest All-Western Night Club," the venue featured live music, square dancing, and southern food, including barbecue ribs, fried chicken, and "Louisiana shrimp a la creole." The crowd of celebrities who attended the grand opening in early November included Joan Crawford, Yvonne De Carlo, Barbara Stanwyck, and John Garfield. In December, his first celebrity guest performer was *Grand Ole Opry* star Roy Acuff. (Like Davis, Acuff caught the political bug. He had briefly entertained running for Tennessee governor in 1944 before deciding against the race. In 1948, he won the Republican primary for governor but lost the general election, receiving 33 percent of the vote.) Davis and his musicians would hold court in Southern California for about eighteen months. In June 1950, after two winters performing in Palm Springs, he and Alvern returned to Shreveport and his regular touring schedule.[14]

While in California, Davis took a few weeks to make another movie. In May 1949, Monogram Pictures released the musical *Mississippi Rhythm.* In the film, Davis plays a young lawyer named Jimmie Davis who rides a steamboat into the small town of Creek City to claim his inheritance: half interest in a land development company. When he arrives, Davis learns that a group of dishonest politicians is trying to defraud Creek City's inhabitants. He encourages the residents to elect honest leaders and expel the charlatans. In late 1949, Davis would make his last movie, *Square Dance Katy,* an undistinguished musical released in 1950 in which he again played himself and sang a few songs but had no significant speaking role.[15]

After several years away from the studio, Davis began recording again. He had not made a record since November 1947. On March 3, 1951, he went to Nashville and recorded four songs: "When They Ring Those Golden Bells," "By and By," "Take My Hand, Precious Lord," and "That Sweet Story of Old." Gone were the steel guitars and fiddles. Replacing them were an electronic organ and an electric guitar.

And singing backup was the Anita Kerr Singers, a vocal ensemble headed by and named for a twenty-three-year-old soprano from Memphis. The year before, Kerr's group sang with country singer Red Foley on "Our Lady of Fatima," a song that reached sixteen on *Billboard*'s pop chart. Over the next few years, besides sessions with Davis, Kerr's singers would back up recordings by Eddy Arnold, Ernest Tubb, and Burl Ives. Before long, the group would become a vital ingredient of the smooth, sophisticated new "Nashville Sound" that would turn country music into something far different from the unadorned styles of Davis's early career.[16]

This was a new style and direction for Davis. Years later, he would explain his decision to record gospel music. Given his penchant for creating origin stories of uncertain authenticity, this one should be read with some skepticism: He didn't specify the year but claimed he and his band were performing at a Texas dance hall when an inebriated soldier asked to speak with him during a break. Davis and the young man found a table where they sat and talked for about fifteen minutes. "I'm drunk now," Davis recalled the man telling him, "but I didn't always drink. I came from a fine home and had good raising." Davis assumed the man needed someone to talk to, and he was prepared to listen but was shocked when the soldier upbraided him for performing in nightclubs. "I don't think this is the kind of place where a man who's been honored by the people of his state should be performing, even though I know it's just a profession to you. It seems to me that a man like you should be an inspiration to people. I know this is strange advice to come from a twenty-one-year-old soldier, and I wouldn't even be offering it if I wasn't full of whiskey."

Davis said that when he returned to the stage, he asked the crowd to draw near. "This will be the last song that Jimmie Davis will ever sing in a dance hall," Davis claimed he said. "It's not that I'm all that good, but perhaps I've got some other things to do with my life." Davis said he sang a hymn, "Lord, I'm Coming Home," and the audience joined him. Afterward, he said he looked for the soldier to thank him "for setting me straight, but he was gone."[17]

It is hard to know if Davis's road-to-Damascus story happened. There was only one advertisement for a performance by Davis at a Texas nightclub in 1950–51, at Dessau Hall (near Pflugerville, northeast of Austin) in August 1951. But this engagement would have occurred *after* Davis redirected his singing career into the gospel music field. Put another way, Davis still booked an appearance in a nightclub after he began making almost nothing but gospel records. Perhaps he encountered the soldier at Dessau Hall and swore off dance halls afterward. One piece of circumstantial evidence for this was that Davis, a month later, performed at Shreveport's Life Tabernacle at a meeting of the Christian Crusaders.[18]

The explanation for Davis's sudden turn to gospel recording may also be as simple as knowing his popularity in country music was fading. Newer, younger artists were on the scene. He was now in his fifties. Fans saw him as much as a dignified statesman as a singer of country tunes. (For his performances, Davis usually wore conservative business suits, not the sequined costumes and Western wear favored by many country stars of the era.) Audiences still enjoyed it when he sang "Sunshine" and "Nobody's Darlin'," but those who attended were older. An astute politician well-trained in reading a crowd, Davis had little trouble discerning that his fans were churchgoing people who would respond well to gospel standards.

And he surely noticed that other country artists were releasing more gospel songs. Popular acts like the Bailes Brothers and Molly O'Day had made gospel records since the late 1940s. Davis's label, Decca, had inaugurated a "Faith Series" in March 1950 featuring gospel recordings by its top stars, including the Andrews Sisters, Ernest Tubb, and Red Foley. Foley's 1950 recording of the gospel standard "Just a Closer Walk with Thee" was a top-ten country hit in July 1950. In February 1951, Eddy Arnold's "May the Good Lord Bless and Keep You" for RCA Victor reached number five on the country chart. And that summer, Foley released another gospel single, Thomas A. Dorsey's "Peace in the Valley." It became the first million-selling gospel record. It's unclear how much these hits influenced Davis, but by 1951, he had gone all in. He would record almost nothing but gospel music for the next two decades. It was a brilliant decision that kept his career alive. Within a few years, as rock and roll exploded in popularity, most of the top country stars of the 1940s and early 1950s saw their careers decline. But, because he had already migrated into a new genre, Davis's career survived and thrived.[19]

Not only were his audiences ready for this new, dignified, upright Jimmie Davis, but his voice was well-suited for gospel. On the first recordings with the Anita Kerr Singers, Davis's voice was pure and smooth, with a revitalized, heartfelt quality. Perhaps it was the new sparer instrumentation. Or maybe it was the support of masterful backup singers. Whatever the case, it was a fresh and appealing sound.

In relaunching his career as a singer of sacred songs, Davis was also a trailblazer. There were few major solo artists in southern gospel. When Davis entered the field, singing groups—mostly quartets—dominated the genre. They roamed the South, performing in churches and other venues. Among the most prominent were the Chuck Wagon Gang, the Speer Family, the Blackwoods, the Statesmen, and the Sunshine Boys Quartet. For Davis, the new emphasis on gospel music boosted his waning career. The decision came with a ready audience that had followed him for years and loved gospel music as much or more than they loved country music. Those already toiling in the southern gospel field regarded his advent not as threatening competition but as an enormous

A Davis gospel album cover. Davis began recording and publishing gospel music in the early 1950s and enjoyed a successful recording career in this field for decades. (Louisiana Digital Library)

compliment. “The gospel music industry profited during the 1950s from a genuine celebrity in its midst,” James R. Goff Jr. wrote of Davis in *Close Harmony: A History of Southern Gospel.*[20]

In short order, Davis recorded an impressive series of popular spiritual songs, including several by famed sacred songwriter Ira Stanphill: “Mansion over the Hilltop” and “I Know Who Holds Tomorrow.” Evidence of the brilliance of Davis’s shift to gospel was his 1953 release of Stanphill’s “Suppertime.” Sung and spoken by Davis, the piece recalls the singer’s boyhood as he played outside until his mother summoned him home at dusk, “Come home, Jimmie, it’s suppertime.” Then, the song transitions into a spiritual realm, with the singer imagining the end of his life when God summons him home for the Great Banquet. It was the perfect blend of country and sacred and, in the pantheon of Davis’s best-loved recordings, “Suppertime” ranks just below “Sunshine.” Other artists who covered the song included Johnny Cash, Jim Reeves, Faron Young, Porter Wagoner, Burl Ives, Conway Twitty, and Pat Boone. (True to form, Davis would later buy the song from Stanphill.)[21]

Davis continued performing secular songs in some of the usual venues. And he teamed up with one of the hottest stars in country music for a songwriting session. In early 1951, Davis and Hank Williams found time to collaborate on three songs, only one of which—"(I Heard That) Lonesome Whistle"—Williams would record. In October 1951, Davis recorded the other two: "Bayou Pon Pon" and "Forever's a Long, Long Time." Davis also performed on the *National Barn Dance* show, broadcast on Chicago's WLS radio, in February 1952. The following month, he was a guest on KWKH's *Louisiana Hayride* and, in September, on WSM's *Grand Ole Opry.* In between, in July, he found his way to Hope, Arkansas, to sing "Sunshine" at a rally for Democratic gubernatorial candidate and former Arkansas attorney general Jack Holt that also featured country stars Al Dexter and Johnny and Jack.[22]

In September, Davis began hosting a weekday, fifteen-minute statewide radio, the *Fillup with Billups Show,* sponsored by the Hammond, Louisiana–based Billups Petroleum Company, and among the nation's largest independent retail service station companies. The company's founder, Rowell Billups, and its CEO, W. L. "Buddy" Billups, were Davis's close friends and devoted supporters and had helped underwrite his gubernatorial campaign.

Davis hosted iterations of the show for the next seven years. (It also aired on some Mississippi radio stations.) In 1955, Billups created a Sunday morning program during which Davis sang hymns. And in 1957, the company added a five-minute daily performance for which he sang a "Billups hymn of the day." Davis stopped the show in 1959 because he was ready to dust off his famous theme song and vie for a second term as governor.[23]

9

A Brilliant Phantom

Davis resisted appeals to run for governor in 1952 and 1956, focusing instead on his successful gospel music career. With Davis absent and Sam Jones unwilling to run, the anti-Long field belonged to Robert Kennon, the state judge and former Minden mayor who won the 1952 race, beating Baton Rouge judge Carlos Spaht in a runoff for the Democratic nomination. Low-key and serious, Kennon passed a series of so-called "good government" initiatives, including spending cuts and a constitutional amendment limiting tax increases. He also created the state's first open-meetings laws and restored a civil service system that Long had dismantled. More controversial was a policy that almost dissuaded Davis from running in 1944: Kennon and his State Police superintendent, Francis Grevemberg, attacked ubiquitous organized gambling in New Orleans and throughout south Louisiana.[1]

In this era, Louisiana voters didn't want an anti-Long government for over four years at a time. In the 1956 election, Long roared back, winning his second governor's race. (It would be his third stint in the office.) The first three years of Long's term were productive but undramatic. He relaxed state enforcement of antigambling laws and, using increased oil and gas revenue, boosted spending on social programs and education, including a significant hike in old-age benefits and a 28 percent teacher pay raise. By the spring of 1959, however, his conduct—always tending toward the outrageous—blossomed into what even some allies and relatives regarded as mental instability. Others, including his close friend and political ally Bill Dodd, argued that "much of his inappropriate behavior and talk was brought on by the influence of drugs and alcohol." Whatever caused it, his troubling conduct included a brief, puzzling dalliance with a French Quarter stripper whose stage name was Blaze Starr. "Earl was trying to act like an eighteen-year-old boy who had just left the family farm and had discovered New Orleans for the first time," a friend remarked. One Long intimate told biographer Jack McGuire that the so-called "affair" was overblown, insisting "she was no more than a friend. If there was anything special between them, I never recognized it."[2]

In May 1959, allies hustled Long out of the House chamber after he made an angry and sometimes incoherent ninety-minute address to a joint legislative session in which he attacked his segregationist detractors. But his bizarre speech only heightened concerns about his mental health. Responding to criticism that he had used profanity with schoolchildren present in the gallery, Long apologized but added, "I got elected saying 'damn' every now and then. I think it's better to say 'damn' in the open than sleep with a n——r woman at night." By week's end, Long's wife, Blanche, and nephew US senator Russell Long had the governor committed to a mental institution in Galveston, Texas. After a protracted legal struggle, Long won his freedom. And, that summer, he hatched an ill-fated plan to secure another four years in office despite the constitutional prohibition against consecutive terms: he planned to resign before the election, allowing Lieutenant Governor Lether E. Frazar to become governor for the last few months of 1959. That meant that, if elected governor, Long would not succeed himself.[3]

The outburst in the House chamber that led to Long's involuntary trip to Galveston emanated from an issue that would overshadow the latter part of the 1960 governor's election: race relations. While he was no civil rights advocate and professed allegiance to white supremacy, Long had supported minority voting rights, viewing Black voters as a reliable part of his base. "I want all the colored votes I can get," he boasted. During his previous term—1948 to 1952—Black voter registration in Louisiana grew from about 7,000 to almost 110,000. Under Long, Louisiana had the largest Black registration in the South. By 1959, however, civil rights opponents—encouraged by a leading segregationist and candidate for governor, state senator William "Willie" Rainach of Claiborne Parish—began tossing thousands of Black voters off parish rolls. Long's anger over this contributed to his outrageous behavior on the House floor in May.

Long's plan to resign and seek another term proved unpopular and too clever by half. When the Democratic State Central Committee ruled in September that Long must resign eight months before his term ended to qualify for the ballot, he surrendered. He ran, instead, for lieutenant governor on a ticket headed by sixty-eight-year-old former governor James A. Noe of Monroe. The crowded field included Rainach, Noe, New Orleans mayor deLesseps "Chep" Morrison, and state comptroller and former lieutenant governor William "Bill" Dodd. Rainach's presence in the race, not to mention the growing civil rights movement in Louisiana and elsewhere in the South, ensured that integration would be a prominent issue. A virulent racist, Rainach had since 1954 chaired the legislature's Joint Legislative Committee, created after the US Supreme Court's 1954 *Brown v. Board of Education* school desegregation decision. Lawmakers charged the committee with crafting legislation to prevent the ruling's implementation in Louisiana.[4]

The burgeoning US civil rights movement in the streets and courtrooms was the backdrop for several governor's races in 1959–60, including in Louisiana. And no court case generated more outrage among white voters in Louisiana and elsewhere than the Supreme Court's *Brown* ruling. President Dwight D. Eisenhower's decision to federalize the Arkansas National Guard and send 1,200 US Army personnel to Arkansas in 1957 to integrate Little Rock Central High School inflamed many Louisiana white voters, who feared "forced integration."

The embryonic desegregation crisis and the exhausting political chaos of 1959 ripened conditions for the candidacy of someone like Davis, for whom "peace and harmony"—and sunshine—were trademarks. However, his opponents were determined to prevent him from singing his way back into the job this time. *Baton Rouge State-Times* columnist Ed Clinton wrote about the developing race, reporting that "the opposition is loaded for bear with propaganda that could prove embarrassing and costly to him." Clinton didn't disclose the nature of the threatened information. But another journalist, Robert Wagner of the *New Orleans*

Times-Picayune, told readers a few days later that it was "politically compromising 'integration' photographs of Davis that his foes allegedly possess." Davis's enemies planned to attack him as a friend and associate of Black people. *Times-Picayune* reporter Shelby Scates recalled meeting in the bar of Baton Rouge's Capitol House Hotel with a political operative who shared photographs he promised would "bust the governor's race wide open." The pictures, which Scates suspected were fake, were of Davis dancing with Black singer and dancer Lena Horne. "I didn't know whether to laugh or to cry," Scates later wrote, adding, "I left him with an unfinished drink." Undeterred by the threats, Davis said in late April that he would run for governor.[5]

While all the leading candidates pledged fealty to segregation, no one could match Rainach's ferocity. "When this campaign started," Rainach would declare in November, "the other major candidates thought they could get by by telling the voters that segregation wasn't an issue or by saying nothing at all. However, they soon found out that the voters wanted to know exactly where they stood and none of them had a record they could be proud of on the segregation issue." Rainach singled out Davis, saying, "Jimmie Davis couldn't untie himself from the entertainment world, which, as everyone knows, is against segregation."[6]

It wasn't long before stories about Davis's alleged associations with Black entertainers resurfaced. Just as his opponents had threatened, doctored photos of him and Horne circulated around the state. As in 1943, the allegation about Davis and Horne was the subject of rumors and whispers. In his first campaign for governor, someone had painted Horne's name on a Davis billboard in Shreveport, suggesting she was his real running mate. This time, a vandal defaced a campaign billboard in Baton Rouge, writing, "Lena Horne, Lt. Gov" and "Satchmo." The *Baton Rouge State-Times* ran a picture of the sign in August 1959. It explained in a caption that the graffiti "refer[s] to allegations that Davis once owned a nightclub in partnership with Lena Horne and had sung with Louis Armstrong's orchestra." Neither suggestion was true.[7]

Horne and Armstrong may not have been Davis's running mates, but segregation would be his constant companion by the campaign's end, no

Davis sings with the Plainsmen Quartet during the 1960 governor's race. (*Shreveport Times* Photos, LSUS Northwest Louisiana Archives)

matter how much he hoped to avoid it. In 1943–44, he ran on "peace and harmony." This time, his theme was "peace, harmony, and progress." Davis pledged not to attack his opponents. He noted he had never done so, "and I am not about to start it now." As in his previous governor's race, Davis would produce his rallies around music. Honky-tonk pianist and former *Grand Ole Opry* star Moon Mullican rejoined the band to help his old friend. And a gospel group from Dallas with whom he had toured for several years, the Plainsmen Quartet, accompanied him.[8]

This time, more so than in the first race, Davis would perform sacred songs, reflecting his decision, almost ten years earlier, to become a gospel artist. But, unlike in 1943–44, Davis could not avoid difficult issues by singing. Still, he tried. At one rally, he made this oblique statement about race relations: "I could argue forever and still not be convinced that integration is the right way." With that, Mullican began pounding his piano, and before anyone could contemplate what Davis meant by that, the Plainsmen were singing "Peace in the Valley."[9]

As much as he tried to distract voters with music, he couldn't escape addressing segregation. An adversary like Rainach would never allow Davis to dodge it by singing a gospel song. While many in Louisiana were ready to jettison the chaos of the Long years, Rainach knew that most white voters also wanted someone who would defend their children's "right" to live and attend school only with other whites.

At first, Davis dodged the issue by focusing on voter fatigue over Long's antics. As he had in 1943–44, he carved out a neutral position between the Long and anti-Long factions. "What your politics have been in the past is not my business," he said in Marksville in September. "I am not prejudiced against any faction or group." He also stressed his commitment to increasing social programs and education spending. "Jimmie Davis will take care of old people, the welfare program, the educational system, and the road program without additional taxes," his running mate, Clarence C. "Taddy" Aycock, said.[10]

From the campaign's early days, his opponents regarded Davis as the front-runner and criticized his fondness for making music and movies while governor in the 1940s. Dodd was especially vitriolic, reminding voters that the former governor had once made records "too vulgar to put on the air." And he challenged Davis to deny that "he used the governor's office to promote his entertainment business." Davis wouldn't take the bait. When, at a gathering of gubernatorial candidates in Monroe in August, Dodd attacked him for his show business career and "for running an integrated nightclub in California," Davis only grinned. Asked later why Dodd had assailed him, Davis replied, "I guess he thought I was in the lead. You know, people throw rocks up, not down."[11]

Dodd wasn't the only opponent to assail Davis's entertainment career. "When Jimmie Davis was last governor of Louisiana," Chep Morrison said in Bunkie in September, "he spent fully 33 percent of his time as governor out of the state making movies or singing with his band, and you can't expect much more from him this time." Addressing a crowd in New Orleans in October, Morrison amplified his attack. "Ladies and gentlemen, you can play 'You Are My Sunshine' on any jukebox for a nickel, and you don't have to hire a governor to sing it." But even Morrison understood the value of music to a campaign. His rally that night

Davis's band at a campaign event in Shreveport during the 1960 governor's race. (*Shreveport Times* Photos, LSUS Northwest Louisiana Archives)

featured a trio from Thibodaux that sang a song, "Chep's Got the Whole State on His Side," to the tune of "He's Got the Whole World in His Hands." By November, Morrison would host rallies with *Grand Ole Opry* stars Minnie Pearl and George Morgan and an unusual calliope on a trailer he called "Morrison's Famous Circus Band Wagon." (Pearl, whose real name was Sarah Ophelia Colley Cannon, counted Davis among her friends. When reporters questioned Davis about her appearances with his opponent, Davis evinced no irritation. "It was a paying job for Minnie Pearl," he explained.)[12]

Noe ridiculed Davis, dubbing him, "Singin', Flingin' Hollywood Jimmie Davis." In mid-October, the former governor said of Davis, "He claims he's going to bring the sweet sunshine back to Louisiana. The last time he ran, he spread the sunshine all over California for more than one-third of his term in office. Sunshine may be all right in its place out there, but its place isn't here in our state government." Later that month, Noe threatened to release what he suggested were incriminating photographs of Davis: the doctored pictures of him dancing with Lena Horne. Davis waved off the attack. "In every race, you have one or two candidates who will stoop mighty low to pick up a few votes," he responded when told of Noe's threat, adding he would not respond in kind: "If I have to do those things to be elected governor, then I don't want the job. Life's too short." Never one to be outdone in the invective department, Long joined the chorus of attacks, telling a reporter Davis "stayed in bed about two-thirds of the time" that he was governor. To another, he said, "Jimmie Davis loves money like a hog loves slop."[13]

In December, at a rally at the Franklin Cotton Gin in Holly Ridge, near Rayville, Davis and Bill Dodd appeared on the loading dock before a crowd of about one thousand. Believing he had Davis cornered, Dodd tore into his opponent, accusing him of "running to Hollywood, making two-bit movies, and grinding out discs of fiddlin' tunes." For good measure, he added, Davis's platform had "no provisions for an old-age pension." Dodd's attacks were so harsh that the crowd heckled him. Heedless of the fact that he was among Davis supporters, Dodd later confessed that when he finished, he thought, "I've got him now; he's got to answer me on all that!" Davis later recalled that "everything [Dodd] said was untrue, but he said it in such a way that I almost believed I'd suffered amnesia and had committed some of the acts he'd talked about."

As always, Davis refused to be baited into a counterattack. "You've already heard my life story," he told the gathering. "You know all about me by this time, and there's not much I can add to it other than to sing you a song or two. So, gather 'round, friends." With that, he sang "You Are My Sunshine," "Suppertime," and "The Old Rugged Cross." Dodd was astonished. "He just took all that criticism and never gave it back, so it never went any further," he said. "He simply could not be suckered into anyone else's ballgame." Dodd later marveled to friends, "That fellow Davis wouldn't be suckered into a street brawl. Old Jimmie just sprinkled the crowd with Sunshine, took them home at Suppertime, and nailed me to the Old Rugged Cross." In 1943, Earl Long complained about the im-

A campaign button from Davis's 1960 governor's campaign. (Robert Mann)

possibility of running against "a song." Dodd's twist on the predicament was to observe, "I was running against a brilliant phantom."[14]

Dodd and the rest were also running against a coalition of New Orleans–area forces backing Davis, including the *New Orleans Times-Picayune,* the Old Regular organization, and the proto-segregationist boss of Plaquemines Parish, District Attorney Leander Perez. When Earl Long heard of the alliance, he said, "The Bible says that before the end of time, all the pussycats, the poodle dogs, the house cats, and lions and tigers are going to lie down and sleep together. Have you seen that bunch hanging around Davis? It looks like the end of time is here already."[15]

Despite its alliance with the racist Perez, Davis's campaign worked through the Old Regulars organization to woo Black voters. Davis had downplayed segregation before the first primary election in December, but he had insisted he stood with the pro-segregation forces whenever he discussed the issue. In mid-September, he announced in a statewide television speech that he was "unqualifiedly in favor of segregation." He added, "In my opinion, the best way to maintain our historic way of life, as well as the harmonious relations between the races, is to provide separate and equal facilities for our school children, not in name only but in actual fact." Shortly before the election, sensing that Rainach's virulent segregationist message resonated with voters, Davis doubled down, insisting he supported segregation "one thousand percent." Davis added there would be "no retreat and no compromise."[16]

On Election Day, December 5, Morrison finished first with 33 percent of the vote to Davis's 25 percent. The two would meet in a January 9 runoff for the Democratic nomination. But Rainach surprised everyone with a strong 17 percentage point third-place finish that guaranteed neither runoff candidate could ignore segregation. Far from it, both men would vie for who could articulate the most potent segregation message. And, in bidding for segregationist votes, Davis broke his promise not to attack an opponent.

Encouraged by Perez, Davis discarded his peace-and-harmony platform in favor of a vitriolic, unadulterated segregationist campaign. The day after the first primary vote, he attacked the National Association for the Advancement of Colored People (NAACP) at a rally of New Orleans supporters. "As for the NAACP," Davis said, "I hope not one of them votes for me because I don't want their vote. I'm not a hater, but there comes a time when you must stand on your principles."[17]

A week before the election, he said Morrison had NAACP ties and was a tool of national Teamster union boss Jimmy Hoffa. Davis's campaign distributed broadsheets with a photo of Morrison dedicating a swimming pool for New Orleans's Black residents. "There has been one sinister and disturbing element injected into this election," Davis said. He meant that Morrison had received the most Black votes. Rainach supporters ran newspaper ads touting the fact that "Davis led with the white voters," adding, "If the N.A.A.C.P. has its way and Morrison is elected, it will be the first time in history that a Governor in the State of Louisiana has been elected with 100,000 more White voters wanting the OTHER candidate." Davis also promised to close state schools before allowing the federal government to integrate them. As journalist A. J. Liebling observed, "Davis was now talking their [the racists'] language, and the violence of 1960 was in the making."[18]

Morrison replied that Davis feared debating him, accused him of writing dirty songs, and said Davis had operated an integrated nightclub in California in the late 1940s. "There is the Jimmie Davis songbook," Morrison said on election eve, "with lyrics so obscene they can't be printed in a family newspaper." Morrison also claimed the NAACP had endorsed Davis. Although the organization's state president said she had voted for him, the NAACP had not endorsed him.[19]

Davis's refusal to attack his opponents in the first primary reaped him rewards in the runoff. Because he had alienated no one, including Long, he earned a grudging endorsement from the governor—who lost his bid for lieutenant governor. "I don't believe Mr. Davis has any rancor or hatred toward any group," Long said, "Italians, French, colored, or anyone." Just as important, Rainach endorsed him. When announcing his support days before the election, the fiery segregationist portrayed his former opponent as a kindred spirit. "We can salvage a great deal we lost when I was not elected governor," Rainach said at a joint appearance with Davis in New Orleans. "[Davis] told me he would go to jail, if necessary, to protect our children." Davis returned the compliment: "Senator Rainach had the most loyal and ardent supporters I've ever seen. I only hope you can be half as enthusiastic for me as you were for Willie." Rainach may not have been persuaded as much by any Davis change of heart as he was by his former opponent's promise to continue funding Rainach's Louisiana Joint Legislative Committee (the panel established to fight federal integration), to create a state sovereignty commission, and to make Rainach its chair. Davis may also have promised to support the creation of Lake Claiborne in Rainach's home parish. And Davis assured Rainach that the image of him with Lena Horne was not genuine. Rainach claimed he had hired a detective agency and was satisfied it was a phony. "Isn't this a fine jambalaya?" Morrison said, complaining about the disparate forces lining up behind Davis: "Earl Long, the *Times-Picayune,* Leander Perez, the *Shreveport Times,* the Monroe papers, the Old Regulars—all together in one pot." In January, Davis won the Democratic nomination, tantamount to victory in the general election, with 54 percent of the vote.[20]

As the Democratic nominee, Davis faced token Republican opposition in the April 19 general election. But everyone knew he was now the presumptive governor. So, he accepted when the producers of CBS's *The Ed Sullivan Show* invited him to sing "Sunshine" on the February 7 broadcast. But when network executives realized he still faced a general

A campaign poster for state senator Willie Rainach's 1960 governor's campaign. The virulent segregationist would endorse Davis in the runoff. (Louisiana Research Collection, Tulane University Archives)

election against a Republican opponent—former State Police superintendent Francis Grevemberg—they withdrew the invitation lest Grevemberg demand equal time on all the state's CBS affiliates.[21]

The peace and harmony Davis promised prevailed at the *Baton Rouge Gridiron Show* in early April, an annual event during which journalists spoofed the state's politicians with songs and skits. Davis, Long, Morrison, and Kennon attended. To show their support of Davis before the crowd of nine hundred, Morrison and the three governors joined arms to sing "Sunshine." Long, never among Davis's biggest fans, told the crowd, "He has a wonderful temper and a wonderful disposition. Sometimes, I wish I had some of that myself."[22]

Davis beat Grevemberg and, on May 10, took office for the second

Davis and outgoing governor Earl Long at Davis's 1960 inauguration. (© Langston McEachern—USA TODAY NETWORK)

time. On his way to the Capitol in the eight-block inaugural parade, several marching bands played "Sunshine" and "Dixie" as his and Long's car rode through downtown Baton Rouge. Later, Davis vowed in a brief speech, "We will preserve segregation. We will maintain our way of life without compromise, without prejudice, and without violence." Among the honored guests were two of the nation's most prominent segregationists, US senator Strom Thurmond of South Carolina and Mississippi governor Ross Barnett. Davis pledged that the state would solve its problems without "interference from those outside our borders." When the ceremony ended, the loudspeakers blared recordings of Davis singing "Suppertime" and "There's a Mansion in the Sky." That night, at the inaugural ball held in LSU's coliseum, he sang "Sunshine" for attendees.[23]

Promises of "peace and harmony" had helped Davis win the governor's office again. However, as he would soon learn, pledging unity was easier sung than done.

10

No "Sunshine" of Moderation

To win Willie Rainach's endorsement, Davis had guaranteed him a voice and some power in the fight against integration. As promised, Davis beefed up funding for the Joint Legislative Committee that Rainach, now a former senator, had chaired for six years. And in June 1960, the legislature approved Davis's proposal to create the Louisiana State Sovereignty Commission. Patterned after a similar body in Mississippi, Davis charged his creation with employing "every legal means to preserve and protect for the state and its people those rights which are legally and traditionally theirs." In other words, keep Black people in their place, as Davis had pledged.

Rainach should have been pleased to have a governor with whom he could work, except that Davis refused to make the commission autonomous. Davis knew a loose cannon like Rainach could create havoc, so he put the new commission on a shorter leash, placing it and its members under the authority of his office. Rainach was outraged by what he perceived as a broken promise. "I would be nothing but a figurehead," he fumed when declining to serve.[1]

At Davis's request, lawmakers converted Rainach's former committee into the Louisiana Joint Legislative Committee on Un-American Activities. With the new governor's support, Louisiana had a legislative body and an executive agency dedicated to fighting federal government efforts to weaken segregation. Chaired by state representative James H. Pfister of Orleans Parish, the committee investigated and harassed pro–civil rights organizations, including the Southern Conference Educational Fund and the American Civil Liberties Union. Also, with Davis's backing, the segregationist forces in the legislature enacted restrictions on Black voting that Rainach and others had wanted but that Earl Long had opposed. From 1960 through 1962, Davis and lawmakers made the voter registration process more confusing for prospective Black voters and threw thousands of them off the rolls.[2]

The most dramatic civil rights showdown during Davis's term happened in New Orleans. He and legislators took charge of Orleans Parish schools after US district court judge J. Skelly Wright ordered the school board to desegregate elementary schools. On May 16, 1960—just days after Davis's inauguration—Wright ruled that first-grade students, Black and white, could attend the school of their choice beginning in the fall. Davis and lawmakers first considered defying the order by pulling state funding from the schools. They thought better of that but concocted something just as egregious: giving Davis authority to shutter every state school if one all-white school enrolled a Black student.

Davis protested that the crisis was thrust upon him. "I would have preferred to have tested the doctrine of state sovereignty using our parks, or our beaches, or some tangible-but-dispensable function of Louisiana government, rather than to see something as vital as our system of education become embroiled in a political tug-of-war," he said in a televised speech in late 1960. "But it has fallen to be my lot, and yours, to become participants in a massive effort to prevent our states from becoming satellites of a supreme and unrestrained central government."[3]

Instead of closing schools, Davis assumed "control, management and administration" of New Orleans public schools in August and ordered them opened on a segregated basis the following month. In late August, the US Fifth Circuit Court of Appeals issued a temporary restraining order against Davis and other state officials, returned the schools to the school board, and ordered members to implement Wright's desegregation order. Judges also found Attorney General Jack Gremillion in contempt for calling the court a "den of iniquity." Davis and segregationist lawmakers retaliated with a special session, passing legislation allowing a legislative committee to run the schools. In November, Wright reached the limits of his patience. He enjoined Davis and legislators and ordered the school board to proceed with integrating its schools. Davis refused and sent a squad of State Police troopers to New Orleans to enforce a state-ordered school holiday. Wright countered by instructing federal marshals to escort four Black girls to the two schools where they would enroll for the year. Despite Davis's efforts to prevent it, the first New Orleans schools were integrated.

During the crisis, those most dedicated to inciting violence among the white residents of New Orleans were Davis's erstwhile supporter Willie Rainach, and a new ally, Plaquemines Parish district attorney Leander Perez. "Let's don't be cowed," the former senator said at a White Citizens Council meeting in New Orleans in November 1960. "Let's use the 'scorched-earth' policy. Let's empty the classrooms where they are integrated." Perez implored the crowd, "Don't wait for your daughter to be raped by these Congolese. Don't wait until the burr-heads are forced into your schools. Do something about it now." Davis begged for calm, but emotions among racist whites in New Orleans ran too high. The anger that Rainach and Perez whipped up overpowered Davis's mild words. The result was a rampage of three thousand white high school students through downtown the following day. They assaulted Black bystanders, and fifty of them invaded City Hall, demanding to see Mayor Morrison. Police extinguished the violence by turning fire hoses on the rioters. (Davis might have distanced himself from a malicious racist like Perez but, instead, made him the administration's chief legislative pro-segregation strategist. Perez's influence over Davis would become so powerful that some insiders at the Capitol began to joke that the governor might propose changing the state flower to the oleander.)[4]

Unable to circumvent Wright's orders, Davis and lawmakers froze state funding for New Orleans schools and advised local banks and businesses against doing business with them. Among the bills Davis proposed to stop school integration was a state-supported bounty system that paid informants who reported to authorities the new crime of offering financial support to parents who sent their children to desegregated schools.

By 1961, the US Justice Department of the new president, John F. Kennedy, took a more forceful approach to integrating New Orleans schools by challenging legislators in court. Wright welcomed the depart-

Plaquemines Parish district attorney Leander Perez (Louisiana Digital Library)

ment's intervention and overruled these new state laws. But other forces made it difficult to keep the school system open: Local banks declined to lend the system funds to meet its payroll. And city officials, intimidated by Davis's actions, wouldn't release tax revenue owed to the schools. In January 1961, the system couldn't pay a third of its employees, while the legislature refused to pay teachers at integrated schools. Threatened with contempt charges, Attorney General Gremillion and state education superintendent Shelby Jackson relented in early March. A fraction of the New Orleans school system was "integrated," but in name only. Few white students remained in the two New Orleans integrated elementary schools.[5]

Even some lawmakers were unwilling to do more to keep schools segregated. Legislators balked when Davis called a special legislative session in December 1960 to propose a new one-cent state sales tax to fund the legal fight against the federal government and to support private school tuition for displaced white students.[6]

It was Davis's mild manner that prevented him from being mentioned in history books alongside the era's most notorious race-baiting governors: Orval Faubus of Arkansas, George Wallace of Alabama, and Ross Barnett of Mississippi. Moon Landrieu, then a state representative who would later serve as New Orleans mayor, claimed Davis was never a firebrand in the anti–civil rights struggle. "There was a great deal of speculation that Jimmie Davis was thrust into a role he did not relish," Landrieu said in 2000, after Davis's death. "I never heard Davis utter any vile or ugly epithets. He just kind of went along."[7]

Davis insisted that his heart wasn't in the fight and that his goal was to keep the peace. "I believe the record will show that we did what had to be done, and it was done within the framework of law and order," he told his biographer and former aide, Gus Weill. "We closed no schools. We lost no lives. We shed no blood. Let those who would find fault with our efforts compare them with some of our sister states who were, perhaps, not as fortunate." Implicit in Davis's defense was that he wasn't a race-baiter or hater and was acting only out of duty to the white majority. Whether he believed in segregation or he was responding out of political expediency may remain a mystery. There is little evidence of his views on matters of civil rights before 1959, but what evidence exists suggests he was a committed white supremacist.

For his 1927 master's thesis, written at Louisiana State University when he was twenty-eight, Davis experimented with seven hundred Baton Rouge white, Black, and mixed-race students, ages nine and ten. Besides administering several sections of the National Intelligence Tests (an IQ exam) to the children, Davis noted he "made a study of color and blood in the negroes" and divided the group into "different shades of 'blackness.'" He reported that his analysis revealed superior reasoning power among white students. "The results indicate," he added, "that among the negroes themselves there are certain individuals who are capable of taking on that type of training which will qualify them for leadership in the betterment of their race, while the large majority of them are not capable of leadership."[8]

In 1930, Davis recorded an ode to Louisiana, "Where the Old Red River Flows," a song he said he wrote on a train from Shreveport to Chicago. It contains the line, "You can hear the darkies singing soft and low." (In a 1978 version of the song, Davis would change it to "You can hear that fiddle playing soft and low.") Describing Black people as "darkies" was common among whites in that Jim Crow era, including those who wrote for white-owned newspapers like the *Shreveport Times*. But it was still degrading, and Davis's use of the term in a song suggested his attitude toward Black people in the early 1930s was consistent with that of the state's white majority. In his favor was that he had recorded and performed with Black musicians in the 1930s when cross-racial collaboration was uncommon.[9]

But those were scattered or minor examples from Davis's younger days before he entered public office. Beyond the overwhelming and deplorable segregationist record of his second term, the best evidence of Davis's views on race would come four years after he left office. On September 11, 1968 (his sixty-ninth birthday), Davis introduced George C. Wallace—a third-party presidential candidate and former governor of Alabama—to an audience at the Roosevelt Hotel in New Orleans. Davis lavished praise on his former colleague, one of the nation's foremost segregationists. "I've never introduced one for whom I had more respect and admiration," he said, adding that Wallace, who had presided over some of the nation's worst racial violence during the early 1960s, was "a man of understanding, a man with deep compassion in his heart and soul for all the people he will serve, regardless of whom they may be, a man through whose veins must flow the milk of human kindness."[10]

Whether Davis's heart was in the effort to keep Black children from attending the state's better-funded all-white school was irrelevant. His private views on race did not matter to Black children or their parents; his official actions did. And those acts supported a racist system that kept Black citizens locked in their second-class status. True, there was no widespread violence or civil unrest, but the relative absence of bloodshed was cold comfort to thousands of young Black citizens denied a decent education besides other human rights. According to historian Glen Jeansonne, by 1964, Davis signed 131 new segregation laws. No state during this era enacted more.[11]

Segregation was not the only contentious issue Davis would face during his second term. Suggestions of cronyism and corruption stained his reputation after news emerged that some of his close associates had chartered the Baker Bank and Trust Company just north of Baton Rouge, where the state government deposited millions at no interest. The associates who created the institution included Davis's friend and top donor, W. L. "Buddy" Billups; Davis's executive secretary, Chris Faser; and the heads of the state's departments of commerce and industry and insurance. By May 1961, $4.9 million of the bank's $8.5 million in deposits were state government accounts on which no interest was being paid. Two months after he left office, Davis would acquire stock in the institution valued at $39,000 ($400,000 in 2024 dollars). Another scandal erupted when the state deposited, interest-free, $23 million ($237 million in 2024 dollars) into the First National Bank of Jefferson Parish in Gretna. Davis downplayed the transactions. "If my colleagues want to buy a Jersey cow or a black stallion, there is nothing for me to say," he told reporters in December 1960.

The scandal over the deals widened when news broke that Faser had received a "finder's fee" for arranging the Gretna bank deposits. Faser, later elected to the Louisiana House, was indicted by a federal grand jury for his role in the alleged bribery scheme. But prosecutors dropped the charges after a key witness died. One state Republican Party official said the questionable banking arrangements were established "for the prime purpose of members of that administration to profit by using state funds to their own advantage." The resulting uproar prompted Davis to propose legislation mandating state funds be deposited in interest-bearing accounts.[12]

Another controversy erupted in 1965 when Capt. William L. Heuer Jr., the former president of the Crescent River Port Pilots Association, told a New Orleans grand jury that during Davis's term, he paid over $100,000 in bribes to legislators and other state officials—including some Davis aides—for their support of legislation favorable to river pilots. Heuer testified he gave Davis a check for $4,000. All the accused denied the allegations, and the investigation ended without indictment. In 1965, Governor John McKeithen denounced the charges as hearsay but acknowledged they had given Louisiana "a black eye."[13]

There was also the matter of the Plainsmen Quartet, a gospel group that had toured with Davis in the late 1950s and accompanied him to campaign rallies in 1959–60. In his first term, Davis found band members state jobs so they could play whenever he needed them. Davis performed the same favor for the singers in 1960, finding a position for Jack Lee Mainord in the Casualty and Surety Division of the Louisiana Insurance Commission. Two other members, Charles Goodman and Thurman Bunch, got jobs as marketing specialists with the Louisiana Strawberry and Advertising Commission. The fourth member, Howard Welborn, found work with the Louisiana Sweet Potato Advertising and Development Commission. In the spring of 1961, state agriculture commissioner Dave Pearce fired Goodman, Bunch, and Welborn after news reports that the quartet had performed in Missouri and Iowa in April and May without taking leave from their state jobs.

The quartet, formed in 1956, had become one of the more popular gospel groups in the country and had toured throughout the South and Midwest in the late 1950s. In early 1960, they would also branch into country music, backing Shreveport's Johnny Horton on his hit recording of "North to Alaska." Considering their popularity, it's unclear why they needed state jobs other than that Davis wanted them to perform with him when needed. News of the group's employment prompted state senator French Jordan of Gretna to ask why Davis's "singing people" were not employed at the state Department of Commerce and Industry "where they can travel all around the country, so the world can appreciate the way they sing. If Jimmie Davis isn't smart enough to get those boys in commerce and industry, he hasn't got sense enough to be governor."

Davis also appointed his longtime friend and piano player, former *Grand Ole Opry* star Moon Mullican, to a $7,000-a-year job with the Louisiana Board of Alcoholic Beverage Control. When Davis had last served as governor, he appointed his brother Henry Davis to a senior position at the Commerce and Industry Department. In May 1960, he did so again, making his younger brother the department's assistant director. The following year, Davis promoted Henry to the department's top job.[14]

On other fronts, Davis's determination to build a new, million-dollar governor's mansion sparked charges of wasteful spending, as did his advocacy for constructing a new $30 million toll bridge across the Mississippi River at Donaldsonville, which opened in October 1964. Named the Sunshine Bridge, the span sparked controversy from its inception, not just because his critics saw its name as a tribute to Davis and his trademark song. Davis and others argued that the state needed a bridge over the river between New Orleans and Baton Rouge, an eighty-mile stretch of river with nothing but ferry crossings. "We couldn't get industry to locate on the west side of the river until we had a bridge," he would explain years later. "We were lagging terribly behind other Southern states in industrial development." One Baton Rouge lawmaker blasted it as a boondoggle that "starts no place and ends no place." Former New Orleans mayor Chep Morrison, running in 1963 to succeed Davis as governor, echoed that refrain. It was a bridge, he said, "that starts nowhere and goes nowhere."

In Baton Rouge, it was no secret that the bridge's name was a tribute to Davis and a vanity project for the outgoing governor that violated the spirit of a state law that prohibited public structures from being named after living individuals. Asked by reporters why he had given the bridge its unusual name, Davis replied, "I think it's because the sun rises in the East and sets in the West." Time would vindicate the decision to build the bridge, although the toll revenue that Davis promised didn't materialize. "The wisdom and the logic behind the construction of this bridge have been borne out," former governor Davis said in October 1964 at the span's dedication. In time, the Sunshine Bridge became a vital link between the east and west sides of the Mississippi downriver from Baton Rouge. It helped spark the industrial development on the west side that Davis had envisioned.[15]

While the bridge named Sunshine may have raised some eyebrows, a horse that Davis owned—also named Sunshine—was the source of the most celebrated visit to his office during the second term. In 1960, Davis had bought a five-year-old white palomino gelding—part quarter horse and part Arabian—for two hundred dollars from a man nicknamed Mexican Pete who lived on Lake St. John near Jonesville. Davis named the horse after his lucrative song. With Davis in the saddle, riding in parades across Louisiana, the gelding became famous. Davis later recalled Sunshine "was a true ham, loved parades, bands and people, and was very gentle with children."[16]

Davis's idea to ride Sunshine up the Capitol steps, through the building's Memorial Hall, and into the Governor's Office was spontaneous. He claimed he was sitting in his office on the morning of Saturday, June 17, 1961, chatting with several reporters when one of them asked about his horse. Sunshine was outside and saddled up for an event later that morning. "Just a minute," Davis said, leaving his office. Then, he rode the horse up the forty-eight steps, through the main entrance, and into his executive office. Tourists and state workers who witnessed the scene were agog. The next day, newspapers around the state carried a photograph of Davis, wearing a cowboy hat and dark bolo tie, sitting on Sunshine outside the Capitol's entrance. Asked by a reporter why he brought the horse into the building, Davis quipped, "Sunshine had never been in the governor's office before." A reporter who witnessed the scene joked, "That's the first time the whole horse was ever in the governor's office." Davis's stunt might have been influenced by memories of singing movie cowboy Roy Rogers, who rode his horse, Trigger, into the lobby and up to room 170 of the Queen's Hotel in Birmingham, England, in February 1954. No matter how the idea occurred to him, the episode attracted statewide and some national attention.[17]

State representative Jack M. Dyer of Baton Rouge, Davis's harshest critic in the legislature, found the stunt offensive. Dyer shipped the governor a bale of hay with a note that explained the straw was "for your horse Sunshine and the jackasses who are advising you." Other critics wondered if Davis had posed atop the horse for the cover of a new album. (He hadn't.)[18]

Years later, critics and admirers alike would see the image of Davis astride Sunshine at the base of the Capitol steps as an act of civil rights defiance. Overseers once rode horses and clutched rifles or whips as they watched enslaved people pick cotton. At the state prison at Angola, corrections officers on horses still minded inmates in the fields. Even if Davis meant his ride as nothing more than a joyous outing with his beloved horse, others saw it as a political statement and a rebellious act to

Davis rode his horse, Sunshine, up the Louisiana Capitol steps and into the governor's office in 1962. (Robert Gentry Louisiana Hayride Collection, LSUS Northwest Louisiana Archives)

support segregation. The authors of a well-regarded book on Louisiana history in 1997 asserted that Davis rode Sunshine into the Capitol "as a symbolic gesture to demonstrate his belief in the supremacy of the white race." After all, the stunt came just months after Judge J. Skelly Wright forced Davis to retreat over the desegregation of New Orleans schools. The only problem with this characterization is that it is difficult to find a contemporaneous account of the incident that viewed it through the lens of defiant pro-segregation.[19]

Still, the idea persisted. Raymond Strother, a campaign advisor to Davis in the early 1970s, would recall people approaching him to say, "Remember when Jimmie rode his horse into the office?" Strother said he nodded as people would add, "He showed 'em, didn't he?" Strother confessed he had "only a vague notion of who the 'them' was, and no concept of what Davis had proved, but this symbolic act of defiance resonated with his red-dirt voters." (The horse would perish in a freak highway accident near Ruston in May 1965.)[20]

The image of Davis as a defiant segregationist was now so vivid in the public mind that even innocent stunts like riding a horse were seen as coded statements about civil rights. As veteran New Orleans journalist Harnett T. Kane wrote in the *New York Times* in January 1961, "bland Jimmie Davis has been pushed into the nervous stance of leader of furious segregationists in a last-stand defiance of the United States government." The reporter added that "the Governor has sided with elements which have threatened to close all schools in the state, which held a mass meeting culminating in the New Orleans street riots and concurred in highly organized campaigns of harassment of white men and women who took their children to desegregated classes."[21]

It was not simply Davis's reputation that had suffered because of his association with segregation and his alliances with ugly racists. "You Are My Sunshine" suffered, too. By the time Davis left office in 1964, the song he had sung to musical, movie, and political fame was now sullied by its association with a segregationist governor. While he was not a malicious race-baiter in the style of Willie Rainach and Leander Perez, he had been their loyal ally in the fight to deny fundamental human rights to a third of Louisiana's population. "Sunshine" had once been a song about lost love. Now, after Davis's 1960 campaign and the racist tenor of his second term, it was the theme song of a prominent segregationist.

Newspaper stories and editorials in Louisiana and throughout the country discussed Davis's fight for segregation. Many identified him as the "writer" or "author" of "Sunshine." In an editorial in November 1960, the *Decatur (IL) Herald* sneered, "Segregationist Gov. Jimmie Davis of Louisiana wrote the ballad 'You Are My Sunshine.' Too bad the country music industry couldn't have kept him too busy to get into politics." An editorial the same month in the student newspaper of the University of North Carolina at Chapel Hill, the *Daily Tarheel,* observed, "Someday, ol' Jimmie, men like you are going to awaken to the fact that the sunshine you sing about isn't the exclusive property of the white people." In another editorial the same day about Davis's segregation efforts, the *Daytona Beach (FL) Morning Journal* referred to him as "Jimmie 'You Are My Sunshine' Davis" and declared that he was "bent on making Orval Faubus look like Caspar Milquetoast in segregationists' eyes." The *Tampa Tribune* that month, in an editorial headlined "No 'Sunshine' for New Orleans," also compared Davis to Faubus, suggesting his "greatest contribution to American life was the composition of that old jukebox favorite 'You Are My Sunshine.'" The editors noted that "the dark clouds of racial conflict again gather in the South. And with Jimmie Davis calling the tune, there is no 'sunshine' of moderation in Louisiana." A few days later, the *Arkansas Gazette* joked about Davis's promise to go to prison before he agreed to school integration. "If Jimmie Davis actually succeeds in landing in [the] pokey there at least will be the consolation that he will have plenty of time for composing some especially lachrymose hillbilly ballads."[22]

That fall, the *New York Post* attacked Davis for a state law denying state and federal welfare assistance to children born to unmarried parents. Davis argued that the legislation would clear the welfare rolls of people "who make it their business" to have babies to collect government funds. The federal government responded by threatening to halt all welfare aid to the state, which the *Post* editorial found monstrous: "This bureaucratic response . . . will accomplish less than nothing to stop the cruelty. One might as well send the frantic unmarried mothers copies of the governor's old hit 'You Are My Sunshine.'"[23]

When Davis had proposed a sales tax increase to support his school segregation initiatives, the Black-owned *Louisiana Weekly* in New Orleans labeled the proposal "the controversial 'You Are My Sunshine' one cent sales tax to maintain segregation in Louisiana." On February 12, 1961, protesters across Texas picketed segregated movie theaters on Abraham Lincoln's birthday. In Austin, a group at one theater rewrote the lyrics to "Battle Hymn of the Republic." They sang, "We'll send Jimmie Davis to an integrated hell" and "We'll hang Orval Faubus to a sour apple tree." A typical example of press commentary about Davis was the observation by a columnist in the *Detroit Free Press* in June 1961 (and carried by other newspapers): "Draw a line east and west, immediately above Alexandria [Louisiana]. To the north are the hard shells, the bitter-end segregationists. They are championed by the Hon. Jimmie H. Davis, he who wrote 'You Are My Sunshine'—governor."[24]

The shadow of racism had descended over one of America's best-loved songs. And Davis, with his disgraceful segregationist record, could do little about it. A progressive white performer could not provide the artistic redemption his song needed. Rescuing "Sunshine" from segregationist purgatory demanded the vision and creativity of a Black artist. Lucky for the song and Davis's bank account, just such an entertainer was ready to breathe new life and popularity into "You Are My Sunshine."

11

A Musical Act of Racial Trespassing

Singer Ray Charles once claimed that the segregation of his rural northern Florida youth hadn't troubled him much. Since childhood, the legendary R&B artist once recalled, "I'd understood that white folks could go wherever the hell they pleased but that we were restricted to our own place and that place had been determined by whites." He acknowledged the system and its rules for white-Black relationships "and knew it was rotten. But I was just too busy trying to stay alive to let it drive me crazy."

Perhaps because he'd been blind as a child, he didn't experience the South's racial divide like his friends. One example he later cited was the months at age seventeen when he briefly played piano in a white country band from Tampa, the Florida Playboys. He said white audiences accepted him because "I could play the music right [and] didn't give 'em anything to laugh at." But he offered another reason: "A lot of the black/white thing in the South was caused by white men worrying about black cats [pursuing] their women. Since I couldn't see—and since they saw I couldn't see—I wasn't much of a threat."[1]

Still, he felt racism's pain and humiliation. Even though Florida had educated him in the Colored Department of the Florida School for the Deaf and Blind, the department was an underfunded stepchild of the larger institution. Black teachers were underpaid. The Black staff grew vegetables in the school's garden that went first to white students. One teacher recalled that even the braille textbooks were hand-me-downs "with the bumps so mashed down the children could hardly read them." Students were trained in menial labor and industrial arts, like broom-making.[2]

Charles also felt racism's sting when touring with his band in the

1950s, an era when driving through the Jim Crow South was a challenge for all Black people. Charles and his musicians couldn't stay at white-owned hotels or motels. They often ate takeout from places that refused them admittance. "We could be hungry as bears and go half a day before we'd find a joint that would serve us," Charles remembered. Bathroom breaks were often roadside. One night outside Natchez, Mississippi, a near-miss on a one-lane bridge led to a confrontation with a white driver. When the police arrived, they ordered everyone off the bus. They lined up alongside the vehicle as an officer shined a flashlight into the men's eyes and spat abusive questions. When a young musician from Pittsburgh forgot to end his answers with "Yes, sir" or "No, sir," the officer erupted. "Don't you know, boy, it's the law in Mississippi a nigger gotta say 'Yes, sir' to a white man?!"[3]

Charles recalled that "the wickedness" of racism "started creeping into our professional life, and I found that I wasn't the right one to tolerate it." He objected when white promoters of his concerts forced Black audience members into the balcony while whites sat downstairs. He refused to play one such date in Augusta, Georgia, in the mid-1950s and lost as much as $2,000 when the promoter sued for breach of contract. Around the same time, he wouldn't play a segregated date in Memphis until the venue allowed whites and Blacks "to mingle." It may have been the first interracial concert audience in the city's history. Charles claimed he reissued that ultimatum in 1962 at a performance in Baton Rouge. "We demanded that the concert be integrated, and it was," he wrote in his autobiography. "I think we were the first band to integrate music events in places like Nashville and Baton Rouge," Charles said. If true, it made no news in the local white or Black Baton Rouge press.

Charles had been making and playing his music in Louisiana for almost a decade. He made several recordings in August 1953 at Cosimo Matassa's J&M Recording Studio on New Orleans's North Rampart Street (the studio where twenty-one-year-old Fats Domino had cut his first hit, "The Fat Man," in 1949). Among his other appearances in the state, Charles played at the Temple Roof Garden, a popular Baton Rouge site for Black audiences, in September 1955 and August 1959. In 1960 and 1961, he gave performances in and around New Orleans.[4]

When asserting that he had first integrated a Baton Rouge venue, Charles might have been remembering one of his 1962 performances in New Orleans. The first two were at Tulane University's McAlister Auditorium on March 2 and another at the city's Municipal Auditorium on July 24, which attracted a sellout crowd of more than 8,700. The fourth would come in December at Loyola University. All were integrated. But Charles was not the first Black performer to play to a mixed-race audience in Louisiana. In April 1956—months before Governor Earl Long signed legislation banning mixed-race concerts, sporting events, and social functions—Domino and Little Richard had performed for integrated audiences at the Loyola Field House. Nat King Cole had sung to what was probably an interracial crowd at New Orleans's Municipal Auditorium the same month. (The US Supreme Court invalidated the Louisiana segregation law in 1959.)[5]

White fans in New Orleans and elsewhere came to hear Charles sing the million-selling hits he had released since the late 1950s, including "What'd I Say" in 1959, "Georgia on My Mind" in 1960, and "Hit the Road Jack" in 1961. In 1962, he would add several recordings to his list of hits after he released two wildly successful volumes of country songs, *Modern Sounds in Country and Western Music.*

Charles grew up listening to country music on the radio, especially the *Grand Ole Opry,* and the songs from that long-running show, he said, "had been performing inside my head since I was a kid in the country." He recorded his first country song in 1959 when he covered Hank Snow's "I'm Movin' On" with an R&B beat. In April 1962, he released the first of two country albums he would make that year. Among the twelve songs on volume 1 were Don Gibson's "I Can't Stop Loving You"; "Bye Bye Love," an Everly Brothers' hit; and three Hank Williams standards, "Half as Much," "You Win Again," and "Hey, Good Lookin'." The album also included two songs that Jimmie Davis had recorded and for which Davis was listed as a coauthor: "Worried Mind" (he shared rights with a Beauregard Parish native, Ted Daffan) and "It Makes No Difference Now" (which Davis bought from Floyd Tillman in 1938).

Charles's interpretations of the twelve country standards were reminiscent of the smooth, modern sound—lavishly orchestrated and arranged—

that he used on "Georgia on My Mind." Most of the recordings (arranged by Marty Paich, Sid Feller, and Gerald Wilson) were, in the words of one music historian, "state-of-the-art country-pop arrangements, string-bejeweled and augmented by a mass of backing vocals." The respected music critic Robert Christgau praised Charles's country project as trail-blazing and historic: "It did nothing less than redefine American pop. Sonically bolder (and schlockier) than, for instance, Owen Bradley's countrypolitan Patsy Cline productions, its massed strings, horns and choruses broke down the walls between classic Tin Pan Alley and déclassé Nashville. In the world it created, not only could a black person sing the American Songbook Ella Fitzgerald owned by then, but a country black person could take it over. Soon Charles' down-home diction, cotton-field grit, corn-pone humor and overstated shows of emotion were standard operating procedure in American music, black and white."[6]

Charles hadn't planned to release any song as a single, regarding the collection as a concept album, not a series of potential hit songs. But when actor/singer Tab Hunter released a version of "I Can't Stop Loving You" using Charles's arrangement, Charles's record company, ABC-Paramount, rushed singles into production for wide distribution, hoping to smother a competitor. Charles's version was an instant and enormous hit. It spent five weeks atop *Billboard*'s Hot 100 and reached the pinnacle of the R&B and adult contemporary charts. *Billboard* deemed it 1962's second-most-popular song. The first album was also a massive success, spending fourteen weeks leading the pop album chart and selling more than 500,000 copies in its first three months. It would become the first million-selling album of country songs. Besides "I Can't Stop Loving You," *Modern Sounds* contained three more big hits: "Born to Lose," "Careless Love," and "You Don't Know Me."[7]

By early September, Charles returned to the studio for a second volume of country songs. Unlike the first, which had alternated between fast and slow tunes, volume 2 featured one side of big-band arrangements (side A, recorded in New York on September 5) sung by Charles and accompanied by the Ray Charles Big Band and his backup singers, the Raelettes. The B-side (recorded in Hollywood on September 7) featured the same lush strings from the first album, backed by the Jack Halloran Singers. The album of twelve recordings included two more Hank Williams songs, "Your Cheatin' Heart" and "Take These Chains from My Heart"; Don Gibson's "Oh, Lonesome Me" and "Don't Tell Me Your Troubles"; and a Ted Daffan song that Jimmie Davis had sometimes sung on the campaign trail in 1943, "No Letter Today."

But the album's first song was the most interesting—a dramatic and distinctive reinvention of "You Are My Sunshine." In the words of one music historian, Charles's rendition was a "transfiguration" of the country standard. He replaced the old melody with a rollicking R&B tune that sounded nothing like the original or any other version. Charles's smooth, melismatic phrasing dominated the early half of the performance. "What Charles has done to it is to transform it into an entirely different thing by applying to it the structure of a gospel song," music critic Ralph J. Gleason marveled about "Sunshine" in a December 1962 review of the album. Gleason observed that the Raelettes and their lead singer, Margie Hendrix, "treat this old hillbilly tune exactly as if it were being sung (and swung) on a Sunday night radio broadcast from a gospel choir with a preacher."[8]

But in Charles's skillful hands, the song became far more than an R&B-suffused gospel-sounding record. It was also a big-band swing song that swelled with the sounds of an impressive, bold brass arrangement. Toward the middle, Hendrix's robust and soulful voice dominates as she sings to Charles about how "you've shattered all of my dreams." As country music scholar Jocelyn R. Neal observed, "Charles's soul-drenched treatment of the song . . . eliminated the straight-ahead three-chord harmonic progression, the largely scalar, identifiable melody, and the vestiges of hillbilly twang that still lingered in contemporaneous country recordings. In Charles's treatment, the lyrics and the album's title alone connected the recording to the country genre."[9]

Nothing about this version of "Sunshine" was like what Davis, Bing Crosby, Carl McVoy, or Richard Berry had produced. It was a dazzling, vibrant, danceable, and engaging recording. And it was no surprise that by November, the song reached number seven on the *Billboard* Hot 100

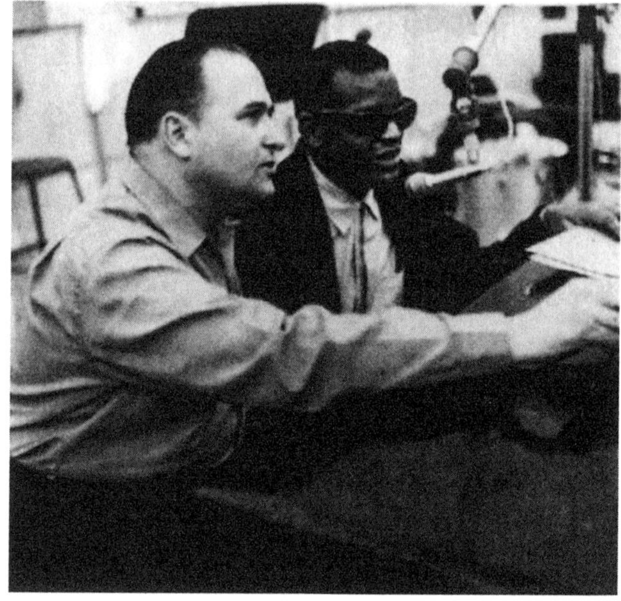

Ray Charles (*right*) with producer Sid Feller, who helped Charles with the groundbreaking country-concept album set *Modern Sounds in Country and Western Music* in 1962. Charles's interpretation of "Sunshine" was a huge national hit. (Wikimedia Commons)

chart and, by December, was number one on the R&B chart. In November, *Billboard* commented on the album's stunning success, "No one could possibly have forecast the huge quantities of records that were sold throughout the South and Southwest."[10]

In December 1962, at the crest of his popularity and fame, Charles returned to New Orleans for a concert at the Loyola University Field House. His appearances and absences had already caused unrest in several cities. In September 1960, a crowd wrecked a ballroom in Portland, Oregon, after learning his plane had been grounded in Seattle and that he wouldn't appear. The following month, police arrested thirty people before a Charles concert in Baltimore after violence erupted when several fans broke in line. This may be why Jimmie Davis phoned Charles after an integrated Louisiana concert in 1962. "I'm proud to say the Negroes acted better than the whites," Charles recalled the governor telling him.

Charles did not say if the implied bigotry in Davis's words offended him, but his response suggests what he thought: "'All right, man. Whatever's fair,' was all I could say in reply." (Davis was having his own successful year in music, releasing a revised version of "Where the Old Red River Flows," which rose to fifteen on *Billboard*'s country chart in June.)[11]

Hours before his appearance at Loyola, heavy fog prevented Charles's plane from landing in New Orleans. The pilots diverted to Baton Rouge, where Davis ordered a State Police escort for Charles and his band. In the throes of heroin addiction, Charles made the troopers wait while he and a musician ducked into an airport bathroom to get high. Despite the high-speed escort, the performance started three hours late. The *Louisiana Weekly* reported that "the audience almost erupted" when Charles sang "Sunshine." One Charles biographer suggested that Davis attended the concert and presented the R&B singer with an award for his hit recording of "Sunshine." If this happened, the local press failed to mention it.[12]

The drastic rearrangement of his song did not bother or offend Davis. And it's unlikely Charles meant to insult him. His first album included several songs that Davis owned. And he featured "Sunshine" as the first song of the second album. *Jet* magazine reported in January 1963 that after Charles had turned his version of "Sunshine" into a lucrative hit, "'Soulful' singer Ray Charles is helping make segregationist Louisiana Gov. Jimmie Davis rich with his rendition of the country and western tune." Asked about Charles's version, Davis said he was happy about the song's success. He seemed bemused by the popularity of the reinterpreted classic, averring that Charles had applied "wilder treatment" than he or other artists who had covered the song. "I don't care how they sing it—just so they sing it!" he told one correspondent. There's no public accounting of Davis's windfall from Charles's 1962 recordings of "Sunshine" and the two other songs he owned. But the royalty income that poured into the account of the late Hank Williams's music publisher, Acuff-Rose, that year offers a clue. Williams's earnings jumped by more than $25,000 for 1962 ($255,000 in 2024 dollars). Charles had recorded three songs written or owned by each artist.[13]

What Davis didn't say—and likely didn't yet perceive—was that Charles gave the world an astonishing, fresh arrangement of the song that had revolutionized it and would place Charles's version on near-equal footing with the traditional tune. It's also remarkable that, of the twenty-four songs on the two *Modern Sounds* albums, only "Sunshine" was a radical departure from the original melody. Charles may have applied his interpretation or sung in a pop or R&B style on all the other songs in the project, but he didn't sing them to a wholly different tune. The only one he revised completely was "Sunshine." Perhaps that's because it was the oldest and best-known song on both albums. Or maybe he was sending a subtle message to the segregationist governor: I'll record your song, but I'll redefine it, and make it mine, too.

The racial prejudice in country radio was a subtext for the whole two-album project. Charles's arrangements for most of the songs differed little from the burgeoning "Nashville Sound" that became popular in the late 1950s and early 1960s. Only those that featured brass instruments would have struck a discordant chord on country radio. The rest would have fit in. Popular country artists like Patsy Cline, Jim Reeves, and Bill Anderson made records in the same style. That country DJs refused to play Charles's records in the early 1960s was almost certainly about his race, not his music. "The absence from country radio of 'You Don't Know Me' and 'I Can't Stop Loving You' was racially motivated," *Rolling Stone*'s David Cantwell declared in a 2019 retrospective about the albums. Music journalist Daniel Cooper reported that only a few northern radio stations that were "experimenting with country programs" would play Charles's songs. "The country old guard, on the other hand, was apparently in one accord that *Modern Sounds in Country and Western Music* had no place on their playlists," Cooper explained, adding, "It's also unlikely ABC bothered to push the single very hard in the country market, given its runaway success in the far more lucrative pop arena."[14]

Charles later insisted he'd had no political agenda when considering whether to make an album of country songs. He had jumped recently from Atlantic Records to ABC-Paramount and was eager to try new styles. ABC-Paramount executives tried to dissuade him, worried that recording country songs might alienate fans. Charles was unconcerned.

"I had no commercial scheme in mind," he wrote later. "I just wanted to try my hand at hillbilly music." He also maintained he wasn't trying to be the first Black country singer: "I only wanted to take country songs and sing them my way, not the country way. I wasn't aware of any bold act on my part or any big breakthrough."[15]

But it was not the first time Charles had reinvented a song associated with racism. His first appearance on the pop charts was in 1957 when he recorded a revised version of Stephen Foster's minstrel song "Old Folks at Home," titled "Swanee River Rock (Talkin' 'bout That River)." As music historian Diane Pecknold observed, Charles transformed the "nostalgic lament into a rollicking hand-clapping gospel stomp that reappropriated the racist stereotypes of the blackface stage in a sly nod both to the historical roles race and racism played in shaping American popular music and to the tenacity and creativity of African Americans who made popular music an important cultural defense against racism." In the liner notes for a compilation of Charles's country records from 1959 to 1986, Daniel Cooper noted that "other blacks had played country music, but none in recent times had so openly claimed it by name. Charles dared whites to object." Cooper added that even in 1962, Charles was often described by reporters "as 'Negro pianist' or 'the blind Negro singer and instrumentalist.'" In making *Modern Sounds,* Cooper concluded, Charles was "audaciously validating the music of the Southern white working class, the very people viewed by many as ready to kill in defense of their determination not to serve lunch to a man of Charles' color."[16]

Music historian and journalist J. Lester Feder argued that regardless of what Charles intended for "Sunshine" and the two volumes of *Modern Sounds,* the R&B artist had encroached on established musical boundaries of the day. "First and foremost, it reveals Charles's use of genre to construct a spatial assault on segregation that paralleled the Civil Rights Movement's most basic tactic: trespassing," Feder wrote. "By the 1950s, segregation had evolved into a system that, at its most material, worked by racializing space. Buses, water fountains, schools, lunch counters—every southern arena was divided into separate-and-unequal black and white zones." Charles's 1962 albums, Feder said, represented "the disruption of segregation's spatial mechanisms," much like Rosa Parks on a Montgomery, Alabama, bus, or the lunch-counter sit-ins by the Student Nonviolent Coordinating Committee (SNCC). "Though he did so in a way that appears to have been non-threatening to his white fans," he explained, "Charles seems to have given a musical form to integrationist trespassing in taking down the barriers that remained in adult-oriented music. He performed the musical equivalent of a sit-in—the black musician trespassing on the whites-only terrain of Good Music." Charles's recording of "Sunshine," Feder concludes, "is a wholesale deconstruction of the barriers erected between black and white music."[17]

Rolling Stone's David Cantwell agreed: "The record was a subtle, and in many ways not subtle at all, embodiment of the integration [Alabama governor George] Wallace and other racists were standing against." Diane Pecknold believed Charles "clearly intended the album as a significant crossing of genre boundaries, and social as well as musical terms." Raul Malo of the Mavericks argued that Charles "not only made a country music record, but did it in his own inimitable way, [and] proved that the genre did not solely belong to white people." Musician and music critic Jimi Calhoun perhaps had the simplest explanation for what Charles accomplished with "Sunshine" and the other country songs on both albums. "My take on Ray Charles's decision," Calhoun wrote in *The Art of God,* "is that he subtly signaled that the past did not matter because the future is yet to be decided."[18]

Charles "trespassed" on Davis's musical property, rearranged the song, and claimed the updated version as his own, giving the music world a fresh and modern recording. Charles's 1962 version of "Sunshine" was the most popular release of the song in twenty years. Before Charles rearranged and recorded "Sunshine," it had been a white country standard associated with a prominent segregationist. Before Charles, the only Black artists to record vocal versions were Nat King Cole in 1955, Richard Berry in 1957, and the Marcels in 1961. After Charles, it became as much a song for Black artists as for whites. The Rivingtons in 1962, Dee Dee Sharp and Marvin Gaye in 1963, Ike & Tina Turner in 1965, and Aretha Franklin and Jackie Shane in 1967—all recorded the song in distinct styles. But each used Charles's melody.

Jimmie Davis had the horse and the bridge named Sunshine, and he still owned the lyrics and melody of his 1940 version of the song and all the royalties accompanying it. But the singer and segregationist governor who had spent much of his early career buying and appropriating the music of others now shared his most famous song with a Black artist.

12

It's a Very Catchy Ditty

Davis turned the new Governor's Mansion over to a charismatic successor in the spring of 1964. A resident of Columbia, forty miles from Davis's birthplace of Beech Springs, John J. McKeithen had spent four years in the state House before winning the job that Davis and Huey Long had used as a stepping stone to the governor's office—north Louisiana's seat on the Public Service Commission.

Despite their similarities, McKeithen and Davis were not allies. Once a House floor leader for Earl Long, the Columbia lawyer resembled Davis in substance and style about as much Davis's version of "Sunshine" sounded like Ray Charles's 1962 recording. And the way McKeithen had campaigned for office only widened the divide between the two men. In appearances across the state, McKeithen attacked Davis and his "Baker Bank crowd," a reference to the scandal involving individuals who formed the bank into which Davis's administration deposited millions in state funds, interest-free.

A tall, imposing man with a natural gift for conversation and making friends, "Big John" had pledged to "move the state forward." The implication was that Davis had produced no such progress. McKeithen charged that under Davis, Louisiana "had no money for school lunches and higher teacher salaries, yet they have plenty of money for the Baker Bank." McKeithen also ridiculed the new Governor's Mansion, joking that "with those eighteen bathrooms in the mansion, Jimmie Davis may not be the best, but he ought to be the cleanest governor in Louisiana history."[1]

None of that campaign enmity between the two men had prevented Governor-elect McKeithen from joining Governors Paul Johnson of Mississippi and Orval Faubus of Arkansas at a dinner at Baton Rouge's

Jack Tar Capitol House Hotel in mid-May 1964 to honor Davis. Among those in attendance to celebrate his second term were his quartet, the Plainsmen, and his longtime friend and campaign piano player, Moon Mullican, who joined the group for two numbers. Finally, Davis rose to sing a series of songs, including "Put on Your Old Gray Bonnet," "The Beginning of the End," and "How Great Thou Art." He concluded with "You Are My Sunshine," or, as the *Baton Rouge Advocate* described it, "his meal ticket." The vice president of Decca Records was there, too, and presented Davis with a lifetime recording contract.[2]

Out of office, Davis returned to singing and recording hymns. He published a 265-page collection of sacred songs, *All-Time Favorite Hymns.* And he presided over constructing a large, comfortable home on the banks of Capitol Lake, behind the Governor's Mansion. Davis took part in another construction project, the 750-seat nondenominational Jimmie Davis Tabernacle at Beech Springs—financed by a group of wealthy supporters and other donors, including W. L. "Buddy" Billups, the head of Billups Petroleum and Davis's chief patron. McKeithen joined 1,500 friends and fans of Davis for the tabernacle's dedication in May 1965, seeming to bury their former enmity.[3]

McKeithen may also have hoped to bury any chance that Davis might oppose a constitutional amendment that lawmakers put on the ballot in November 1966 and that would allow him and future governors to serve two consecutive terms. The forty-eight-year-old McKeithen had proved a well-liked leader almost three years into his term. Much of his popularity rested on his and lawmakers' significant investments in health, education, and public works programs. But his administration was far more than a return to the big-spending Long years. He passed a tougher ethics code and established a state ethics commission to enforce it, among other initiatives. In no area, however, did he leave a more meaningful legacy than in race relations. Unlike Davis, he accepted the inevitability of school desegregation, worked to tamp down racial violence, appointed Blacks to important state jobs, and supported enforcing the Civil Rights Act of 1964. All this put him in a favorable position to woo Black voters as he argued for changing the constitution to permit him another term.

Louisiana governor John McKeithen, a sometime adversary of Davis, vetoed legislation in 1968 to make "You Are My Sunshine" the state song. (Louisiana Digital Library)

Louisiana governors had dreamed for decades of amending the constitution or bending the law to give them more or longer terms. In 1950, Earl Long tried to persuade lawmakers to convene a constitutional convention during which he hoped delegates would give governors one six-year term. He abandoned the effort in the face of public opposition. Ten years later, Long hatched a short-lived plan to succeed himself as governor by turning the office over to his lieutenant governor for the last months of his term. But, of all Louisiana governors since Huey Long, McKeithen's popularity put him in the strongest position to argue for the constitutional change.

Davis, who made it no secret he might run for governor again, opposed the amendment. In a thirty-minute statewide television speech in mid-October, he listed his reasons, including that an eight-year tenure might allow a governor to accumulate too much power. In that time, he said, a chief executive could "gain control of the LSU Board of Supervisors, local elections, blue ribbon boards, and probably the legislature." He said if he were governor "and could run for a second term, I wouldn't do it." Unpleasant memories of McKeithen's attacks on him during the 1964 campaign might have influenced Davis's position. And McKeithen seemed to have decided such attacks were still compelling arguments. By the last month of the referendum campaign, he framed the amendment as a choice between his record and Davis's, asking at one press conference if Louisiana voters wished to return to the days of the "Sunshine Bridge gang." In the November election, 69 percent of voters backed the amendment, almost guaranteeing McKeithen another term and making it unlikely Davis or any other politician could mount a viable challenge.[4]

As they had after McKeithen's 1964 election, the two men appeared to abandon their campaign acrimony. In April 1967, McKeithen attended the annual *Capitol Correspondents Association Gridiron Show.* During his rebuttal to the journalists' ribbing, McKeithen invited former governors Davis, Noe, Jones, and Kennon to join him onstage. Noting that Davis, still a potential opponent in the 1967 election, lived near the Governor's Mansion, McKeithen joked, "He is my nearest neighbor, and I hope he stays that way." Davis summoned the Plainsmen to the stage and sang, with apparent irony, "It's a Hard Row to Travel to That Mansion on the Hill." Then, Davis and McKeithen led the audience in "You Are My Sunshine."[5]

Davis could read polls and election returns better than a sheet of music, and the constitutional amendment's passage was persuasive evidence that McKeithen was unbeatable. Davis surprised no one by declining to run for governor. In November 1967, McKeithen won a landslide election for the Democratic Party's nomination, beating an unwavering segregationist, US representative John Rarick of St. Francisville. Because Republicans ran no candidate for governor that year, McKeithen was guaranteed a second term. Days later, McKeithen appointed Davis to the LSU Board of Supervisors to fill the unexpired term of former first lady Alvern Davis, who died of cancer in July 1967 and whom Davis had put on the university board in 1960. McKeithen insisted to reporters that appointing Davis and a New Orleans insurance executive whose party affiliation was unknown to him proved he was not trying to control the LSU Board, as Davis had suggested the year before.[6]

Davis was no longer a political threat to McKeithen, and maybe the reelected governor rested easier knowing that the former governor would tour the country singing gospel songs and "Sunshine" for adoring audiences far from the Louisiana Capitol. Still, he may not have welcomed news in May 1968, during the first legislative session of his second term, that two House members, Carl Dawson of Zachary and Parey Branton of Shongaloo, had introduced legislation to make "Sunshine" the Louisiana state song.

Dawson, a former East Baton Rouge Parish School Board president, was the lead sponsor. If he and Davis were intimate friends, such was not apparent, although they had some business dealings, their paths crossed occasionally, and they had friends in common. Davis and the Plainsmen had provided the entertainment in December 1963, when Dawson had presided over the installation of Congressman-elect John Rarick as "worshipful master" of a St. Francisville Masonic lodge. Since early 1965, Dawson served on the Baker Bank and Trust Company board, the controversial institution that Davis intimates had established.[7]

When asked during a House debate why "Sunshine" should be Louisiana's song when it didn't mention the state, Dawson replied, "Whenever anyone asks what Louisiana's state song is, no one ever knows. But everybody in the nation knows 'You Are My Sunshine.'" Some representatives complained that making "Sunshine" the state song would be an implied endorsement of a 1971 Davis gubernatorial campaign. Another proposed making the Cajun standard "Jole Blon" the song of south Louisiana, while "Sunshine" would become the song of north Louisiana. And Representative Jesse McClain of Covington wondered why "Tiger Rag" was not the state song. "That's the state fight song," Dawson quipped.[8]

In the Senate, Jules Mollere of New Orleans complained, "This is like changing the national anthem and substituting a song that is number one on the *Hit Parade*. The song doesn't even mention Louisiana." Senator Jesse Knowles of Lake Charles praised "Sunshine" as "one of the most pretty songs ever written by a Louisianan. It has won a man an election twice, but I do not think it is appropriate for the state song of Louisiana."[9]

The strongest argument against the bill was that Louisiana already had a state song: "Song of Louisiana," written in 1928 by Vashti Robertson Stopher of Baton Rouge, a poet, LSU graduate, and the wife of Henry Wallace Stopher, director of LSU's School of Music from 1915 to 1940.

Louisiana! Louisiana!
Where the mocker sings the sweetest,
And the land is filled with flowers.
With hearts and voices lifted,
In our joyous way.
We sing to Louisiana
Forever and a day.

The legislature and Governor O. K. Allen made it the state song in 1932. In 1952, Governor Bob Kennon signed legislation making another song, "Louisiana, My Home Sweet Home," the state "march song." With words by Sammie McKenzie and Lou Lavoy and music by Castro Carazo, the LSU band had played it at home football games for years. Carazo became LSU's band director in 1934, when US senator Huey Long recruited him from the Fountain Room of New Orleans's Roosevelt Hotel. Some of Long's political instincts must have rubbed off on the former band director. Carazo reportedly persuaded McKenzie and Lavoy to offer their song, not as the state song but as the Louisiana march, reasoning that future lawmakers would not add another march. It was a wise decision, as "Louisiana, My Home Sweet Home," remained the state march into the twenty-first century.[10]

In early July, House members voted 73–23 to supplant "Song of Louisiana" with "Sunshine." A few weeks later, the Senate followed suit, voting 20–16 for Dawson's bill. Several of the state's daily newspapers weighed in before McKeithen announced his position on the legislation. The song, the *New Orleans States-Item* observed, "conjures memories of a dreadful administration (1960–64), marked by horse rides up the Capitol steps, hidden payrolls, construction of a bridge from nowhere to nowhere, a $1 million governor's mansion and a state deficit so huge that a bond issue had to be passed to cure it. No thanks. If it comes down to having 'You Are My Sunshine' or nothing for our official state song, we'll take nothing." The *New Orleans Times-Picayune* pointed out, like many others, that "there is nothing in its lyrics about Louisiana."[11]

McKeithen vetoed the bill the day after Senate passage. Louisiana governors seldom rejected legislation so quickly. "Although I have great esteem for the composer and the song," the governor said in a statement released to reporters, "I don't believe it is appropriate for the state song of Louisiana." To soften the blow, McKeithen proclaimed July 7–13 as "You Are My Sunshine Week." He also suggested lawmakers appoint a "small committee" chaired by Davis to "compose or select an appropriate song to be submitted to the Legislature for approval as the official state song of Louisiana." By one account, McKeithen had labored over four versions of his veto message.[12]

While McKeithen did not frame his veto as slighting Davis, one reporter could not avoid considering the political implications. An Associated Press correspondent observed that Davis "is not numbered among McKeithen's friends." And Adras LaBorde of the *Alexandria Town Talk* noted that McKeithen rejected the bill with unusual speed, "as if an earth-shaking emergency were involved." LaBorde wrote that one Capitol reporter said, "Perhaps the governor was disturbed by the prospect that a band would play 'Sunshine' when his name is offered as a favorite-son presidential candidate at the Democratic national convention next month." The *Shreveport Times* pointed out it was doubtful Davis had written "Sunshine," suggesting "Paul or Hoke Rice" were the authors. Davis made no public remarks about McKeithen's decision.[13]

Few noted the obvious: when McKeithen had wanted a constitutional amendment to allow him to seek a second term, Davis campaigned against it and implied that McKeithen and others might use the new constitutional provision to remain in office for decades. Why anyone thought McKeithen should reward Davis's antagonism by making the singer's biggest hit the state song is unclear. Two years later, McKeithen signed legislation making "Give Me Louisiana," by Doralice Fontane of Baton Rouge, the state song. This time, there was no controversy over the composition. The House approved it 78–6; the Senate, unanimously.[14]

Davis's decision to run for governor again in 1971 might have suggested to McKeithen that he was justified in viewing his Capitol Lake neighbor as a potential rival. Davis still wanted the job. But now, in his early seventies, he was no longer regarded as a sunny compromise candidate who could bridge the tumultuous gap between Longs and anti-Longs. By the early 1970s, such political divisions had faded. Huey Long had been dead for more than thirty-five years.

Davis announced his candidacy in late July 1971 on the steps of the Beech Springs sharecropper's cabin where he was born. Touting his experience, he said that although he didn't have "all the answers, I have many more than one who has never served." Davis campaigned the only way he knew—he sang. The one change was that music was even more critical to his message. "The Davis campaign rolls with the smoothness of a Grand Ol' Opry performance," Allan Katz of the *New Orleans States-Item* observed in October. *Shreveport Times* reporter Wiley Hilburn, who covered Davis's campaign launch in Jonesboro in July, recalled, "He had the routine down to the last detail. He would sing and play a lot; maybe brushstroke an issue here or there, almost an afterthought."[15]

Davis had a new singing partner for his rallies, the former Anna Carter Gordon, whom he married after Alvern died in 1967. If Davis was a gospel music star, Anna (whose first husband also died in 1967) was gospel music royalty. For decades, she sang alto with her family's legendary country-gospel group, the Chuck Wagon Gang. Joining them to round out the entertainment for voters at rallies was a legendary Nashville-based gospel group, the Speer Family, and a former truck driver and rising country singer from Lafayette, Eddy Raven (his real name was Edward Futch). From 1984 to 1990, Raven would score six number-one singles on *Billboard*'s country charts.[16]

As always, Davis held most of his rallies in small towns. He spoke for about ten minutes, and his message had not changed since 1943: "You know, if being governor means I have to lambast some fine man or his wife or fine children, then I don't want the job. When this election is over, and everyone has said their 'amens' and gone home, I want to come back to your fine city and walk your highways and byways. I want to be able to look every man, woman, and child in the eye, for I know that life is short, but eternity is long." As his thirty-one-year-old campaign manager and media consultant, Raymond Strother, recalled, "The speech lasted about twelve minutes, loaded with platitudes and cliches, not a single word of which related to any concern a voter might have—or even to the second half of the twentieth century." The rest of the rallies were music and song.[17]

His music was still entertaining, but many voters saw Davis as a political relic. And he did little to persuade voters he was anything other than the ardent segregationist of his second term. "Busing is the most damaging, most destructive thing that has ever happened to our nation since it became a nation," he told audiences. If anyone countered with an argument about slavery's more deleterious influence on American life, the reporter covering the event didn't mention it.[18]

For all the ways he could still entertain a crowd, Davis was better suited for the pretelevision era. He could stump for votes by making a quick speech before singing a few hymns, capped off with a rousing rendition of "You Are My Sunshine," but his bromides did not land as effectively as before. "Our campaign was an antique museum of the political past, a 78-rpm recording with all the scratches and warps of time," Strother observed. "I felt like a cultural anthropologist studying the rituals, speech patterns, and political techniques of some vanished tribe." In failing to adopt modern campaign methods, Davis appeared lost. He was no match for his younger opponents, including the charismatic US representative Edwin W. Edwards of Crowley; an effective young reformer, state senator J. Bennett Johnston of Shreveport; two younger members of the Long family, US representative Speedy O. Long of Jena and a cousin, former US representative Gillis Long of Alexandria; and state senator John G. Schwegmann of New Orleans. The race also included one of Davis's closest political allies, Lieutenant Governor Clarence "Taddy" Aycock.

Despite his age and the hackneyed feel of his campaign, some Davis opponents regarded him as a strong contender and attacked him by dredging up the scandals and alleged corruption that had marked his second term. To the Baker Bank and Chris Faser bribery allegations, they added one charge that touched Davis directly: after leaving office, he accepted a $5,000-a-month lobbying job with a company that sold $3 million in voting machines and driving simulators to Louisiana agencies during his term. Davis insisted he hadn't lobbied for the company in Louisiana, but news of the arrangement only tarnished him more. Gillis Long was blunt in his criticism. "Jimmie Davis can call it lobbying fees if he wants," he said, "but the rest of the people in Louisiana think that $5,000 a month looks more like a kickback for buying equipment from that firm." In 1972, a federal prosecutor explained that his office had not investigated the case because the federal statute of limitations had expired.[19]

Beyond ignoring reporters' questions about the scandals, Davis did little to assure voters that his attitude toward the state's ethics laws would be different in a third term. To the contrary, Davis said he opposed legislation requiring public officials to resign when charged with a felony. And he scoffed at legislation to force candidates to disclose their funding sources. "If the contributor himself objected," he said, "well, you see, it wouldn't be fair to him."[20]

Decades later, reflecting on the ill-fated campaign, Raymond Strother scoffed at Davis's reputation for integrity and described his candidate's method of raising campaign cash: "Davis would rent a suite [at the Fairmont Hotel in New Orleans] and call in all of the people who had profited from his previous administrations. The people who built the bridges to nowhere, constructed the redundant buildings, warehoused voting machines, sold the cheap food to the schools, built highways that potholed months after completion, poked holes in the earth for oil, soiled the air with pollution, and poisoned the bayous—all those grifters came at regular intervals through the lobby of the elegant old hotel and up to the suite. They understood that although checks were acceptable, cash was the commodity that would win favor with the past and future governor."[21]

At times, the campaign was less a music show and more a circus sideshow. At one stop in Bossier City in September 1971, Davis's refusal to respond to questions about alleged corruption boiled over into violence. As he tried to escape a scrum of reporters at a campaign stop, an overly enthusiastic supporter punched *Shreveport Journal* reporter Carl Liberto when he asked Davis for an interview. Strother said that when he urged Davis to meet with reporters and address their questions, Davis threw him off the campaign bus—at night on a lonely country road. Few were surprised by Davis's fourth-place finish in the Democratic Party primary—at 12 percent, behind Edwards, Johnston, and Gillis Long. Edwards would win the Democratic Party nomination and beat Republican David Treen in the general election.[22]

Davis's election in 1972 to the prestigious Country Music Hall of Fame eased the sting of his only election loss. In winning the honor, he had earned more votes than five other nominees: artists Chet Atkins, Pee Wee King, Kitty Wells, comedian Minnie Pearl, and former *Billboard* music editor Paul Ackerman. He was only the twentieth person ushered into the pantheon of country music greats, and the honor was a recognition of his significant role in the 1930s and 1940s as a pioneer of an American musical genre now popular worldwide. (The year before, he was inducted into the Nashville Songwriters Hall of Fame. In 1993, he would be elected to the Gospel Music Hall of Fame.)[23]

In December 1972, Davis's longtime former band leader/steel guitar player and political aide, Charles Mitchell, died in Shreveport at sixty-seven. Mitchell, who many still believed was the coauthor of "Sunshine," had tried to follow Davis into politics, running unsuccessfully for the Louisiana Public Service Commission in 1948. He returned to Shreveport after helping Davis manage the Stables nightclub in Palm Springs, California, in the late 1940s. After working as deputy clerk of the Shreveport City Court, he became Caddo Parish registrar of voters in 1958, a job he held until his death. He would not live to see "Sunshine" become a Louisiana state song. (Years earlier, he sold his interest in it to Davis for less than fifty dollars.) But decades after his death, journalists and historians still credited the steel guitar player with co-writing "Sunshine" and helping Davis make it world famous.[24]

On March 16, 1974, two years after Mitchell died and Davis entered the Country Music Hall of Fame, "Sunshine" would earn the distinction of being the second song sung from the stage of the new Grand Ole Opry House in Nashville. The show's top star and Davis's longtime friend, Roy Acuff, sang it after he opened with his theme song, "Wabash Cannonball."[25]

Davis's plaque in the Rotunda of the Country Music Hall of Fame. (Robert Mann)

By the mid-1970s, the cause of making "Sunshine" the state song had a new leader: state representative Robert "Bobby" Freeman of Plaquemines Parish. Freeman, who would be elected lieutenant governor in 1979 with Davis's support, was an unabashed country music fan. His first effort to persuade lawmakers to replace "Give Me Louisiana" with "Sunshine" failed in 1976, when House members voted it down 41–35. A bill needed at least 53 votes in the House to become law, meaning not only did "Sunshine" fall short by 12 votes, but only 76 of the 105 House members voted on the bill.[26]

Freeman pushed the measure again the following year, getting it through the House, 57–42. But the bill encountered Senate opposition, only clearing that body after Senators Jim Brown of Ferriday and John

Saunders of Ville Platte offered an amendment making "Sunshine" one of *two* official songs. (Louisiana would not be the only state with more than one state song. As of 2024, six states had two or more state songs. Tennessee had twelve. Each of them—including "Tennessee Waltz," written in 1946 by Pee Wee King and Redd Stewart—mentioned Tennessee.) Not forcing lawmakers to choose between "Sunshine" and "Give Me Louisiana" was the key to getting "Sunshine" approved. The Brown-Saunders amendment passed only after Shreveport senator Virginia Shehee added two Louisiana-specific verses. After over four decades, the song about faded love finally had words associated with Louisiana:

> Louisiana, My Louisiana,
> The place where I was born.
> White fields of clover,
> The best fishing and long, tall corn.
>
> Crawfish gumbo and jambalaya,
> The biggest shrimp and sugar cane.
> The finest oysters and sweet strawberries,
> From Toledo Bend to New Orleans.

With those unrelated additions to a song about lost love, both houses passed the bill. Governor Edwin Edwards, with Davis present, signed it at a press conference on July 14. He told his predecessor that "the high regard many legislators have for you made this possible." Although she was expected to attend the ceremony, Doralice Fontane, the author of the other state song, was absent. She spent months working to keep her composition the sole state song, spending thousands of dollars on the effort, which included hiring a band to record it and sending hundreds of copies to radio stations and school districts. She insisted she harbored no ill will toward "Sunshine." "It's a very catchy ditty," she said, noting, as most opponents did, that it originally had no lyrics about Louisiana. (In 2021, the Louisiana Legislature would retire "Give Me Louisiana," making "Sunshine" Louisiana's sole state song.) Perhaps it was an oversight, or it would have been a distraction from the important business of his press conference, but no one asked Davis to sing his world-famous song on this momentous day. Davis did not complain. "I'm very grateful," he said. "This is quite an honor."[27]

Two years later, in March 1979, Ray Charles—who had redefined "You Are My Sunshine" and released what may have been the best-selling recording of the song—was accorded the honor denied to Davis in 1977: he had the joy of singing his 1960 version of the Hoagy Carmichael–Stuart Gorrell standard "Georgia on My Mind" to a packed Georgia House chamber. Days earlier, lawmakers had made Charles's version the official song of his native state.[28]

13

A Song beyond Politics

Jimmie Davis kept singing "Sunshine" into his late nineties, sometimes performing it at the close of legislative sessions and at other official gatherings of lawmakers and former governors. He recorded it for the last time in 1998 with a children's choir. By his tenth decade, Davis and his music underwent a renaissance. Some younger audiences honored him as a blues and country music pioneer and recognized him as one of the most celebrated politician-entertainers in US history.

At a remarkable appearance in 1993, Davis and his wife, Anna, sang for a large crowd that included many African Americans at the New Orleans Jazz and Heritage Festival. Journalist Jason Berry noted that the presence of many Black fans had underscored that "a generation had passed since the desegregation battles. People were spellbound at the man in his 90s, singing and spinning yarns. He reminded them that he had recorded and performed with black bluesmen in the '20s. Who could revile a guy like that?"[1]

Not only was Davis's reputation as an unwavering segregationist softened by three decades' passage, but Ray Charles and others had reinvented his famous song. From 1963 through 2024, more than 220 artists recorded it, including the Righteous Brothers (1965), Trini Lopez (1965), Count Basie with the Alan Copeland Singers (1966), Burl Ives (1968), Anita Bryant (1969), Jerry Lee Lewis (1970), Mickey Gilley (1975), Chuck Berry (1975), Doug Kershaw (1975), Anne Murray (1977), Duane Eddy (1977), Willie Nelson and Leon Russell (1979), Johnny Cash (1989), Michael Bolton (1993), Delbert McClinton (2006), Carly Simon (2007), the Dead South (2021), and Tom Petty and the Heartbreakers (recorded in

1997 and released in 2022). And that doesn't include dozens of instrumental recordings of "Sunshine" during those years.

Among memorable recordings in the latter twentieth and early twenty-first centuries was renowned jazz vocalist and pianist Mose Allison's version, included in his acclaimed 1968 album, *I've Been Doin' Some Thinkin'.* A 1952 LSU graduate, Allison gave the song a new modern jazz-and-blues minor-key melody. His spare, whimsical rendition used only three instruments: Allison's piano, Red Mitchell's bass, and Bill Goodwin's drums. Aretha Franklin's 1998 version featured a two-minute introduction that leaves the listener wondering when the familiar refrain might begin. When it does, it's a clever and distinctive interpretation of Charles's 1962 recording. Also notable was Johnny Cash's simple, earthy, and poignant 1989 rendition (but released in 2003 after his death). Musicians Norman Blake and Marty Stuart accompanied the country legend at his Cash Cabin Studio near Hendersonville, Tennessee. "It's a distillation of 'You Are My Sunshine' to the very essence, Cash even conflating the second and third verses," musicologists Andrew Ford and Anni Heino wrote. "But through his shaky wreck of a voice, the tune remains intact, and perhaps for the first time, the tune makes sense of the words. It's still major key, still simple—in fact never simpler—and it's definitely not a blues, but it is heartbreaking." In the mid-2010s, appliance manufacturer Whirlpool cheapened Cash's exquisite version by using it in a series of television commercials.[2]

Country star Chris Stapleton and his wife, Morgane, collaborated on a remarkable cover of "Sunshine" in 2016. Morgane sang lead while her husband harmonized on the chorus and contributed an energetic, bluesy guitar accompaniment and solo. The recording earned them a 2016 CMA Awards nomination for "Vocal Collaboration of the Year." Morgane loved the song so much that she had "You Are My Sunshine" engraved inside her husband's wedding ring. A version of "Sunshine" recorded in 2021 by the folk-bluegrass group the Dead South was a powerful and mournful minor-key interpretation that contained hints of the original tune. It sounds modern and fresh, paying tribute to the song's country roots.[3]

Johnny Cash recorded a raw, emotional version of "Sunshine" in 1989. It would be released in 2003, after his death. (Wikimedia Commons)

Nothing gave "Sunshine" more notoriety in the early twenty-first century than its inclusion in a popular 2000 film by Joel and Ethan Coen, *O Brother, Where Art Thou?* The movie earned two Academy Award nominations, and the soundtrack, which included "Sunshine" sung by Norman Blake, won a Grammy for Album of the Year in 2002. On "Sunshine," Blake provided the voice-over for Charles Durning, the actor playing Pappy O'Daniel, a character based on Davis and the real singing Texas governor, W. Lee "Pappy" O'Daniel. The song would appear in other movies. In 1998's *Primary Colors,* guitarist Ry Cooder arranged a country instrumental recording of "Sunshine." A rock version of the song by singer

Stine J. appeared in the 2005 movie *Mr. & Mrs. Smith,* starring Brad Pitt and Angelina Jolie. And a cover of "Sunshine," sounding almost identical to Davis's 1940 recording, was on the soundtrack of a 2017 horror/mystery, *Annabelle: Creation.*[4]

In addition to Johnny Cash's version in Whirlpool commercials, "Sunshine" has been the soundtrack for products and causes over the decades, including a popular TV spot in the early 1980s for French's mustard; a 2008 Greenpeace ad in the UK; a Children's Tylenol spot in 2012; a 2013 Coca-Cola commercial; a television advertisement in 2014 for BC Children's Hospital Foundation in Vancouver; and, using a riotous cover by the indie-rock band the Next Great American Novelist, a commercial for the diabetes drug *Rybelsus* in 2020.[5]

"Sunshine" became so popular in Japan in the 1980s that when First Lady Nancy Reagan visited a Tokyo school in 1986, the children enticed her to join them in an enthusiastic performance of the song. The song's popularity in his country fascinated Japanese scholar Toru Mitsui so much that he resolved to discover its author. When he interviewed Davis in 1983, the former governor boasted about the handsome royalties from "Sunshine" and claimed that "in the last statement quarter, the biggest check in there came from Japan." In October 1989, when Nancy Reagan returned to Japan with her husband, the performers at a Yokohama concert to raise money for Ronald Reagan's presidential library serenaded the couple with a version of "Sunshine." To the original tune, the crowd sang, "You are our sunshine, our only sunshine. You worked for friendship and brought us peace. You'll never know, Ron, how much we need you. Please come here with Nancy to stay."[6]

Besides serving as a beloved lullaby for generations of parents settling a grumpy child into slumber, the title became a popular greeting card theme and is featured on various items in American gift shops, including jewelry, coffee mugs, plaques, and posters. It even inspired another hit recording: a number-one country song by the Statler Brothers in 1978, "Do You Know You Are My Sunshine?" And it may have influenced a number-one pop hit for Stevie Wonder in 1973, "You Are the Sunshine of My Life," which he wrote and won him four Grammy Awards, including Song of the Year. The following year, Davis released an album, *Walking in the Sunshine,* which included a gospel version of "Sunshine." He sang "Christ Is My Sunshine" to the song's original tune. One of the more exciting iterations of "Sunshine" came in 2020 in the UK in the depths of the coronavirus pandemic, when Gareth Malone, host of a popular BBC television program, *The Choir,* created an online show, *The Great British Home Chorus.* The program allowed tens of thousands to join a virtual choir. On the broadcast's last show in July 2020, Malone led viewers in singing "Sunshine." Accompanied by the London Symphony Orchestra, more than eleven thousand people sang from their homes and offices. Malone released a recording from the YouTube broadcast, and by early August, it moved into fifth place on *Billboard*'s UK chart.[7]

Toward the end of the twentieth century and into the next, "Sunshine" earned accolades for its cultural and historical influence. *Country America* magazine placed it among the "Top 100 Country Songs of All Time" in 1999. The same year, Davis's 1940 version entered the Grammy Hall of Fame, a distinction created in 1973 "to honor recordings of lasting qualitative or historical significance that are at least 25 years old." In 2000, the Songwriters Hall of Fame awarded Davis's rendition its Towering Song Award. And in 2013, the Library of Congress added his 1940 record to its National Recording Registry, a list of sound recordings that "are culturally, historically, or aesthetically significant, and/or inform or reflect life in the United States."[8]

On September 10, 1999, the night before Davis's one-hundredth birthday, Louisiana governor Mike Foster and former governors Edwin Edwards, Dave Treen, and Buddy Roemer joined a crowd of eight hundred in a Baton Rouge hotel ballroom to honor Davis's political and musical careers. He arrived late, looking frail as he shuffled across the stage, pushing a walker. "It seemed unlikely he would be able to sing," one reporter observed. "I don't know if I'll make it through the program," Davis told the audience. "At one hundred years, there's not much feeling left. You've had it." But, with his wife, Anna, by his side, Davis

Davis at his one-hundredth birthday celebration in Baton Rouge in September 2000. *Left to right:* Former Louisiana governors David Treen, Edwin Edwards, Davis, and Buddy Roemer, and then-governor Mike Foster. (Photo courtesy David R. Kors)

summoned the strength for one last try. His weak voice grew stronger as he sang. Everyone in the ballroom accompanied him. Some dabbed tears, probably knowing it was his last public appearance. Or, maybe as an observer wrote, they were "moved by memories rocking their babies to sleep to 'Sunshine.'"[9]

Davis lived another year, dying at his Baton Rouge home on November 5, 2000. At his funeral at the Jimmie Davis Tabernacle near his Beech Springs birthplace, hundreds of mourners—including Lieutenant Governor (and future governor) Kathleen Blanco—gathered in stormy weather. Former Louisiana Senate president Randy Ewing of nearby Quitman eulogized him as a man "who grasped the unreachable star" but "whose feet never left the ground." About Davis's famous song, Ewing said, "It is a special sunshine that Governor Davis spread to warm the heart and cause our spirits to grow. It is his song 'Sunshine' that became the universal language—the language of goodwill, of happiness." To the surprise of some, Davis's most famous song, "Sunshine"—the one he often called his "meal ticket"—was not what mourners sang at his funeral.

Instead, they sent him to his eternal reward with another song for which he was well known and was more appropriate for a funeral—even Jimmie Davis's: "Suppertime."

> Come home, come home,
> It's suppertime.
> We're going home at last.[10]

As pallbearers carried Davis's casket to the small cemetery behind the tabernacle, the rain stopped and the sun pierced the dark clouds. Without prompting, the crowd broke into song: "You are my sunshine, my only sunshine. You make me happy when skies are gray."[11]

As journalists and editors assessed his lengthy career in politics and music, the *Baton Rouge Advocate* may have captured the prevailing, conflicted view of Davis. Noting that his failures as governor in the 1940s and 1960s had earned him "justifiable criticism," the paper concluded, "Like most of us, he will be remembered as a man who was not always right, but who wasn't always wrong, either." It was a forgiving take and one not wholly justified given Davis's deplorable civil rights record, for which he never apologized. In its editorial about Davis's passing, the *New Orleans Times-Picayune* was also kind, if somewhat less forgiving. "One has to wonder: How would history have turned out if Mr. Davis had used his position and his popularity for more progressive ends?" Among those eulogizing Davis in print was columnist Wiley Hilburn of the *Shreveport Times.* Like the rest, Hilburn minimized Davis's segregationist past. "The segregation issue turned on Davis," he wrote. "He just couldn't cope with it, coming as he did from another culture." But Hilburn noted that whatever Davis's politics, his famous song would be "forever imprinted on the national consciousness" and was enough "to justify his place in history; a song beyond politics."[12]

Decades after his passing, memories of Davis faded. While his plaque hangs in the rotunda at the Country Music Hall of Fame in Nashville, he is rarely mentioned among country music pioneers. In 2017, three years before Davis's death, *Rolling Stone* magazine ranked the top hundred country artists of all time. Several Davis contemporaries made the list: Hank Williams (2), the Carter Family (5), Jimmie Rodgers (11), Bob Wills and His Texas Playboys (14), Ernest Tubb (23), Bill Monroe (27), Hank Snow (40), and Roy Acuff (66). Davis's successful musical career had stretched from the late 1920s to the late 1990s—longer than any country artist—but that earned him no mention.[13]

But the popularity of the song Davis made famous in the early 1940s has not waned. As *New Orleans Times-Picayune* columnist Jerry Estopinal noted shortly after the singer's death, many young voters in Louisiana could "barely" comprehend Davis's era, finding his music "at best quaint." Estopinal, however, identified the lasting contribution of Davis's seventy-year music career: He had immortalized a song. "Without a doubt," the writer asserted, "people will be singing and listening to 'You Are My Sunshine' a millennium from now, when memories of a rural sharecropper's son, who taught school, sang, wrote, acted and served two terms as Louisiana's governor, will be as distant as the Middle Ages are today."[14]

NOTES

ABBREVIATIONS

ATT	*Alexandria Town Talk*
BRA	*Baton Rouge Advocate*
BRST	*Baton Rouge State-Times*
CMHFM	Country Music Hall of Fame and Museum
NOI	*New Orleans Item*
NOS	*New Orleans States*
NOTP	*New Orleans Times-Picayune*
SJ	*Shreveport Journal*
ST	*Shreveport Times*

1. JIMMIE DAVIS NEEDED A SONG

1. "Cobb Records," *Dallas Morning News,* August 23, 1939; "Cards, Slowed Down," *Knoxville News-Sentinel,* August 23, 1939; "Eminent Spanish Educator," *Beaumont Enterprise,* August 23, 1939.

2. Daniel, *Pickin' on Peachtree,* 149; Pine Ridge Boys, "You Are My Sunshine," Bluebird, B-8263-A, 1939, 78 rpm.

3. Green, "The Blue Sky Boys on Radio," *Journal of Country Music,* 108–10, 134.

4. Rice Brothers Gang, "You Are My Sunshine," Decca, 66432, 1939, 78 rpm; Russell, *Country Music Records,* 746.

5. Wayne W. Daniel, "The Rice Brothers: Hillbillies with Uptown Ambitions," Hillbilly-Music.com, http://www.hillbilly-music.com/groups/story/index.php?groupid=11764; Kingsbury, McCall, and Rumble, *Encyclopedia of Country Music,* s.v. "The Rice Brothers," 424; KTBS radio programming in *ST,* December 16 and 24, 1935; "Program Previews," *ST,* December 7, 1939. KWKH programming in the *Shreveport Times* first mentions the Rice Brothers' Gang show on September 29; Daniel, *Pickin' on Peachtree,* 140–41.

6. Bañagale, "You Are My Sunshine," *Musicological Explorations,* 18; photocopy of December 16, 1939, contract between Davis and Rice in author's possession; "Background of a $17.50 Song," *ST,* September 16, 1956; *Catalog of Copyright Entries, 1930 Musical Compositions,* vol. 5, no. 1 (Washington, DC: Library of Congress, Copyright Office, 1940).

7. "Background of a $17.50 Song," *ST,* September 16, 1956; Russell, *Country Music Records,* 746.

8. Daniel, "The Rice Brothers," Hillbilly-Music.com, http://www.hillbilly-music.com/groups

/story/index.php?groupid=11764; Atcher to Daniel, February 2, 1981, Wayne W. Daniel Collection, Box 10: Series III, Special Collections and Archives, Georgia State University; Atcher oral history, May 1, 1987, CMHFM; "Bonnie Blue Eyes," SecondHandSongs.com, https://secondhandsongs.com/artist/59267/all. In the 1981 letter and his 1987 interview, Atcher claimed Satherley told him Davis was at the Pine Ridge Boys' August 22, 1939, session when the group recorded "You Are My Sunshine." Davis was in Shreveport ("Work on Parking," *ST,* August 23, 1939).

9. Mitsui, "You Are My Sunshine," *Old Time Country.*

10. Daniel, *Pickin' on Peachtree,* 150; "Family Claims 'Sunshine,'" *Cannon Falls (MN) Republican Eagle,* December 4, 2013.

11. "For My Alumnae," *Memphis Commercial Appeal,* May 27, 1900; ads in *Dayton Herald,* December 26, 1919, May 14 and April 9, 1920; "Never Knew It!" *Atlanta Constitution,* March 16, 1924; "Song She Wrote," *New York Daily News,* April 13, 1928; "Contributed Verse," *Franklin (IN) Evening Star,* September 5, 1932; "You Are My Sunshine," *Missoulian,* December 29, 1935; *Catalog of Copyright Entries, 1930 Musical Compositions,* new series, vol. 25, pt. 3 (Washington, DC: US Government Printing Office, 1931), 929; *Catalog of Copyright Entries, 1935 Musical Compositions,* new series, vol. 30, pt. 3 (Washington, DC: US Government Printing Office, 1936), 228; *Catalog of Copyright Entries, 1936 Musical Compositions,* new series, vol. 31, pt. 3 (Washington, DC: US Government Printing Office, 1937), 559.

12. Carter Family, "Little Darling, Pal of Mine," Victor, BVE-45021, 1928, 78 rpm; Carter Family, "When the World's on Fire," Victor, BVE-59984, 1930, 78 rpm.; Bañagale, *Musicological Explorations,* 18–19.

13. Pappas, "The 'Theft' of an American Classic," *Chronicles;* Crook, *The Oliver Hood Sessions;* 1940 US Census records for Troup County, Georgia, LaGrange, 141–49, 8-A; Pappas and Hood Family histories compiled by Tracey Pappas, April 1976, Rock Valley Family History Collection, Rock Valley College, 1981; David Crook correspondence with author, November 27, 2023. Hood family members have reported that Oliver's birth year was 1894 or 1896. On the 1940 US Census form, however, he indicated he was born in 1897.

14. Pappas, "The 'Theft' of an American Classic," *Chronicles;* Crook, *The Oliver Hood Sessions.*

15. Pappas, "The 'Theft' of an American Classic," *Chronicles;* WGST and WSB radio schedules in *Atlanta Journal,* June 24 and December 15, 1937.

16. Crook, interview by author, October 15, 2023; Crook correspondence with author, November 27, 2023; "Tarheels Plan Great Tour of State," *Atlanta Journal,* November 20, 1932; Carlin, *American Popular Music: Folk,* 29.

17. Daniel, *Pickin' on Peachtree,* 261n61; Moman, interview by Crook, 2014, in *The Oliver Hood Sessions.*

18. Crook, *The Oliver Hood Sessions;* Pappas, "The 'Theft' of an American Classic," *Chronicles.*

19. Crook, *The Oliver Hood Sessions; Catalog of Copyright Entries, Unpublished,* January–December 3, 1955 (Washington, DC: US Government Printing Office, 1956), 635.

20. Rose, "Stories," 6; Fontenot, "Sing It Good, Sing It Strong, Sing It Loud," in Lornell and Laird, *Shreveport Sounds in Black and White,* 48.

2. THE ONLY WAY I EVER PLAY POLITICS

1. Matthiessen, *Looking for Magical Country,* 24–25.

2. Dick Tate, "News in the Classifieds," *Houston Chronicle,* August 25, 1948; Davis oral history,

1990, CMHFM archives; "Davis Claims He, Mitchell Wrote Theme," *ST,* May 10, 1977; Hannusch, "You Are My Sunshine," *Offbeat.*

3. Davis, interview by Bob Allen, June 9, 1987, CMHFM digital archives; Russell, *Country Music Records,* 298–99; "The Sunshine Singing Governor," *BRA,* May 19, 1985.

4. Ginell, *Milton Brown,* 132.

5. Davis, interview by Biff Collie, May 22, 1989, CMHFM digital archives; Birk, *Unfurrowed Ground,* 37.

6. Mitsui, "You Are My Sunshine," *Old Time Country,* 15–17; Davis oral history, 1990, CMHFM archives.

7. Russell, *Country Music Records,* 298.

8. Wynne to author, July 9, 2023.

9. James H. Davis, "Comparative Intelligence of Whites, Blacks, and Mulattoes" (master's thesis, LSU, 1927); "Questionnaire, Country, Western and Gospel Music, September 20, 1959," and Jimmie Davis Capitol Records biography, undated, CMHFM archives; Weill, *You Are My Sunshine,* 10; "US Census, 1910," Samuel J. Davis, Police Jury Ward 3, Jackson, LA, GenealogyBank.com, https://genealogybank.com/#.

10. Weill, *You Are My Sunshine,* 1–29; McWhiney and Mills, "Jimmie Davis and His Music," *Journal of American Culture,* 54–55; "The Sunshine Singing Governor," *BRA,* May 19, 1985.

11. Weill, *You Are My Sunshine,* 35–47; "Jimmie Davis: The Early Years," *Louisiana Trooper,* n.d., 49; Davis, *Louisiana, This One's for You,* 15.

12. "List of Teachers for the Year of 1925–26," *Jackson Independent,* September 17, 1925; "L.S.U. Glee Club off on Tour," *Monroe News-Star,* February 7, 1927; "Select Dean and Faculty," *ST,* July 17, 1927; ad for Dodd College in *ST,* August 21, 1927.

13. "Inspired At Court," *Staunton (VA) Daily News Leader,* May 8, 1931; "Entertainer," *SJ,* March 19, 1928; "To Make Tour," *ST,* May 24, 1928; "Rural Electrification Discussed," *SJ,* September 28, 1928; Stedman Gunning interview, June 18, 1981, LSU Shreveport Oral History Collection, OH 60; Laird, *Louisiana Hayride,* 71–72; Mazor, *Meeting Jimmie Rodgers,* 77.

14. Russell, *Country Music Records,* 298.

15. "Takes New Post," *SJ,* February 14, 1929; "Holmes Is Named," *SJ,* April 1, 1929; Fontenot, "You Can't Fight a Song," *Journal of Country Music,* 52; Weill, *You Are My Sunshine,* 49–50; Tosches, *Country,* 123.

16. Pecknold, *The Selling Sound,* 22; Malone and Laird, *Country Music USA,* 121; Ginell, *Milton Brown,* xxviii; Pugh, *Ernest Tubb,* 43–46; Hall, *Hell-Bent for Music,* 29.

17. Russell, *Country Music Records,* 299–301, 804; Tony Russell's liner notes, Jimmie Davis, *Barnyard Stomp,* Bear Family Records, 1988; Stacey and Henderson, *Encyclopedia of Music in the 20th Century,* 752; Russell, *Blacks, Whites, and Blues,* 83–85; Pecknold, *Hidden in the Mix,* 36–37; Uncle Dave Lewis, "Buddy Woods Biography," AllMusic.com, https://www.allmusic.com/artist/buddy-woods-mn0000524696/biography; McWhiney and Mills, "Jimmie Davis and His Music," *Journal of American Culture* 56; Troutman, *Kīkā Kila,* 167; Ginell, *Milton Brown,* 61; Townsend, *San Antonio Rose,* 72. Some music historians claim that Jimmie Rodgers was the first country artist to record with Black musicians, on July 16, 1930. Tony Russell's *Country Music Records* points to Davis recording with Woods and Schaffer in Memphis on May 20, 1930, almost two months before Rodgers's session with Louis Armstrong (Russell, *Country Music Records,* 299, 804; Tosches, *Country,* 210–11).

18. Tosches, *Country,* 202–3; Malone and Laird, *Country Music USA,* 122.

19. "Inspired at Court," *Staunton* (VA) *Daily News*, May 8, 1931; Russell, *Country Music Originals*, 161; Russell, *Blacks, Whites, and Blues*, 81; Russell, *Country Music Records*, 299–300; Wolfe and Akenson, *The Women of Country Music*, 141.

20. Jimmie Davis, "High Behind Blues, Bluebird, BVE-70655–1, 1934, 78 rpm.

21. Jimmie Davis, "Bed Bug Blues," Decca, 60837, 1936, 78 rpm.

22. Mazor, *Meeting Jimmie Rodgers*, 78; Peterson, *Creating Country Music*, 146–49; Two songs Acuff recorded in 1936—"When Lulu's Gone" and "Doin' It the Old Fashioned Way"—were so risqué that he released them under a pseudonym, the Bang Boys (Schlappi, *Roy Acuff*, 28). Mikelbank, "Places in the Sun," *Journal of Country Music;* Davis interview by Bob Allen, June 9, 1987, CMHFM digital archives.

23. Tony Russell liner notes, Jimmie Davis, *Barnyard Stomp*, Bear Family Records, 1988.

24. Russell, *Country Music Records*, 300; Tucker, "Louisiana Saturday Night," 154.

25. Kenney, *Recorded Music in American Life*, 151; Tucker, "Louisiana Saturday Night," 156; "The Rock & Roll Encyclopedia & Discography," Rocky-52.net, https://www.rocky-52.net/chanteursn/nettles_b.htm; *The Encyclopedia of Country Music*, ebook ed. (Oxford: Oxford University Press, 2004), s.v. "Bill Nettles"; Davis and Nettles, "Agreement and Transfer of Copyright," June 23, 1937, Robert Gentry's Louisiana Hayride Collection, Box 1, Northwest Louisiana Archives, Louisiana State University Libraries.

3. BULL MARKET IN CORN

1. Whitburn, *Joel Whitburn's Pop Memories*, 121; Russell, *Country Music Records*, 303; "Folk Music Finds Its Way," *Billboard 1944 Music Year Book*, 353.

2. Bob Atcher oral history, May 1, 1987, CMHFM archives; Ward and Huber, *A&R Pioneers*, 93, 97; Peterson, *Creating Country Music*, 114; Lange, *Smile When You Call Me a Hillbilly*, 42–43.

3. "Governor's Band," *State-Times*, May 10, 1944; Wills, *The King of Western Swing*, 115–16; "Charles Mitchell," Hillbilly-music.com; "Registrar U. C. Mitchell Dead," *ST*, December 28, 1972; Troutman, *Kīkā Kila*, 159; Ginell, *Milton Brown*, 186–87; "Ball Club in Cedar Grove," *ST*, April 2, 1935; "Harrison Speaks," *SJ*, April 3, 1935; "Jimmy Davis," *ST*, September 13, 1936; "Jimmie Davis Is Given Writeup," *SJ*, August 8, 1936; "Today's Radio Programs," *ST*, September 15, 1936; Russell, *Country Music Records*, 301.

4. Sackheim, *The Blues Line*, 484; Dicaire, *Blues Singers*, 235; Davis, *The Songs of Jimmie Davis*, 44; Obrecht, *Early Blues*, 95; *Columbia Supplementary Record Catalogue 1931*, 21, https://archive.org/details/columbia-1931-supplementary-catalogue/mode/2up?q="Come+on+around+to+my+house"; *Catalog of Copyright Entries, 1937 Musical Compositions*, new series, vol. 32, pt. 3 (Washington, DC: US Government Printing Office, 1938), 11420.

5. Tosches, *Country*, 126; Russell, *Country Music Records*, 302–4.

6. Lange, *Smile When You Call Me a Hillbilly*, 86; Russell, *Country Music Originals*, 237; "Former Post Resident," *Lubbock Morning Avalanche*, January 13, 1939; "People You Know," *Pampa Daily News*, January 2, 1939; "Scatterings," *Lubbock Avalanche-Journal*, January 8, 1939.

7. Floyd Tillman interview, CMHFM Oral History Project, October 13, 1986; Hudson, *Telling Stories, Writing Songs*, 19; Pugh, *Ernest Tubb*, 42.

8. Russell, *Country Music Records*, 104, 140, 303, 316; Russell, *Country Music Originals*, 161, 237; "Hillbilly and Foreign Record Hits," *Billboard*, August 26, 1939, 129.

9. "Bull Market," *Time*, October 4, 1943.

10. Mazor, *Ralph Peer and the Making of Popular Roots Music*, 80.

11. Ward and Huber, *A&R Pioneers*, 91–95. Here and throughout the book, I have used the Bureau of Labor Statistics' CPI Inflation Calculator (https://www.bls.gov/data/inflation_calculator.htm) to estimate inflation-adjusted amounts.

12. Peterson, *Creating Country Music*, 114; Zwonitzer, *Will You Miss Me When I'm Gone?*, 171, 176; Mazor, *Ralph Peer and the Making of Popular Roots Music*, 81–83; Kenney, *Recorded Music in American Life*, 151; Tucker, "Louisiana Saturday Night," 161–62.

13. Pugh, *Ernest Tubb*, 27; Davis and Nettles, "Assignment and Transfer of Copyright," June 23, 1937, Robert Gentry's Louisiana Hayride Collection, Box 1, Northwest Louisiana Archives, LSUS; "Elsie McWilliams," Nashville Songwriters Hall of Fame, https://nashvillesongwritersfoundation.com/Site/inductee?entry_id=2490; Mel Foree interview, April 30, 1972, CMHFM archives; Ward and Huber, *A&R Pioneers*, 96.

14. Ginell, *Milton Brown*, xxvii; Cusic, *The Cowboy in Country Music*, 113.

15. "What Matter Who Writes the Laws," *Progress* (Hammond, LA), June 30, 1939.

4. I BELONGED IN LOUISIANA

1. "Thar's GOLD," *Collier's*, April 30, 1938.

2. Weill, You Are My *Sunshine*, 54–55.

3. "Jimmie Davis Enters Race," *ST*, July 18, 1938; "More Candidates," *SJ*, July 19, 1938; "Davis Submits," *ST*, September 4, 1938; "Music, Politics Mixed," *NOI*, April 2, 1946.

4. Weill, *You Are My Sunshine*, 55. "Large Crowd," *SJ*, August 13, 1938; "Davis Speaks," *SJ*, August 23, 1938; "Final Drive," *ST*, September 6, 1938; "On the Air Tonight," Davis/KRMD ad in *ST*, September 6 and 8, 1938; Davis campaign ads in *SJ*, August 22, September 1, September 7, 1938; "Political Rallies Tonight," *SJ*, October 12, 1938; "Davis Wins," *SJ*, October 19, 1938.

5. Russell, *Country Music Records*, 303–5; "Hillbilly," *Billboard*, May 27, 1939, 82; "Hillbilly," *Billboard*, August 5, 1939, 77; "Hillbilly," *Billboard*, September 30, 1939, 78; "Hillbilly," *Billboard*, November 25, 1939, 68; "Hillbilly," *Billboard*, December 30, 1939, 146.

6. Bañagale, "You Are My Sunshine," *Musicological Explorations*, 12.

7. Russell, *Country Music Records*, 304; Laird, *Shreveport's KWKH*, 108–10; Oral Memoirs of Jimmy Thomason, July 27, 1993, Baylor University Institute for Oral History, 20.

8. "'You Are My Sunshine,'" *Salon*, May 26, 2013; Bañagale, "You Are My Sunshine," *Musicological Explorations*, 13.

9. Stanbridge, "Of Sunshine and Happy Endings," *Critical Studies in Improvisation;* "G. I.'s Platter," *Sioux Falls Argus-Leader*, December 20, 1942; "Harrison in Hollywood," *Hope Star*, April 15, 1942; "15 Best Sheet Music Sellers," *Variety*, May 21, June 11, and June 25, 1941; "Sing America First," *NAB Reports*, August 1, 1941.

10. "Billboard Top 100 of 1940," http://billboardtop1000f.com/1940-2/; "Billboard Top 100 of 1941," http://billboardtop1000f.com/1941-2/; "Songs from the Year 1940," Tsort.com: https://tsort.info/music/yr1940.htm; "Songs from the Year 1940," Music ID: http://impact.musicid.academicrightspress.com/music/yr1940.htm.

11. "Folk Music Finds Its Way," *Billboard 1944 Music Year Book*, 353; Jones, *The Songs That Fought the War*, 50.

12. "Hillbilly," *Billboard,* July 27, 1940, 84; "Hillbilly and Foreign Record Hits," *Billboard,* September 28, 1940, 70; "Hillbilly," *Billboard,* October 26, 1940, 64; "Hillbilly," *Billboard,* May 31, 1941, 83; "Hillbilly," *Billboard,* January 31, 1942, 91; Russell, *Country Music Recordings,* 52.

13. Gardner, *Popular Songs of the Twentieth Century,* 229; "On the Records," *Billboard,* August 23, 1941, 13; "Hillbilly and Foreign Record Hits," *Billboard,* October 25, 1941, 62; Montana Slim, "You Are My Sunshine," Bluebird, B-8491, 1940, 78 rpm.

14. Russell and Laird, *Country Music USA,* 213–14, 232; Ward and Huber, *A&R Pioneers,* 144; "'Sunshine' Favorite," *Spokane Chronicle,* August 8, 1941.

15. "Music Items," *Billboard,* March 7, 1942, 23; "Letter Box," *Billboard,* April 18, 1942, 63; Whitburn, *Joel Whitburn's Pop Memories,* 40, 108, 258.

16. *Take Me Back to Oklahoma,* Albert Herman (Los Angeles: Monogram Pictures, 1940), Prime Video; Cusic, *Gene Autry,* 98; *Stardust on the Sage,* William Morgan (Los Angeles: Republic Pictures, 1942), Prime Video.

17. Giddins, *Bing Crosby: Swinging on a Star,* 138; Discography, *Governor Jimmie Davis: Nobody's Darlin' But Mine,* Bear Family Records, 1997; Bing Crosby, "You Are My Sunshine," Decca, DLA 2515, 1941, 78 rpm; "Jimmie Davis: The Early Years," *Louisiana Trooper,* n.d., 55; Cusic, *Discovering Country Music,* 56; "On the Records" and "Record Buying Guide—Part 2," *Billboard,* August 23, 1941, 13, 78.

18. Tucker, "Louisiana Saturday Night," 168; Ward and Huber, *A&R Pioneers,* 143–44; Giddins, *Bing Crosby: A Pocketful of Dreams,* 367–68; Whitburn, *Joel Whitburn's Pop Memories,* 108.

19. Mikelbank, "Places in the Sun," *Journal of Country Music,* 31; "Harrison in Hollywood," *Lancaster (OH) Eagle-Gazette,* April 7, 1942.

20. "Know Shreveport Radio," *ST,* March 4, 1942; Russell, *Country Music Records,* 304–5; "The Hollywood Roundup," *Muskegon (MI) Chronicle,* June 3, 1942; "Jimmy Davis and Band," *Minden Herald,* July 24, 1942; Weill, *You Are My Sunshine,* 57–58; 32; Mikelbank, "Places in the Sun," *Journal of Country Music,* 32, 49; "Harrison In Hollywood," *Lancaster (OH) Eagle-Gazette,* April 7, 1942; "Jimmie Sings," *ST,* April 8, 1942; *Strictly in the Groove,* Vernon Keays (Los Angeles: Universal Pictures, 1942), https://ok.ru/video/1949977938527; "Royal Theater Film," *Birmingham News,* April 25, 1943; Hajduk, *Music Wars,* 32; Mazor, *Ralph Peer and the Making of Popular Roots Music,* 82, 86; Pugh, *Ernest Tubb,* 76–77.

21. Quoted in Hajduk, *Music Wars,* 27; Lange, *Smile When You Call Me a Hillbilly,* 84.

22. Austin, "Hollywood Barn Dance," *Southern Quarterly,* 111–22; Schlappi, *Roy Acuff,* 174–76; Weill, *You Are My Sunshine,* 58–59.

23. Weill, *You Are My Sunshine,* 59; "Jimmie Davis Files," *NOS,* July 16, 1942; "The Hollywood Roundup," *Muskegon (MI) Chronicle,* June 3, 1942; "Jimmy Davis and Band," *Minden Herald,* July 24, 1942; "War-Bond Parade," *SJ,* July 30, 1942; "Jimmie Davis Swept," *BRA,* September 10, 1942; "New Member of Public Service," *BRA,* January 12, 1943.

24. "Grand Ole Opry," *Arkansas Gazette,* August 15, 1942; "MGM to Hand Name," *Billboard,* August 15, 1942, 21; "Hillbilly Jamboree Attendance," *Memphis Commercial Appeal,* December 1, 1942; ad for Hillbilly Jamboree in *Commercial Appeal,* November 22, 1942.

5. EASIER TO SING THAN TO TALK

1. "Looking Davy Jones Straight in the Eye," *Baltimore Sun,* November 22, 1942.

2. White, *Tamarack White, Orygun Seabee in War and Peace,* 110; Eriksen, *Dennis Olson Story,*

144–46; Bender, *You Are Not Forgotten,* 98; Magnan, *Letters from the Pacific Front,* 66; Cloud, *Biography of a Grunt,* 118; Smith, *The Do-or-Die Men,* 80; "Music Hath Charms," *Central New Jersey Home News,* May 3, 1945; "'You Are My Sunshine' Is Hit," *ST,* December 1, 1945.

3. *The Garland Encyclopedia of World Music: Australia and the Pacific Islands,* 25; Gonzales, *Let Freedom Ring,* 6; "Nurses Waiting," *London Sunday Dispatch,* February 21, 1943.

4. Warner and Centro, *World War II,* 59.

5. Cohen and Capaldi, *The Pete Seeger Reader,* 73–76.

6. Castro, *Without a Penny in My Pocket,* 80–81.

7. Kenney, *Recorded Music in American Life,* 168.

8. "'You Are My Sunshine,'" *Akron Beacon Journal,* March 7, 1943; "'That Sunshine Song,'" *ST,* March 11, 1943; Meacham, *Franklin and Winston,* 207; Atkinson, *An Army at Dawn,* 287.

9. "Hull Police Entertain," *Daily Mail* (Hull, UK), December 16, 1942; Leitch, *Great Songs of World War II,* 142–43; Hyams, *Bomb Girls,* 128; "Music Goes Round," *Shepton Mallet Journal* (Somerset, UK), August 20, 1943; "Rise of Davis," *NOS,* May 9, 1944; "Journals from England," *Lincoln Journal Star,* October 29, 1943.

10. Leitch, *Great Songs of World War II,* 63.

11. "Séance Sang,'" *Manchester Evening News* (UK), March 24, 1944; "'Sunshine' Frowned On!" *Whitstable Times and Tankerton Press* (UK), April 14, 1945; "Sunshine or Moonshine?" *Bucks Examiner* (Chesham, UK), March 16, 1945.

12. "'You Are My Sunshine,'" *Akron Beacon Journal,* March 7, 1943.

13. "Engines of Plane Sing," *Greenville (SC) News,* May 9, 1944.

14. Lewis, *D-Day,* 93; "Keeping Alive," *Eastern Daily Press* (Newport, Wales), November 12, 2017; "'You Are My Sunshine" Has Appeal," *Harper County Journal* (Buffalo, OK), September 6, 1945.

15. Duncan and Burns, *Country Music,* 114–15.

16. Cusic, *Discovering Country Music,* 55–57.

17. Sears, *V-Discs,* 162.

18. Schoening and Kasper, *Don't Stop Thinking about the Music,* 30; Dunaway, "Music and Politics in the United States," *Folk Music Journal,* 280; Miles, *Songs, Odes, Glees and Ballads,* 1; Lohman, *Hail Columbia! American Music and Politics in the Early Nation,* 2.

19. Harrison, *Kentucky's Governors,* 55–57; Clark, *The Rampaging Frontier,* 270–71; Peter La Chapel, "Senator Glen H. Taylor: Radio's Utopian Singing Cowboy," in *The Honky Tonk on the Left,* ed. Jackson, 50; Fontenot, "You Can't Fight a Song," *Journal of Country Music.*

20. Owenby and Wilson, *The Mississippi Encyclopedia,* 720; Fontenot, "You Can't Fight a Song," *Journal of Country Music;* "The Life Story of W. Lee O'Daniel," *Paris (TX) News,* August 26, 1938; Malone and Laird, *Country Music USA,* 191–92; Redlawsk, *The American Governor,* 209–10.

21. "New Member of Public Service," *BRA,* January 12, 1943; "Dilemma of the Crooner-Governor," *New York Times Magazine,* January 1, 1961.

6. HOW IN THE DEVIL CAN YOU FIGHT A SONG?

1. *Discography of American Historical Recordings,* s.v. "Davis, Jimmie," https://adp.library.ucsb.edu/names/105055.

2. Carleton, "Four Anti-Longites," *Louisiana History.*

3. Liebling, *Earl of Louisiana,* 178; Kurtz and Peoples, *Earl K. Long,* 48; Carleton, "Four Anti-Longites," *Louisiana History.*

4. "Jimmie Davis Looms," *SJ*, February 25, 1943; "Places in the Sun," *Journal of Country Music*, 49; Weill, *You Are My Sunshine*, 61–63.

5. Sindler, *Huey Long's Louisiana*, 182–83; "Morrison Raps," *SJ*, December 17, 1943; Clay, *Coozan Dudley LeBlanc*, 146.

6. Ad in *Houston Post*, May 6, 1943, 8; "Hillbilly Jamboree," *Houston Post*, May 9, 1943.

7. "Jimmie Davis in Governor's Race," *SJ*, September 11, 1943; "J. H. Davis Is Candidate," *Lafayette Daily Advertiser*, September 11, 1943; "Jimmie Davis Enters Race," *BRST*, September 11, 1943; "Jimmie Davis in Governor's Race," *SJ*, September 11, 1943; "J. H. 'Jimmie' Davis to Run," *NOS*, September 11, 1943; "Hon. Jimmie Davis Announces," *Bossier City Planter's Press*, September 23, 1943.

8. Glen Jeansonne, "Sam Houston Jones and the Revolution of 1940," in *The Age of the Longs: Louisiana*, ed. Haas, 361; Sanson, *Louisiana during World War II*, 21; Sanson, "A History of Louisiana," 202; "Morrison Raps Jones," *SJ*, December 17, 1943.

9. Sanson, "A History of Louisiana," 203–4.

10. "Places in the Sun," *Journal of Country Music*, 49; Davis oral history with Biff Collie, May 22, 1989, CMHFM archives.

11. "Hear Jimmie H. Davis," ad in *SJ*, October 13, 1943; "Davis Opens Tour with Talk, Songs," *NOTP*, October 24, 1943; "Davis Speak at Ruston," *NOTP*, October 24, 1943; "Davis Will Make Opening Speech," *SJ*, October 21, 1943. Davis made a similar claim about this rally in another interview in which he also recalled it happening in 1943, not 1938 ("Jimmie Davis: The Early Years," *Louisiana Trooper*, n.d.).

12. "Candidates Speak," *SJ*, August 5, 1938; "Large Crowd Attends Rally," *SJ*, August 13, 1938.

13. Mikelbank, "Places in the Sun," *Journal of Country Music*, 51; "Sunshine Boys of Shreveport," *Ruston Daily Leader*, October 14, 1935; Jerome Beatty, "How to Win an Election," *American Magazine*, August 1944; "Governor Davis' Hill-Billy," *Eunice New Era*, May 10, 1944; "Davis Running on Own Ticket," *NOS*, November 13, 1943. "Davis Opens Tour," *NOTP*, October 24, 1943.

14. Weill, *You Are My Sunshine*, 64; Fontenot, "You Can't Fight a Song," *Journal of Country Music*, 58; Mikelbank, "Places in the Sun," *Journal of Country Music*, 51; "Davis Made Fine Impression," *Bogalusa Bulletin*, November 15, 1943; "Davis Impresses Voters," *Franklinton Era-Leader*, November 18, 1943; "Jimmie Davis in Political Rally," *Opelousas Clarion-News*, November 18, 1943.

15. Fontenot, "You Can't Fight a Song," *Journal of Country Music*, 54–55; "Jimmie Davis: The Early Years," *Louisiana Trooper*, n.d., 51.

16. "Jimmie Davis Is Going Fishing," *NOS*, March 2, 1944; Townsend, *San Antonio Rose*, 356; *Discography of American Historical Recordings*, "Thomason, Jimmy" and "Perrin, Curly," https://adp.library.ucsb.edu/.

17. Bragg, *Jerry Lee Lewis*, 72; Kingsbury et al., *The Encyclopedia of Country Music*, s.v. "Moon Mullican," 342–43; Fontenot, "You Can't Fight a Song," *Journal of Country Music*, 58; Whitburn, *Joel Whitburn's Top Country Singles*, 239; "Moon Mullican," AllMusic.com, https://www.allmusic.com/artist/moon-mullican-mn0000594267/biography; "Folk Talent and Tunes," *Billboard*, June 23, 1951, 32; Fox, *King of the Queen City*, 74–77; Don Helms, interview by Paul R. Nail, June 17, 1997, and Jimmie Davis oral history with Biff Collie, May 22, 1989, CMHFM archives; "Jambalaya (On the Bayou)," Sullivan, *Encyclopedia of Great Popular Song Recordings*, 381; Broven, *South to Louisiana*, 34; Bomar, *Southbound*, 6; Coffey, *Cliff Bruner*, 25–31; Boyd, *Dance All Night*, 84–85; "Jimmie Davis: The Early Years," *Louisiana Trooper*, n.d., 51.

18. Fontenot, "You Can't Fight a Song," *Journal of Country Music*, 58.

19. "Davis Opens Tour," *NOTP,* October 24, 1943; "Complete Home Rule Favored," *BRST,* December 2, 1943; Fontenot, "You Can't Fight a Song," *Journal of Country Music,* 59; Sam Houston Jones OH, T. Harry Williams Center for Oral History, LSU.

20. "Davis Pledges," *NOS,* November 8, 1943; Davis oral history interview with Biff Collie, May 22, 1989, CMHFM archives.

21. "Jones Too Busy," *NOTP,* October 3, 1943; "Caldwell Hits Morgan," *NOS,* November 29, 1943; "Caldwell Scores Davis," *BRA,* December 9, 1943.

22. "Davis and Caldwell," *ST,* November 28, 1943.

23. "Davis Invades Morgan's Town," *NOS,* November 29, 1943.

24. "Unkind Cut," *SJ,* December 17, 1943; Fontenot, "You Can't Fight a Song," *Journal of Country Music,* 54.

25. Fontenot, "You Can't Fight a Song," *Journal of Country Music,* 54; "Unkind Cut," *SJ,* December 17, 1943.

26. "Singing Candidate," *Monroe Times,* December 31, 1943, Logan "Tex" Congor Collection, Louisiana State Archives.

27. "Attention Ladies" ad in *BRA,* January 11, 1944; Anti-Davis flier, Richard W. Leche Papers, Box 67, LSU Special Collections; Lewis Morgan ad in *BRST,* January 17, 1944; "Clements Points to Bills," *NOS,* January 12, 1944.

28. Weill, *You Are My Sunshine,* 69; Davis speech text, Louisiana Bandmasters Convention, July 21, 1970, Davis Papers, SLU.

29. "Jimmie Davis Looms," *SJ,* February 25, 1943.

30. "Just Fiddlin' Around," *Kansas City Star,* October 17, 1948.

31. Laird, *Louisiana Hayride,* 73.

32. Sanson, *Louisiana during World War II,* 227–33; Wall and Rodrigue, *Louisiana,* 337.

33. "Harmony His Watchword," *Omaha World-Herald,* March 5, 1944; "Louisiana's New Crooner Governor," *Milwaukee Journal,* March 10, 1944; untitled editorial, *St. Louis Post-Dispatch,* March 6, 1944; "Music as a Vote Lure, *Grand Rapids Press,* March 14, 1944.

34. "Entire Davis Ticket Wins," *Bunkie Record,* March 3, 1944.

7. WE JUST HUNG AROUND JIMMIE

1. "Jimmie Davis Becomes Governor," *ST,* May 10, 1944; "J. H. 'Jimmie' Davis Takes Oath," *Eunice New Era,* May 10, 1944.

2. "With Inaugural Hubbub," *BRST,* May 10, 1944; "Governor's Band," *BRST,* May 10, 1944.

3. "Present OCD Payroll," *NOI,* December 20, 1944; "Civilian Defense Pay Roll," *NOTP,* December 31, 1944; "Hillbillies Fiddled," *NOI,* January 12, 1945; "Davis Band," *ST,* January 12, 1945; "Davis Band Leader," *ST,* February 20, 1945; "Davis Band Boys," *ST,* January 12, 1945.

4. "Louisiana Voters Who Thought," *BRA,* March 5, 1944; "Governor and Recording Band," *BRST,* June 6, 1944; "Legislators Trip," *BRST,* June 9, 1944; "The Washington Merry-Go-Round," *Provo (UT) Daily Herald,* October 10, 1944; "State Legislative Session," *NOS,* July 6, 1944.

5. "Jimmy Davis and His Songs," *NOS,* July 19, 1944; "Jones Praises Fight," *NOS,* July 22, 1944; "Stand of South," *NOTP,* July 23, 1944; "Remembering Jimmie Davis," *BRA,* May 19, 1985.

6. Whitburn, *Joel Whitburn's Top Country Singles, 1944–1997,* 100; "Broad Dixie Plan," *NOTP,* November 26, 1944; "Jimmie Davis," Discogs.com, https://www.discogs.com/artist/570696-Jimmie-Davis; "Governor Davis in New Picture," *Bossier City Planter's Press,* November 23, 1944.

7. "Corn Fed Music," *NOI,* January 10, 1945.

8. "Gov. Davis Sings," *ST,* February 25, 1945.

9. "Davis Returning," *NOTP,* May 31, 1945; "Of Interest," *BRST,* June 22, 1945; Weill, *You Are My Sunshine,* 73; "Davis Will Take Band," *NOTP,* January 19, 1946; "'You Are My Sunshine,'" *NOI,* January 24, 1946.

10. *Discography of American Historical Recordings,* s.vv. "Recordings Made on Monday, February 18, 1946," https://adp.library.ucsb.edu/index.php/date/browse?date=1946-02-18, and "Recordings Made on Tuesday, February 19, 1946," https://adp.library.ucsb.edu/index.php/date/browse?date=1946-02-19; "The Little Signal," *Crowley Post-Signal,* February 21, 1946; "Jimmie Davis in Hollywood," *ST,* February 18, 1946; *Songs by Sinatra,* CBS Radio, February 20, 1946, https://www.youtube.com/watch?app=desktop&v=QPj7SKCAKPs; "Gov. Jimmie Davis to Make Movie," *NOTP,* August 5, 1946; "Davis' Life Story," *NOTP,* September 19, 1946; "Davis Film," *NOTP,* October 3, 1946.

11. "Jimmie Davis Not Interested," *BRA,* March 17, 1944; "Davis Absences," *NOTP,* May 24, 1947; "New Iberia Is 'State Capital,'" *Daily Iberian,* September 19, 1947; "Governor Returns," *NOTP,* September 28, 1947.

12. Weill, *You Are My Sunshine,* 80; "Cut State Costs," *NOTP,* November 13, 1947.

13. Whitburn, *Joel Whitburn's Top Country Singles, 1944–1997,* 523; "Most-Played Juke Box Folk Records," *Billboard,* March 31, 1945, 21; Most-Played Juke Box Folk Records," *Billboard,* May 12, 1945 25; "American Folk Tunes," *Billboard,* June 9, 1945, 66; "Most-Played Juke Box Folk Records," *Billboard,* March 2, 1946, 31; "Album Reviews," *Billboard,* May 17, 1947, 36; Whitburn, *Joel Whitburn's Top Country Singles,* 100.

14. Wall, *Louisiana,* 337; "Davis' Help Sought" and "Anti-Closed Shop," *NOI,* July 8, 1946; Kurtz and Peoples, *Earl K. Long,* 121; Sindler, *Huey Long's Louisiana,* 190–97; "Good-Government Crops," *NOTP,* November 29, 1947; "Long Discusses Platform," *BRA,* January 17, 1948; "Paving, Blacktop," *NOTP,* November 16, 1947; "Kennon Lashes," *NOS,* December 22, 1947.

15. Sindler, *Huey Long's Louisiana,* 196.

16. Carleton, "Four Anti-Longites," *Louisiana History,* 258.

17. "Jimmie Davis in Hollywood," *ST,* February 18, 1946; "Gov. Jimmie Davis to Make Movie," *NOTP,* August 5, 1946; "Davis' Life Story," *NOTP,* September 19, 1946; "Davis Film," *NOTP,* October 3, 1946; "Private Car," *NOTP,* March 1, 1947; Call sheets for *Louisiana* and "Program and Schedule of World Premiere, 'Louisiana,'" Logan "Tex" Congor Collection, Louisiana State Archives; Hanson, *American Film Institute Catalog of Motion Pictures,* s.v. *Louisiana,* 1417; "Gov. Davis Entertains," *NOI,* October 7, 1947; "Davis Film Will Open," *BRA,* October 8, 1947; "Premiere of 'Louisiana'" *SJ,* October 7, 1947; "30,000 Watch Parade," *ST,* October 8, 1947.

18. "Ex-Governor Jimmie Davis Plays Himself," *Louisville Courier-Journal,* March 12, 1948.

19. Text of Davis radio address, November 27, 1947, Jimmie Davis Collection, Box 1, Louisiana State Archives; "Jones Voices His Thanks" and "Jones Says Davis Assures Victory," *NOTP,* November 29, 1947; "Jones Slates 20 Speeches," *NOTP,* November 16, 1947; "Kennon Pledges to Halt," *NOS,* November 21, 1947; ad for Jones rally in *NOI,* January 15, 1948.

20. "Jones Challenges Long," *NOS,* January 16, 1948.

21. "Kennon Lashes Out," *NOS,* December 22, 1947; "The Town Crier," *Chicago Daily News,* July 10, 1948.

22. "Earl Says Foes," *NOTP,* January 17, 1948.

23. "Hospital Plan Advocated," *Crowley Post-Signal,* November 8, 1947; "Long and Jones in Radio," *SJ,* October 21, 1947; Kurtz and Peoples, *Earl K. Long,* 120–28; "Earl Is Defended," *NOTP,* November 14, 1947; "Long and Jones in Radio," *SJ,* October 21, 1947; "Long Is Losing Ground," *NOS,* December 3, 1947.

24. "Davis Blows Kisses," *NOI,* May 11, 1948.

8. COME HOME, JIMMIE

1. Harry Roy and His Orchestra, "You Are My Sunshine," Regal Zonophone, MR-3653, 1942, 78 rpm.

2. Big Bill Campbell and His Rocky Mountain Rhythm, "You Are My Sunshine," Rex, R-6002, 1942, 78 rpm; Albert Ammons and His Rhythm Kings, "You Are My Sunshine," Mercury, 8070, 1948, 78 rpm.

3. The Ames Brothers, "You Are My Sunshine," Coral, 9–60886, 1952, 45 rpm.

4. Nat King Cole, "You Are My Sunshine," Capitol Records, CAP F-15, 1955, 45 rpm; Friedwald, *Straighten Up and Fly Right,* 338.

5. Faron Young, *Sweethearts or Strangers,* Capitol Records, T-778, 1957, 33$^{1}/_{3}$ rpm; Keikamn, *Live Fast, Love Hard:* 7, 51.

6. Richard Berry and the Pharaohs, "You Are My Sunshine," Flip Records, 45–360, 1962, 45 rpm; Stanton, *The Tombstone Tourist,* 30–31.

7. Marsh, *Louie Louie,* 33–34.

8. "Reviews of New R&B Records," *Billboard,* April 13, 1957, 87; Stanton, *The Tombstone Tourist,* 31.

9. Andre Williams, "You Are My Sunshine," Fortune Records, 834, 1957, 45 rpm; "On the Beat," *Billboard,* May 6, 1957, 69.

10. Carl McVoy, "You Are My Sunshine," Hi Recording, 1957, 45 rpm; McDonough, *Soul Survivor,* 42; Bragg, *Jerry Lee Lewis,* 75–76; Talevski, *Knocking on Heaven's Door,* 419; "Reviews of New Pop Records," *Billboard,* December 9, 1957, 50; Burke and Griffin, *The Blue Moon Boys,* 134–35; Escott, *Tattooed on Their Tongues,* 77–83; Sims, *The Next Elvis,* 87; "New Record Label," *Memphis Press-Scimitar,* November 14, 1957; "Top Tunes," *Memphis Press-Scimitar,* December 3, 1957; Peter Silverton, "Hi Records," *Encyclopedia Britannica,* https://www.britannica.com/topic/Hi-Records.

11. Zak, *I Don't Sound Like Nobody,* 116, 137; "The 50s: A Decade of Music," *Rolling Stone,* April 19, 1990, https://www.rollingstone.com/feature/the-50s-a-decade-of-music-that-changed-the-world-229924/.

12. "You Are My Sunshine," SecondHandSongs.com, https://secondhandsongs.com/work/45675/all; Johnny and the Thunderbirds, "You Are My Sunshine," Clover Records, 45–1001, 1959, 45 rpm.

13. Weill, *You Are My Sunshine,* 83; "Davis Prefers," *San Angelo Standard-Times,* June 16, 1948; "Jimmie Davis Calls," *SJ,* July 20, 1948; "Jimmy Davis Wows," *NOI,* July 16, 1948; "Voters More Interested," *Louisville Courier-Journal,* September 24, 1948; "Jimmie Davis Here," *Camden News,* December 14, 1948; "In Person," Davis ad in *Grand Rapid Press,* July 23, 1948.

14. Ad for the Stables, *Palm Springs Limelight-News,* December 3, 1948; "Skelton Eyes 'Harvey'" *Grand Rapids Press,* November 27, 1948; "Dining, Dancing," *Palm Springs Desert Sun,* De-

cember 10, 1948; "Stables Jammed for Great Opening Event," *Palm Springs Desert Sun,* November 23, 1948; Oral Memoirs of Jimmy Thomason, July 27, 1993, Baylor University Institute for Oral History, 8; "Folk Talent and Tunes," *Billboard,* June 17, 1950, 35; Laird, *Shreveport's KWKH,* 111; "Roy Acuff, 89, Singer, Dies," *New York Times,* November 24, 1992.

15. "Former Governor Big Star," *Rocky Mount (NC) Telegram,* October 9, 1949.

16. "Jimmie Davis," Discogs.com, https://www.discogs.com/artist/570696-Jimmie-Davis; Whitburn, *Joel Whitburn's Top Country Singles,* 124.

17. Weill, You Are My *Sunshine,* 85–86.

18. Dessau Hall ad in *Austin American,* August 11, 1951; "Former Solon to Speak," *ST,* September 16, 1951.

19. Bailes Brothers and Molly O'Day discographies, Discogs.com; Whitburn, *Joel Whitburn's Top Country Singles,* 32, 124; "Tri-Speeds Gain," *Denver Post,* March 14, 1950; McNeil, *Encyclopedia of American Gospel Music,* s.v. "Red Foley," 126.

20. Goff, *Close Harmony,* 157–61, 167–72, 181.

21. Jimmie Davis with the Anita Kerr Singers, "Supper-time," Decca, 9–28799, 1953, 45 rpm.

22. Escott, *I Saw the Light,* 177–79; "3 Crack Entertainers," *Fort Worth Star-Telegram,* February 13, 1952; "'Hayride' Books Jimmie Davis," *ST,* March 9, 1952; "Louisiana's Ex-Governor Sings," *Madison (WI) Capital Times,* September 6, 1952; Holt for Governor ad in *Hope Star,* July 18, 1952.

23. "Folk Singer Jimmie Davis," *ATT,* December 17, 1952; Billups ad in *ATT,* September 19, 1952; Billups ad in *Jackson Clarion-Ledger,* March 24, 1953; Billups ad in *Lafayette Daily Advertiser,* November 22, 1954, January 9, 1955, March 4, 1956, July 4, 1957, and February 23, 1958; Billups ad in *ATT,* April 1, 1955; "Radio Log," *Greenwood (MS) Commonwealth,* August 29, 1959; "Affairs of State," *Jackson (MS) Clarion-Ledger,* August 5, 1960; "Billups Proposes," *ATT,* July 7, 1962.

9. A BRILLIANT PHANTOM

1. Wall and Rodrigue, *Louisiana,* 351–55.

2. Wall and Rodrigue, *Louisiana,* 355; Kurtz and Peoples, *Earl K. Long,* 184–85, 214; Dodd, *Peapatch Politics,* 39; McGuire, *Win the Race or Die Trying,* 82–83.

3. Kurtz and Peoples, *Earl K. Long,* 211–29; McGuire, *Win the Race or Die Trying,* 61–64; "Long Still Pushing," *BRST,* May 27, 1959; "Paper Says Long's 'Foul Mouth,'" *BRST,* May 28, 1959; "Stinging Defeat," *BRA,* May 27, 1959; "Long Again Blasts," *BRST,* May 28, 1959.

4. "Long Says Davis May Take Look," *BRA,* April 21, 1959; McGuire, *Win the Race or Die Trying,* 93; "Gov. Long Must Resign," *Opelousas Daily World,* September 6, 1959; Stowe, "Willie Rainach and the Defense of Segregation in Louisiana," 16.

5. "Just Plain Politics," *BRST,* January 7, 1959; "Davis Often," *NOTP,* January 11, 1959; Scates, *War and Politics by Other Means,* 64. "Jimmie Davis Is Candidate," *BRST,* April 20, 1959.

6. "Rainach Says Segregation," *ST,* November 3, 1959.

7. "Something New Has Been Added," *BRST,* August 21, 1959; "Davis Often in Gubernatorial Talk," *NOTP,* January 11, 1959.

8. "Clean Campaign Is Promised," *BRST,* July 9, 1959; "Tempo of Campaign Increases," *BRST,* September 19, 1959; Jack Gremillion Oral History, October 17, 1995, T. Harry Williams Center for Oral History.

9. "Jimmie Davis Takes Office," *Bridgeport (CT) Post,* May 8, 1960.

10. "Davis Promises," *BRA,* September 7, 1959; "Davis Speaks," *NOTP,* September 7, 1959.

11. "Five Candidates Swap," *BRA,* August 30, 1959; Jeansonne, *Leander Perez,* 215.

12. "Morrison Says Long 'Sold Out,'" *BRST,* September 10, 1959; "Morrison Raps Tune," *NOTP,* October 23, 1959; Morrison ads in *BRA* and *Monroe Morning World,* November 15, 1959; "Morrison Lists Saturday Tour," *NOTP,* November 21, 1959; "Mayor Morrison and Group," *Lake Providence Banner-Democrat,* September 18, 1959; Fontenot, "You Can't Fight a Song," *Journal of Country Music,* 56.

13. "Noe Claims Segregation Issue," *ATT,* October 10, 1959; "Morrison Says He Will Bring," *SJ,* October 30, 1959; Peoples, "Earl Kemp Long."

14. Weill, *You Are My Sunshine,* 118–19; "Five Gubernatorial Candidates," *Richland Beacon-News,* September 5, 1959; "Nearness of Election," *Crowley Post-Signal,* November 19, 1959; Davis in Dodd, *Peapatch Politics,* x–xii.

15. "Major Candidates Working," *BRST,* November 30, 1959.

16. "Left Surplus," *NOTP,* September 18, 1959; Liebling, *Earl of Louisiana,* 179; "Dodd and Noe Separately Slap," *BRA,* November 26, 1959.

17. "NAACP Target of Davis Talk," *NOTP,* December 12, 1959.

18. Jeansonne, "*Racism and Longism in Louisiana,*" *Louisiana History,* 264–65; ad, "Who Got the Negro Vote?" *BRA,* January 3, 1960; Jeansonne, *Leander Perez,* 215–16; Liebling, *Earl of Louisiana,* 195.

19. "Gubernatorial Candidates Make Final Appeals," *BRA,* January 9, 1960; "Candidates Entering Last Week," *BRA,* January 3, 1960; Jeansonne, "*Racism and Longism in Louisiana,*" *Louisiana History,* 266.

20. "Long Backs Davis," *NOSI,* January 5, 1960; Liebling, *Earl of Louisiana,* 212, 214–15; "Back Davis," *NOSI,* January 7, 1960; Jeansonne, "*Racism and Longism in Louisiana,*" *Louisiana History,* 262; William M. Rainach oral history interviews, August 19 and October 7, 1977, LSU Oral History Collection, LSUS; "Davis Camp Is Jambalaya," *NOS,* January 6, 1960; "Lake Dedication," *Homer Guardian-Journal,* May 8, 1969.

21. "CBS Drops Plan," *Columbus (GA) Inquirer,* January 16, 1960.

22. "Governor Long Sings," *Lafayette Daily Advertiser,* April 4, 1960; "It May Be So," *Natchitoches Enterprise,* April 21, 1960.

23. "Thousands See Davis," *ST,* May 11, 1960; "Davis Hints Austerity," *Crowley Post-Signal,* May 11, 1960; "Davis' Inaugural Address," *ATT,* May 11, 1960; "10,000 Hear Davis," *NOSI,* May 11, 1960.

10. NO "SUNSHINE" OF MODERATION

1. "Rainach Claims," *BRA,* June 1, 1960; "Rainach Hints," *NOTP,* June 1, 1960.

2. Katagiri, *Black Freedom, White Resistance, and Red Menace,* 90–91; Webb, *Massive Resistance,* 68; Jack Gremillion oral history, May 24, 1996, T. Harry Williams Center for Oral History, LSU.

3. "Backing Asked," *NOTP,* November 22, 1960.

4. Fairclough, *Race and Democracy,* 234–46; "N.O. School Ruling," *BRA,* August 27, 1960; Haas, *DeLesseps S. Morrison,* 259–267; "Rowdiness Marks Mixing," *NOTP,* November 16, 1960;

Jack Gremillion oral history, January 31, 1996, T. Harry Williams Center for Oral History, LSU; Carleton, Howard, and Parker, *Readings in Louisiana Politics,* 362, 388.

5. Fairclough, *Race and Democracy,* 244–47; "More Segregation Bills Pressed," *Baltimore Sun,* February 19, 1961; "Contempt Move Set Aside," *Newport News (VA) Daily Press,* March 4, 1961.

6. Bartley, *The New South, 1945–1980,* 252; "Panelists Rap Tax," *NOTP, January 3, 1961.*

7. "Final Verse," *Chicago Tribune,* December 24, 2000.

8. Weill, *You Are My Sunshine,* 126; Davis, "Comparative Intelligence of Whites, Blacks, and Mulattoes" (master's thesis, LSU, 1927).

9. Horstman, *Sing Your Heart Out, Country Boy,* 29.

10. Davis speech text, September 11, 1968, Davis Collection, Louisiana State Archives, Box 3.

11. Jeansonne, "Leander Perez," *Louisiana Studies.*

12. Wall and Rodrigue, *Louisiana,* 382; "Davis Sings," *BRA,* October 23, 1971; "Legislature to Scan," *NOSI,* May 9, 1961; "U.S. Asks to Drop Faser Fraud Case," *NOSI,* July 23, 1970; "Baker Bank's Growth," *NOTP,* August 3, 1961; "Chris Faser No Longer," *BRST,* January 19, 1961; "Highway Agency Viewing Suit," *Lafayette Daily Advertiser,* October 8, 1971; "Davis Got Bank Stock," *ST,* August 8, 1971; "Davis Answers," *NOTP,* December 3, 1960; "Rep. Faster Seeking Dismissal," *BRST,* April 29, 1969; "Drive Urged," *NOSI,* December 30, 1960. "Agency May Try," *BRA,* October 8, 1971.

13. "Heuer Testimony," *BRST,* October 2, 1965; "N.O. Mayor Subpoenaed," *BRA,* October 5, 1965; "Heuer Subpoenaed," *BRST,* September 28, 1965; "Jimmie Davis: The Truth," *NOSI,* October. 26, 1971.

14. "Davis Quartet Reported," *ST,* January 12, 1961; "Davis Quartet Members on Leave," *ST,* May 20, 1961; "McNeil, *Encyclopedia of American Gospel Music,* s.v. "Plainsmen Quartet," 302; Goff, *Close Harmony,* 205–6; "Civil Service Eyes Record," *NOSI,* May 18, 1961; "Henry Davis Is Named," *BRST,* May 20, 1960; "Davis Musician Has State Job," *NOTP,* May 27, 1961; "Davis Brother," *BRA,* August 2, 1961; "Work for Davis' Singers Urged," *NOTP,* May 25, 1961.

15. "Solons Sound Public Opinion," *NOSI,* May 12, 1961; "Dyer Continues Mansion Attack," *BRST,* August 17, 1961; "Bridge to Open," *Lake Charles American Press,* October 12, 1964; "Rep. Dyer, in Pineville Talk," *ATT,* January 9, 1963; "Long and Morrison in Friday Stump Speeches," *Crowley Post Signal,* October 19, 1963; Weill, *You Are My Sunshine,* 128–29; Sunshine Bridge speech text, October 12, 1964, Davis Collection, Louisiana State Archives, Box 3; "Jimmie Davis: The Bridges," *BRST,* February 22, 1975.

16. Weill, *You Are My Sunshine,* 131; "Davis Plans to Ride," *Lake Charles American Press,* April 23, 1963.

17. Weill, *You Are My Sunshine,* 131; "Davis' Horse Visits," *Lake Charles American Press,* June 18, 1961; "'Sunshine' Goes," *NOTP,* June 18, 1961; "Davis Rides Sunshine," *Opelousas Daily World,* June 20, 1961; "A Little Hay," *ATT,* June 23, 1961; "Twin City Chit-Chat," *Monroe News-Star,* June 30, 1961; "Remembering Jimmie Davis," *BRA,* May 19, 1985; "5,000 Wait Two Hours," *Birmingham Gazette* (UK), March 1, 1954.

18. "Davis Receives Hay," *Lafayette Daily Advertiser,* June 25, 1961.

19. Wall and Rodrigue, *Louisiana,* 378.

20. Strother, *Falling Up,* 71; "When Skies Are Gray," *Gambit,* November 28, 2000; "Traffic Crash," *ST,* May 11, 1965.

21. "Dilemma of the Crooner-Governor," *NOTP,* January 1, 1961.

22. Untitled editorial, *Decatur (IL) Herald,* November 21, 1960; "'You Are My Sunshine' Ol' Jimmie," *Daily Tar Heel,* November 15, 1960; "No Road Back," *Daytona Beach Morning Journal,* November 15, 1960; "No 'Sunshine," *Tampa Tribune,* November 13, 1960; untitled editorial, *Arkansas Gazette,* November 17, 1960.

23. *New York Post* editorial quoted in "Louisiana Draws Brickbats," *Eugene (OR) Guard,* October 1, 1960.

24. "Sales Tax Stampede," *Louisiana Weekly,* January 1, 1961; "Movie Theater Protests," *SJ,* February 13, 1961; "New Orleans Divided," *Detroit Free Press,* June 9, 1961.

11. A MUSICAL ACT OF RACIAL TRESPASSING

1. Charles and Ritz, *Brother Ray,* 87–88; "Ray Charles and the Florida Playboys, A Short Adventure," RayCharlesVideoMuseum.blogspot.com, https://raycharlesvideomuseum.blogspot.com/2016/12/ray-charles-and-florida-playboys-short.html.

2. Lydon, *Ray Charles,* 14.

3. Lydon, *Ray Charles,* 75–76; Charles, *Brother Ray,* 164.

4. Lydon, *Ray Charles,* 98; "Sensational Ray Charles," *Baton Rouge News Leader,* September 17, 1955; Duggleby, *Uh Huh!,* 102; Charles and Ritz, *Brother Ray,* 165; "Ray Charles Is in Town—Chronology 1959," RayCharlesVideoMuseum.com, https://raycharlesvideomuseum.blogspot.com/2010/08/ray-charles-is-in-town-chronology-1959.html.

5. "2 Concerts Slated," *NOSI,* March 1, 1962; "The Fabulous Ray Charles," ad in *Louisiana Weekly,* July 7, 1962; "Dig Me!," *Louisiana Weekly,* July 21 and December 29, 1962; "Ray Charles Sought," *Louisiana Weekly,* August 18, 1962; "In Person," Ray Charles concert ad in *NOTP,* February 25, 1962; "Mixed Sports Ban," *Louisiana Weekly,* October 13, 1956; "Fats Domino Show," *Louisiana Weekly,* April 21, 1956; "Record Crowd," *Louisiana Weekly,* April 7, 1956; "Court Rules State Sport," *ST,* May 26, 1959.

6. "Ray Charles and Country's Color Barrier," *Rolling Stone,* February 22, 2019; Jarrett, *Producing Country,* 74; Robert Christgau, "The Genius at Work: A Critical Discography: Five Decades of Blues, Soul, R&B, Jazz, Country and Classic Schmaltz," *Rolling Stone,* July 8, 2004.

7. Pecknold, *Hidden in the Mix,* 82, 88–90.

8. Bogdanov, *All Music Guide to the Blues,* 107; "If Ray Charles Does It," *Las Vegas Review-Journal,* December 2, 1962; Sid Feller liner notes, *Modern Sounds in Country and Western Music,* vol. 2, ABC-Paramount, 1962.

9. Jocelyn R. Neal, "The Twang Factor in Country Music," in *The Relentless Pursuit of Tone,* ed. Fink, 43–64.

10. Whitburn, *The Billboard Book of Top 40 Hits,* 857; Whitburn, *Across the Charts,* 79; "Ray Charles Carried the Ball," *Billboard,* November 10, 1962, 34.

11. "Rioters Wreck Ballroom," *BRA,* September 5, 1960; "30 Arrested in Theater Riot," *BRA,* October 16, 1960; Charles and Ritz, *Brother Ray,* 165; Whitburn, *Joel Whitburn's Top Country Singles,* 100.

12. Lydon, *Ray Charles,* 222; "Dig Me!" *Louisiana Weekly,* December 29, 1962.

13. "Talking About," *Jet,* January 19, 1963; "'Sunshine' Platter," *BRSI,* November 15, 1962; Davis to Charles Sullivan, December 3, 1962, Collection of the Smithsonian National Museum of Africa American History and Culture; Escott, *I Saw the Light,* 293.

14. "Ray Charles and Country's Color Barrier," *Rolling Stone,* February 22, 2019; Daniel Cooper in liner notes for *Ray Charles: The Complete Country & Western Recordings, 1959–1986,* Rhino Entertainment Co., 1998, CD.

15. Charles and Ritz, *Brother Ray,* 223.

16. Pecknold, *Hidden in the Mix,* 84; Ray Charles, "Swanee River Rock," https://www.youtube.com/watch?v=nC-vaI53t_4; Daniel Cooper in liner notes for *Ray Charles: The Complete Country & Western Recordings, 1959–1986,* Rhino Entertainment Co., 1998, CD.

17. Feder, "Song of the South," 171–91.

18. Pecknold, *Hidden in the Mix,* 86; "Ray Charles and Country's Color Barrier," *Rolling Stone,* February 22, 2019; Raul Malo in liner notes for *Ray Charles: The Complete Country & Western Recordings, 1959–1986,* Rhino Entertainment Co., 1998, CD; Calhoun, *The Art of God,* 109.

12. IT'S A VERY CATCHY DITTY

1. "McKeithen Assails," *ATT,* October 19, 1963; "McKeithen Hits," *Lake Charles American Press,* December 28, 1963.

2. "Testimonial Dinner," *BRST,* March 13, 1964.

3. "Jimmie Davis in Nashville," *Clarksville (TN) Leaf-Chronicle,* April 24, 1963; "Ballads, Horses," *BRA,* May 16, 1964; "Davis Tabernacle," *BRA,* May 17, 1965.

4. "Balladier-Politico," *ATT,* January 7, 1965; Jimmie Davis, *All-Time Favorite Hymns,* Shreveport: Jimmie Davis Music Co., 1965; "Reason Triumphs," *SJ,* November 9, 1966; "Long Favors 6-Year," *ATT,* August 12, 1950; "Too Early, Says Davis," *BRA,* November 5, 1966; "Jimmie Davis to Attack," *Lafayette Daily Advertiser,* October 18, 1966; "Davis Says He Opposes," *BRST,* October 19, 1966; "Jimmie Davis Cites Dangers," *SJ,* October 18, 1966; "McKeithen Endorsed," *ATT,* November 9, 1966.

5. "'April Fools' Scorched," *BRA,* April 2, 1967.

6. "McKeithen Sweeps," *Lafayette Advertiser,* November 5, 1967; "Jimmie Davis Named," *BRST,* November 6, 1967.

7. "Dawson Enters Race," *BRST,* August 26, 1963; "Rarick Installed," *BRA,* December 13, 1966; "Carl Dawson Is New Director," *BRST,* January 13, 1965.

8. "Tenor Seems to Be Right," *BRA,* June 19, 1968.

9. "'You Are My Sunshine' Is Now," *Alexandria Town Talk,* July 4, 1968; "'Sunshine' Is Voted," *BRST,* July 3, 1968.

10. "Act. No. 187," *BRST,* July 26, 1932; "Writes State Song," *BRA,* July 17, 1932; "New State Song,'" *Opelousas Daily World,* June 10, 1952; "Jeff David: State Marches to 'Louisiana,'" *Livingston Parish News,* August 3, 2006; "Issue of State's Official Song," *BRST,* August 21, 1968.

11. "Tenor Seems to Be Right," *BRA,* June 19, 1968; "'Sunshine' Weathers," *BRA,* July 4, 1968; "No Sunshine," *NOSI,* June 20, 1968; "A Good Veto," *NOTP,* July 8, 1968; "Anthem! Anthem!" *BRA,* July 9, 1968.

12. "'You Are My Sunshine' Is Vetoed," *NOTP,* July 5, 1968; "'You Are My Sunshine' Gets Lightning," *SJ,* July 5, 1968; *Capitol Report,* Louisiana News Bureau, July 5, 1968, in Davis Collection, Louisiana State Archives, Box 3.

13. "Talk of the Town," *ATT,* July 12, 1968; "State Song for Louisiana," *ST,* July 6, 1968; "'You Are My Sunshine' Gets Lightning," *SJ,* July 5, 1968.

14. "New Song for State," *BRST,* June 18, 1970; "Legislative Digest," *Lafayette Daily Advertiser,* July 9, 1970.

15. "Official Announcement," *Ringgold Record,* July 30, 1971; "Jimmie Davis: A Personal Perspective," *ST,* November 6, 2000.

16. Strother, *Falling Up,* 72–73.

17. "Davis' Singing Effective," *NOSI,* October 8, 1971; "Davis Pushes," *NOTP,* October 24, 1971; "Davis Sings," *BRA,* October 23, 1971; Strother, *Falling Up,* 72, 77

18. "Davis Pushes," *NOTP,* October 24, 1971; "Former Gov. Davis," *ST,* September 18, 1971; "Gillis Long Asks," *BRA,* August 8, 1971; "Gremillion Says," *BRST,* January 29, 1972; "Shoup Firm Hit," *BRST,* January 25, 1972.

19. Strother, *Falling Up,* 70; "Speedy Long Asks," *NOTP,* September 19, 1971; "Former Gov. Davis," *ST,* September 18, 1971; "Aycock Eyeing," *NOTP,* October 1, 1971; "Downs Refuses," *NOSI,* January 31, 1972.

20. Davis, "Aycock Present," *BRST,* October 27, 1971.

21. "Jimmie Davis," *Monroe News-Star,* April 13, 2008; Strother, *Falling Up,* 77–78.

22. "Davis Avoids," *SJ,* September 18, 1971; "Former Gov. Davis," *ST,* September 18, 1971; "Jimmie Davis Breaks," *SJ,* September 21, 1971; Strother, *Falling Up,* 79–80.

23. "Awards in Country Music," *Richmond Times-Dispatch,* October 15, 1972; "Loretta Lynn Wins," *Anchorage Daily News,* October 19, 1972; "Jimmie Davis," GospelMusicHallofFame.com, https://gospelmusichalloffame.org/jimmie-davis/.

24. "Registrar U. C. Mitchell Dead," *ST,* December 28, 1972.

25. "March 16, 1974—Grand Opening of the Grand Ole Opry House," *Fayfare's Opry Blog,* fayfare.blogspot.com, March 16, 2012, https://fayfare.blogspot.com/2012/03/march-16-1974-grand-opening-of-grand.html.

26. "Solons Shun 'Sunshine,'" *BRST,* June 26, 1976; "Writer of State Song," *BRA,* June 9, 1976; "Freeman Says He'll Win," *NOTP,* September 13, 1979.

27. "Song Bill Signed," *ST,* July 15, 1977; "State Song Battle," *BRST,* April 7, 1977; "House Oks 'Sunshine,'" *NOTP,* June 22, 1977; "Senate Bill Adds 'You Are My Sunshine,'" *BRST,* July 10, 1977; "State Songs," TN.gov, https://www.tn.gov/about-tn/state-songs.html; "Edwards Says Carter's View," *BRA,* July 15, 1977.

28. "Singer Ray Charles Croons," *Atlanta Journal,* March 6, 1979; "'Georgia on My Mind,'" *Macon Telegraph,* February 23, 1979.

13. A SONG BEYOND POLITICS

1. "Jimmie Davis Dies," *BRA,* November 6, 2000; "Ex-Governor Regales House with Songs," *BRST,* June 28, 1983; "Smiley Anders' Baton Rouge," *BRA,* December 12, 1983; "Treen Shines at Gospel Sing," *NOTP,* October 28, 1982; "The Legacies of Jimmie Davis," *Gambit Weekly,* November 28, 2000.

2. "Atlantic Records Catalog: 1500 Series," JazzDisco.org, https://www.jazzdisco.org/atlantic-records/catalog-1500-series/#sd-1511; Aretha Franklin, *Aretha Arrives,* Atlantic Records, 1967, 33⅓ rpm; Stanbridge, *Rhythm Changes,* 114–18; Ford and Heino, *The Song Remains the Same,* 68.

3. "Dave Cobb on Chris and Morgane Stapleton's 'You Are My Sunshine,'" *The Boot,* April 12, 2016, theboot.com, https://theboot.com/dave-cobb-chris-morgane-stapleton-you-are-my-sun

shine/; The Dead South, *Easy Listening for Jerks, Parts 1 & 2,* Six Shooter Records, 2022, 33⅓ rpm.

4. Adams, *The Cinema of the Coen Brothers,* 143; SoundTrackCollector.com.

5. French's Mustard spot, https://www.youtube.com/watch?v=pKGRBrMwMDI; Greenpeace spot, https://tinyurl.com/dbe8wm5m; Children's Tylenol spot, https://www.ispot.tv/ad/77Gt/childrens-tylenol-you-are-my-sunshine; Coca Cola spot, https://www.ispot.tv/ad/7Zmf/coca-cola-you-are-my-sunshine-song-by-stine-j; BC Children's Hospital Foundation spot, https://tinyurl.com/zufbjw7u; "You Are My Sunshine," by The Next Great American Novelist, https://www.youtube.com/watch?v=v82nLvjKWpw.

6. "Nancy Reagan 'Links,'" *Jersey Journal* (Jersey City, NJ), May 6, 1986; "Reagan's Ultimate Political Junket," *Oakland Tribune,* November 1, 1989; Mitsui, *You Are My Sunshine,* 15.

7. Jimmie Davis, "Walking in the Sunshine," https://www.youtube.com/watch?v=Phwj0W2f9t8; "11,000 Voices Sing 'You Are My Sunshine,'" ClassicFM.com, July 31, 2020, https://www.classicfm.com/artists/gareth-malone/you-are-my-sunshine-home-chorus/; "You Are the Sunshine of My Life, AllMusic.com, https://www.allmusic.com/song/you-are-the-sunshine-of-my-life-mt0001787985; "Billie Eilish on Track for U.K. Top 5 Debut with 'My Future,'" August 3, 2020, Billboard.com, https://www.billboard.com/pro/billie-eilish-uk-top-5-my-future/.

8. "Grammy Hall of Fame Awards," Grammy.com, https://www.grammy.com/awards/hall-of-fame-award#y; "You Are My Sunshine," Songwriter's Hall of Fame, songhall.com, https://www.songhall.org/awards/winner/You_Are_My_Sunshine; "Library of Congress National Recording Registry," https://www.loc.gov/static/programs/national-recording-preservation-board/documents/registry-by-alpha.pdf.

9. "Former Singer-Actor-Governor," *Atlanta Journal,* September 12, 1999; "Crowd Gathers," *BRA,* September 11, 1999.

10. "Jimmie Davis Dies," *BRA,* November 6, 2000; "Gov. Davis Laid to Rest," *BRA,* November 9, 2000; "Politics with a Song," *Baltimore Sun,* November 17, 2000; Ewing eulogy text and "A Celebration of Life" for Davis's funeral service, November 8, 2000, Randy Ewing personal papers.

11. Randy Ewing, interview by the author, February 27, 2024.

12. "Jimmie Davis Left Two Legacies," *BRA,* November 8, 2000; "The Singing Governor," *NOTP,* November 7, 2000; "Jimmie Davis: A Personal Perspective," *ST,* November 6, 2000.

13. "100 Greatest Country Music Artists," *Rolling Stone,* June 15, 2017, Rollingstone.com, https://www.rollingstone.com/music/music-lists/100-greatest-country-artists-of-all-time-195775/hank-williams-jr-6-195613/.

14. "100 Years of Life," *NOTP,* November 16, 2000.

BIBLIOGRAPHY

LIBRARIES AND ARCHIVAL COLLECTIONS

Baylor University Institute for Oral History, Baylor University Libraries
Digital Collections
Center for Southeast Louisiana Studies, Southeastern Louisiana University
Jimmie Davis Collection
Country Music Hall of Fame and Museum, Frist Library and Archives
Oral History Collection
Printed Material Collection
Georgia State University Library, Special Collections and Archives
Wayne W. Daniel Collection
Harry Ransom Center, University of Texas at Austin
Harry Pennington Photography Collection
Jackson Parish Museum, Jonesboro, Louisiana
Jimmie Davis Collection
Louisiana State Archives
Logan "Tex" Congor Collection
Jimmie Davis Collection
J. Dawson & Mark Cordes Gasquet Collection: 1920–1970
Louisiana State University Libraries
Richard W. Leche Papers, Special Collections, Hill Library
T. Harry Williams Center for Oral History
Noel Memorial Library, Northwest Louisiana Collection, Louisiana State University–Shreveport
LSU Oral History Collection
Henry Langston McEachern Photographic Collection
Robert Gentry's Louisiana Hayride Collection
Shreveport Times Photo Negatives

BOOKS, BOOK CHAPTERS, AND DISSERTATIONS

Adams, Jeffery. *The Cinema of the Coen Brothers: Hard-Boiled Entertainments.* New York: Columbia University Press, 2015.

Atkinson, Rick. *An Army at Dawn: The War in North Africa, 1942–43.* New York: Owl Books, 2002.

Bartley, Numan V. *The New South, 1945–1980.* Baton Rouge: LSU Press, 1995.

Bender, Bryan. *You Are Not Forgotten.* New York: Anchor Books, 2014.

Birk, Carl S. *Unfurrowed Ground: The Innovators of Country Music.* Infinity, 2005.

Bogdanov, Vladimir. *All Music Guide to the Blues: The Definitive Guide to the Blues.* Essex, CT: Backbeat Books, 2003.

Bomar, Scott B. *Southbound: An Illustrated History of Southern Rock.* Lanham, MD: Backbeat Books, 2014.

Boyd, Jean A. *Dance All Night: Those Other Southwestern Swing Bands, Past and Present.* Lubbock: Texas Tech University Press, 2012.

Bragg, Rick. *Jerry Lee Lewis: His Own Story.* New York: HarperCollins, 2014.

Broven, John. *South to Louisiana: The Music of the Cajun Bayous.* New Orleans: Pelican, 1992.

Burke, Ken, and Dan Griffin. *The Blue Moon Boys: The Story of Elvis Presley's Band.* Chicago: Chicago Review Press, 2006.

Calhoun, Jimi. *The Art of God: Reflections on Music, Diversity, and the Beauty in You.* Eugene, OR: Cascade Books, 2015.

Carleton, Mark T., Perry H. Howard, and Joseph B. Parker. *Readings in Louisiana Politics.* 4th ed. Baton Rouge: Claitor's, 1988.

Carlin, Richard, ed. *American Popular Music: Folk.* New York: Facts on File, 2006.

Castro, Marie S. C. *Without a Penny in My Pocket: My Bittersweet Memories before and after World War II.* Pittsburgh, PA: Dorrance, 2014.

Charles, Ray, and David Ritz. *Brother Ray: Ray Charles' Own Story.* New York: Dial, 1978.

Clark, Thomas D. *The Rampaging Frontier: Manners and Humors of Pioneer Days in the South and the Middle West.* Westport, CT: Greenwood, 1975.

Clay, Floyd Martin. *Coozan Dudley LeBlanc: From Huey Long to Hadacol.* New Orleans: Pelican, 1973.

Cloud, Jay T. *Biography of a Grunt.* San Jose, CA: Writers Club Press, 2000.

Coffey, Kevin. *Cliff Bruner and His Texas Wanderers.* Hambergen, Germany: Bear Family Records, 1996.

Cohen, Ronald D., and James Capaldi, eds. *The Pete Seger Reader.* Oxford: Oxford University Press, 2014.

Crook, David. *The Oliver Hood Sessions.* Self-published, 2019.

Cusic, Don. *The Cowboy in Country Music: An Historical Survey with Artist Profiles.* Jefferson, NC: McFarland, 2011.

———. *Discovering Country Music.* Westport, CT: Praeger, 2008.

———. *Gene Autry: His Life and Career.* Jefferson, NC: McFarland, 2007.

Daniel, Wayne W. *Pickin' on Peachtree: A History of Country Music in Atlanta.* Urbana: University of Illinois, 2001.

Davis, Jimmie. *Great Gospel Songs of Jimmie Davis.* Milwaukee: Hal Leonard Corporation, undated.

———. *Louisiana, This One's for You.* Baton Rouge: Ed Cheshire, 1985.

———. *Songs of Jimmie Davis.* New York: Southern Music Publishing Co., 1938.

Dicaire, David. *Blues Singers: Biographies of 50 Legendary Artists of the Early 20th Century.* Jefferson, NC: McFarland, 1999.

Dodd, William J. *Peapatch Politics: The Earl Long Era in Louisiana Politics.* Baton Rouge: Claitor's, 1991.

Duggleby, John. *Uh Huh! The Story of Ray Charles.* Greensboro, NC: Morgan Reynolds, 2005.

Duncan, Dayton, and Ken Burns. *Country Music: An Illustrated History.* New York: Knopf, 2019.

Eriksen, Karl. *The Dennis Olson Story: Hand to Hand in the Pacific.* iUniverse, 2011.

Escott, Colin. *I Saw the Light: The Story of Hank Williams.* Boston: Back Bay Books, 2004.

———. *Tattooed on Their Tongues: A Journey through the Backrooms of American Music.* New York: Schirmer Books, 1996.

Fairclough, Adam. *Race and Democracy: The Civil Rights Struggle in Louisiana, 1915–1972.* Athens: University of Georgia Press, 1995.

Feder, J. Lester. "Song of the South": Country Music, Race, Region, and the Politics of Culture, 1920–1974." PhD diss., University of California Los Angeles, 2006.

Fink, Robert Wallace, ed. *The Relentless Pursuit of Tone: Timbre in Popular Music.* New York: Oxford University Press, 2018.

Ford, Andrew, and Anni Heino. *The Song Remains the Same: 800 Years of Love Song, Laments and Lullabies.* Bundoora, Australia: La Trobe University Press, 2019.

Fox, John Hartley. *King of the Queen City: The Story of King Records.* Champaign: University of Illinois Press, 2009.

Friedwald, Will. *Straighten Up and Fly Right: The Life and Music of Nat King Cole.* New York: Oxford University Press, 2020.

Gardner, Edward F. *Popular Songs of the Twentieth Century. Vol. 1: Chart Detail and Encyclopedia, 1900–1949.* St. Paul, MN: Paragon House, 2000.

Giddins, Gary. *Bing Crosby: A Pocketful of Dreams: The Early Years, 1903–1940.* Boston: Little, Brown, 2001.

———. *Bing Crosby: Swinging on a Star: The War Years, 1940–1946.* Boston: Little, Brown, 2018.

Ginell, Cary. *Milton Brown and the Founding of Western Swing.* Urbana: University Press of Illinois, 1994.

Goff, James R., Jr. *Close Harmony: A History of Southern Gospel.* Chapel Hill: University of North Carolina Press, 2002.

Gonzales, Virgilio I. *Let Freedom Ring.* Bloomington, IN: Author House, 2016.

Haas, Edward F., ed. *The Age of the Longs: Louisiana, 1928–1960.* Vol. 7. Lafayette: Center for Louisiana Studies, University of Louisiana at Lafayette, 2001.

———. *DeLesseps S. Morrison and the Image of Reform.* Baton Rouge: LSU Press, 1974.

Hajduk, John C. *Music Wars: Money, Politics, and Race in the Construction of Rock and Roll Culture, 1940–1960.* Lanham, MD: Lexington, 2018.

Hall, Wade. *Hell-Bent for Music: The Life of Pee Wee King.* Lexington: University Press of Kentucky, 1996.

Hanson, Patricia King, ed. *American Film Institute Catalog of Motion Pictures Produced in the United States, Feature Films, 1941–1950* (Film entries, A–L). Berkeley: University of California Press, 1999.

Harrison, Lowell H., ed. *Kentucky's Governors.* Lexington: University Press of Kentucky, 2004.

Horstman, Dorothy. *Sing Your Heart Out, Country Boy: Classic Country Songs and Their Inside Stories by the People Who Wrote Them.* New York: E. P. Dutton, 1975.

Hudson, Kathleen. *Telling Stories, Writing Songs: An Album of Texas Songwriters.* Austin: University of Texas Press, 2000.

Hyams, Jacky. *Bomb Girls—Britain's Secret Army: The Munitions Women of World War II.* London: Kings Road, 2013.

Kingsbury, Paul, Michael McCall, and John Rumble, eds. *The Encyclopedia of Country Music.* 2nd ed. New York: Oxford University Press, 1998.

Jackson, Mark Allan, *The Honky Tonk on the Left: Progressive Thought in Country Music.* Amherst: University of Massachusetts Press, 2018.

Jarrett, Michael. *Producing Country: The Inside Story of the Great Recordings.* Middletown, CT: Wesleyan University Press, 2014.

Jeansonne, Glen. *Leader Perez: Boss of the Delta.* Jackson: University Press of Mississippi, 2006.

Jones, John Bush. *The Songs That Fought the War: Popular Music and the Home Front, 1939–1945.* Waltham, MA: Brandeis University Press, 2006.

Kaeppler, Adrienne L., and J. W. Love, eds. *The Garland Encyclopedia of World Music: Australia and the Pacific Islands. Vol. 9.* New York: Garland, 1998.

Katagiri, Yasuhiro. *Black Freedom, White Resistance, and Red Menace: Civil Rights and Anticommunism in the Jim Crow South.* Baton Rouge: LSU Press, 2014.

Keikamn, Diane. *Live Fast, Love Hard: The Faron Young Story.* Champaign: University of Illinois Press, 2007.

Kenney, William Howland. *Recorded Music in American Life: The Phonograph and Popular Memory, 1890–1945.* New York: Oxford University Press, 1999.

Kurtz, Michael L., and Morgan D. Peoples. *Earl K. Long: The Saga of Uncle Earl and Louisiana Politics.* Baton Rouge: LSU Press, 1990.

Laird, Tracey E. W. *Louisiana Hayride: Radio and Roots Music along the Red River.* New York: Oxford University Press, 2005.

———. "Shreveport's KWKH: A City and Its Radio Station in the Evolution of Country Music and Rock-and-Roll." PhD diss., University of Michigan, 2000.

Lange, Jeffery J. *Smile When You Call Me a Hillbilly: Country Music's Struggle for Respectability, 1939–1954.* Athens: University of Georgia Press, 2004.

Liebling, A. J. *The Earl of Louisiana.* Baton Rouge: LSU Press, 2008.

Leitch, Michael. *Great Songs of World War II.* London: Wise, 1975.

Lewis, Jon E., ed. *D-Day: As They Saw It.* New York: Carroll & Graf, 2004.

Lohman, Laura. *Hail Columbia! American Music and Politics in the Early Nation.* New York: Oxford University Press, 2020.

Lornell, Kip, and Tracey E. W. Laird. *Shreveport Sounds in Black and White.* Jackson: University Press of Mississippi, 2008.

Lydon, Michael. *Ray Charles: Man and Music.* New York: Riverhead Books, 1998.

Magnan, Philip J. *Letters from the Pacific Front: My Father's Adventures from Guadalcanal to Okinawa.* New York: Writers Advantage, 2003.

Malone, Bill C., and Tracey E. W. Laird. *Country Music USA, 50th Anniversary Edition.* Austin: University of Texas Press, 2018.

Marsh, Dave. *Louie Louie: The History and Mythology of the World's Most Famous Rock 'n' Roll Song.* Ann Arbor: University of Michigan Press, 2004.

Matthiessen, Maria von. *Looking for Magical Country: A Gathering of Savory Southern Characters.* Macon, GA: Mercer University Press, 2001.

Mazor, Barry. *Meeting Jimmie Rodgers: How America's Original Roots Music Hero Changed the Pop Sounds of a Country.* New York: Oxford University Press, 2009.

———. *Ralph Peer and the Making of Popular Roots Music.* Chicago: Chicago Review Press, 2016.

McDonough, Jimmy. *Soul Survivor: A Biography of Al Green.* New York: Da Capo, 2017.

McGuire, Jack B. *Win the Race or Die Trying: Uncle Earl's Last Hurrah.* Jackson: University Press of Mississippi, 2016.

McNeil, W. K., ed. *Encyclopedia of American Gospel Music.* New York: Routledge, 2005.

Meacham, Jon. *Franklin and Winston: An Intimate Portrait of an Epic Friendship.* New York: Random House, 2003.

Miles, William. *Songs, Odes, Glees and Ballads: A Bibliography of American Presidential Campaign Songsters.* New York: Greenwood, 1990.

Obrecht, Jas. *Early Blues: The First Stars of Blues Guitar.* Minneapolis: University of Minnesota Press, 2015.

Owenby, Ted, and Charles Reagan Wilson, eds. *The Mississippi Encyclopedia.* Jackson: University Press of Mississippi, 2017.

Pecknold, Diane, ed. *Hidden in the Mix: The African American Presence in Country Music.* Durham, NC: Duke University Press, 2013.

———. *The Selling Sound: The Rise of the Country Music Industry.* Durham, NC: Duke University Press, 2007.

Peterson, Richard A. *Creating Country Music: Fabricating Authenticity.* Chicago: University of Chicago Press, 1997.

Pugh, Ronnie. *Ernest Tubb: The Texas Troubadour.* Durham, NC: Duke University Press, 1996.

Redlawsk, David P., ed. *The American Governor: Power, Constraint, and Leadership in the States.* New York: Palgrave Macmillan, 2015.

Rose, Jessica. "Stories I Have Always Heard: The Rhetorical Life of an American Song." PhD diss., Georgia State University, 2021.

Russell, Tony. *Blacks, Whites, and Blues.* New York: Stein and Day, 1970.

———. *Country Music Originals: The Legends and the Lost.* New York: Oxford University Press, 2010.

———. *Country Music Records: A Discography, 1921–1942.* New York: Oxford University Press, 2004.

Sackheim, Eric. *The Blues Line: A Collection of Blues Lyrics.* New York: Grossman, 1969.

Sanson, Jerry Purvis. "A History of Louisiana, 1939–1945." PhD diss., Louisiana State University, 1984.

———. *Louisiana during World War II: Politics and Society, 1939–1945.* Baton Rouge: LSU Press, 2020.

Scates, Shelby. *War and Politics by Other Means: A Journalist's Memoir.* Seattle: University of Washington Press, 2000.

Schlappi, Elizabeth. *Roy Acuff: The Smoky Mountain Boy.* New Orleans: Pelican, 1997.

Schoening, Benjamin S., and Eric T. Kasper. *Don't Stop Thinking about the Music: The Politics of Songs and Musicians in Presidential Campaigns.* Lanham, MD: Lexington Books, 2001.

Sears, Richard S. *V-Discs: A History and Discography.* Westport, CT: Greenwood, 1980.

Sims, Barbara Barnes. *The Next Elvis: Searching for Stardom at Sun Records.* Baton Rouge: LSU Press, 2014.

Sindler, Allan P. *Huey Long's Louisiana: State Politics, 1920–1952.* Baltimore, MD: Johns Hopkins University Press, 1968.

Smith, George W. *The Do-or-Die Men: The 1st Marine Raider Battalion at Guadalcanal.* New York: Pocket Books, 2003.

Stacey, Lee, and Lol Henderson, eds. *Encyclopedia of Music in the 20th Century.* London: Routledge, 1999.

Stanbridge, Alan. *Rhythm Changes: Jazz, Culture, Discourse.* New York: Routledge, 2023.

Stanton, Scott. *The Tombstone Tourist: Musicians.* New York: Gallery Books, 2003.

Stowe, William McFerrin, Jr. "Willie Rainach and the Defense of Segregation in Louisiana, 1954–1959." PhD diss., Texas Christian University, 1989.

Strother, Raymond D. *Falling Up: How a Redneck Helped Invent Political Consulting.* Baton Rouge: LSU Press, 2003.

Sullivan, Steve. *Encyclopedia of Great Popular Song Recordings.* Vol. 1. Lanham, MD: Scarecrow, 2013.

Talevski, Nick. *Knocking on Heaven's Door: Rock Obituaries.* London: Omnibus, 2006.

Tosches, Nick. *Country: The Twisted Roots of Rock 'n' Roll.* Cambridge, MA: Da Capo, 1977.

Townsend, Charles R. *San Antonio Rose: The Life and Music of Bob Wills.* Urbana: University of Illinois Press, 1976.

Troutman, John W. *Kīkā Kila: How the Hawaiian Steel Guitar Changed the Sound of Modern Music.* Chapel Hill: University of North Carolina Press, 2016.

Tucker, Stephen R. "Louisiana Saturday Night: A History of Louisiana Country Music," PhD diss., Tulane University, 1995.

Wall, Bennett H., and John C. Rodrigue. *Louisiana: A History.* Malden, MA: John Wiley & Sons, 2014.

Ward, Brian and Patrick Huber. *A&R Pioneers: The Architects of American Roots Music.* Nashville, TN: Vanderbilt University Press, 2018.

Warner, Linda, and Bill Centro. *World War II: One Little Boat.* New York: Page, 2019.

Webb, Clive, ed. *Massive Resistance: Southern Opposition to the Second Reconstruction.* New York: Oxford University Press, 2005.

Weill, Gus. *You Are My Sunshine: The Jimmie Davis Story.* New Orleans: Pelican, 1998.

Whitburn, Joel. *Across the Charts: The 1960s.* Menomonee, WI: Record Research, 2008.

———. *The Billboard Book of Top 40 Hits.* 9th ed. New York: Billboard Books, 2010.

———. *Joel Whitburn's Pop Memories: The History of American Pop Music.* Menomonee, WI: Record Research, 1986.

———. *Joel Whitburn's Top Country Singles, 1944–1997.* 4th ed. Menomonee, WI: Record Research, 1998.

White, Robert J. *Tamarack White, Orygun Seabee in War and Peace.* Baker, OR: Sagebrush Heritage, 1990.

Wills, Rosetta. *The King of Western Swing: Bob Wills Remembered.* New York: Billboard Books, 1998.

Wolfe, Charles K., and James E. Akenson. *The Women of Country Music: A Reader.* Lexington: University of Kentucky Press, 2003.

Zak, Albin J., III. *I Don't Sound Like Nobody: Remaking Music in 1950s America.* Ann Arbor: University of Michigan Press, 2010.

Zwonitzer, Mark. *Will You Miss Me When I'm Gone? The Carter Family & Their Legacy in American Music.* New York: Simon & Schuster, 2002.

JOURNAL ARTICLES

Austin, Wade. "Hollywood Barn Dance: A Brief Survey of Country Music in Films." *Southern Quarterly* 22, no. 3 (Spring 1984): 111–23.

Bañagale, Ryan Raul. "You Are My Sunshine: The Record Pedigree of an American Song." *Musicological Explorations* 6 (Spring 2005): 7–24. University of Victoria, British Columbia.

Berry, Jason. "The Sunshine Man: A Tale of Stardom, Political Heart, and Legendary Music." *Reckon* 3 (Fall 1995): 48–57.

Carleton, Mark T. "Four Anti-Longites: A Tentative Assessment." *Louisiana History* 30, no. 3 (Summer 1989): 249–62.

Dunaway, David King. "Music and Politics in the United States." *Folk Music Journal* 5, no. 3 (1987): 268–94.

Fontenot, Kevin. "You Can't Fight a Song: Country Music in the Campaigns of Jimmie Davis." *Journal of Country Music* 25, no. 2 (2005): 50–59.

Green, Douglas. "The Blue Sky Boys on Radio, 1939–1940: A Newly Discovered Log of Their Daily Program, Kept By Ruth Walker." *Journal of Country Music* 4, no. 4 (1973): 108–58.

Hannusch, Jeff. "You Are My Sunshine." *Offbeat,* October 2009, 24.

Jeansonne, Glen. "Leander Perez: A Southern Demagogue and Reformer." *Louisiana Studies* 14 (Fall 1975): 315–23. Louisiana Studies Institute, Northwestern State University.

———. "Racism and Longism in Louisiana: The 1959–60 Gubernatorial Elections." *Louisiana History* (Summer 1970).

McWhiney, Grady, and Gary B. Mills. "Jimmie Davis and His Music: An Interpretation." *Journal of American Culture* 6, no. 2 (Summer 1983): 54–57.

Mikelbank, Peter. "Places in the Sun: The Many Splendored Careers of Jimmie Davis." *Journal of Country Music* 10, no. 3 (1985): 30–31.

Mitsui, Tori. "You Are My Sunshine: A Question of Authorship." *Old Time Country* 6, no. 4 (Winter 1990): 14–19. University of Mississippi, Center for the Study of Southern Culture.

Pappas, Theodore. "The 'Theft' of an American Classic." *Chronicles: A Magazine of American Culture,* November 1990, 14–19.

Peoples, Morgan D. "Earl Kemp Long: The Man from Pea Patch Farm." *Louisiana History* 17, no. 4 (Autumn 1976): 365–92.

Stanbridge, Alan. "Of Sunshine and Happy Endings: Jazz, Parody, and the Limits of Interpretation." *Critical Studies in Improvisation* 1, no. 1 (2004).

INDEX

Note: Page numbers in *italics* refer to illustrations; those followed by "n" indicate endnotes.

ABC-Paramount Records, 132, 136

Acuff, Roy, 28, 30, 49, 57, 161; friendship with Davis, 77, 96; sings "Sunshine" on *Grand Ole Opry,* 77, 150, 166n13

Acuff-Rose Music, 135

Albert Ammons and His Rhythm Kings, 90

All-Time Favorite Hymns (Davis), 141

Allen, Bob, 16

Allen, Oscar K., 88, 145

Allen Park (Shreveport), 65

Allison, Mose, 155

American Federation of Musicians, 84; 1942 strike by, 57, 61

American Samoa: popularity of "Sunshine" in, 51–52

Ames Brothers, 91, 95

Andrews Sisters, 47, 99

Anita Kerr Singers: as part of "Nashville Sound," 97; recording with Davis, 97, 99

Annabelle: Creation (motion picture), 157

Armstrong, Lillian Hardin, 25

Armstrong, Louis, 25, 77, 105

Arnold, Eddy, 29, 49, 97, 99

Art of God, The (Calhoun), 138

Atcher, Bob, 41; on early recording industry, 30; records "Sunshine," 7, 43, 164n8

Atkins, Chet, 94, 150

Austin, Gene, 59

Autry, Gene, 23, 26, 29, 41, 46, 53, 57; as early country star, 28, 38, 48–49; records "Sunshine," 43, 44, 45, 48, 95

"Away Out on the Mountain" (song), 23

Aycock, Clarence C. "Taddy": and 1960 governor's race, 107; and 1971 governor's race, 148

"Baby Your Mother" (song), 40

"Baby's Lullaby, The" (song), 25

Back in the Saddle (motion picture), 45

Baker Bank and Trust Company, 121, 141; as issue in the 1971 governor's race, 148. *See also* First National Bank of Jefferson Parish

Bañagale, Ryan, 6, 9, 41

"Bang, Bang" (song), 82, 85

"Baptizing of Sister Lucy Lee, The" (song), 72

Barlow, Joel, 58

Barnett, Ross, 114, 118

"Barroom Message, The" (song), 25

Baton Rouge Gridiron Show, 113

Bayeux Tapestry, xi–xii

"Bayou Pon Pon" (song), 101

"Bear Cat Mama from Horner's Corners" (song), 27–28

"Bed Bug Blues" (song), 27; attacks on in 1944 governor's race, 75–76; Davis regrets recording, 28

Bell's Court (now Pomander Walk), 55

Bermejo, Juan José Arévalo, 82

Berry, Jason, 154

Berry, Richard, 133, 138; records "Sunshine," 92–93

Beytia, José González, 82

Bibb, George M., 58

Big Bill Campbell and His Rocky Mountain Rhythm, 90

"Big Mamou" (song), 69

"Big Texas" (song), 71

Billboard (magazine), 42–45, 49, 81, 93, 134, 150; musical categories in, 42; song rankings in, 34, 39, 46, 81, 83–84, 91, 97, 132, 133, 135, 147, 158

Billups, Rowell, 101
Billups, W. L. "Buddy," 141; relationship with Davis, 101, 121
Billups Petroleum Company, 101, 141
Bissmeyer, Ollie E., Jr., 85, 87
Blake, Norman: accompanies Johnny Cash on "Sunshine," 155; sings "Sunshine" in *O Brother, Where Art Thou?* 156
Blanco, Kathleen B., 159
"Blessed Be the Tie That Binds" (hymn), 68
Blue Goose, the, 25
Blue Ridge Playboys, the, 70
Blue Sky Boys, the 3–4
"Blue Yodel No. 9" (song), 25
Bluebird (record label), 1, 3, 28
Bob Wills and His Texas Playboys, 57, 70, 161. *See also* Wills, Bob
Bolick, Bill, 3–4
Bolick, Earl, 3–4
Botkin, Perry, 46
Bottoms, The (Shreveport neighborhood), 27
"Boy Who Never Grew Too Old to Comb His Mother's Hair, The," (song), 69
Branton, Parey, 144
Brown, James "Jim" (state senator), 151
Brown, Jimmy (baseball player), 1
Brown, Milton, 59
Brown, T. E. "Sleepy," 40
Brown v. Board of Education, 104
Bruner, Cliff, 33, 34, 70, 72
Bunch, Thurman, 122. *See also* Plainsmen Quartet

Caldwell, Sam S., 65; attacks on Davis, 122
Calhoun, Jimi, 138
Camp Susupe (Saipan), 53
Campaign songs, 58; music in politics, 59
Cantwell, David, 136, 138
Capital Correspondents Association Gridiron Show, 143
Carazo, Castro, 145
Carleton, Mark T., 62, 85
Carlisle, Cliff, 23, 26, 32
Carolina Sunshine Girl, 12
Carolina Tarheels, 12
Carson, Fiddlin' John, 4, 38
Carter, A. P., 9. *See also* Carter Family, the
Carter, Wilf "Montana Slim," 44
Carter Family, the, 9, 17, 30, 35, 38, 161
Cash, Johnny: records "Sunshine," 101, 154, 155, *156,* 157
Castro, Marie S. C., 52
Centenary College, 22
Centro, Bill, 52
Chappelear, Leon, 40
Charles Mitchell's Texans, 33, 40. *See also* Mitchell, Charles
Charles, Ray, xii, 140; and 1962 performance at Loyola University, 131, 134–35; call from Davis about Loyola performance, 134; concerts in Baton Rouge, 130–31; concerts in New Orleans, 130–31, 134–35; country disc jockeys ignore his country recordings, 136; desegregates concerts in South, 130–31; drug use by, 135; experience with racism in childhood, 129–30; hit records by, 131, 132, 133, 134; hit status of his "Sunshine" recording, 133; interpretation of "Sunshine" by, 133–34; *Modern Sounds* album, 131–39; "racial trespassing" of his "Sunshine" version, 137–39; records "Sunshine," 133–39; reinterprets songs associated with racism, 137; royalties for Davis from his "Sunshine" version, 135
"Christ Is My Sunshine" (song), 158
Chuck Guillory and His Rhythm Boys, 71
Chuck Wagon Gang, 99, 147. *See also* Davis, Anna Carter Gordon (wife of Davis)
Churchill, Winston: love of "Sunshine," 53–54
Civil rights: Black voters registered under Earl Long, 103, 116; Davis and, 110–12, 114–20, 124–28, 135–36, 138–39, 148, 154; Earl Long and, 103–4, 131; Federal courts and, 116–18, 125; Louisiana Legislature and, 112, 115–18, 127; and Ray Charles's music, 133–34; state laws on integration, 131
Clemons, Zeke, 69
Cliff Bruner and His Texas Wanderers, 33, 70. *See also* Bruner, Cliff
Cline, Patsy, 132, 136
Clinton, Ed, 104
Close Harmony: A History of Southern Gospel (Goff), 100
Cobb, John, 1
Coffman, Wanna, 16

Cole, Nat King, 91, 131; as first Black vocalist to record "Sunshine," 91; records "Sunshine," 91, 138

Columbia Pictures, 48, 49, 81

Columbia Records, 7, 24

Cooder, Ry, 156

Cooper, Daniel, 136, 137

Country: The Twisted Roots of Rock 'n' Roll (Tosches), 26

Country music, 5, 7, 25, 28, 39, 40, 57, 59, 60, 63, 67, 69, 78, 90, 95, 97, 99, 101, 122, 126–27, 131, 133, 136–38, 150–51, 160; Bing Crosby's role in early popularity of, 34, 36; Davis's role in early popularity of, 6, 19–20, 28, 33–34, 36–38; early artists of, 1–4, 6, 9, 11, 16–17, 23–24, 26–27, 30–36, 38, 41, 43–49; early reputation of, 34, 36–38, 41–42, 46, 49–49, 67, 78, 127, 137; earnings by early artists, 34–37; growth of, 30, 34; radio as a prime venue for early artists, 24–25, 59; Ralph Peer's importance to early success of genre, 17, 25, 34–35, 38

Country Music Hall of Fame, xii, 7, 33, 70; Davis's induction, 150–51, 160

Country Music Records: A Discography, 1921–1942 (Russell), 7, 25, 40

Country Music USA (Malone and Laird), 44

Crook, David, 11, 12, 13

Crosby, Bing, 29, 32; records "Sunshine," 44–47, 57, 91, 95, 133; role in acceptance of country music, 34, 36–37; V-Disc recording of "Sunshine," 57

Crowley, Harriet Hughes, 55

Cuoghi, Joe, 94

Cyclone Prairie Rangers (motion picture), 81

Daniel, Wayne, 8, 12

Darling, Denver, 90

Davis, Alvern Adams (wife of Davis), 80, 96, 143, 147; Davis's marriage to, 38

Davis, Anna Carter Gordon (wife of Davis), 154, 158; Davis's marriage to, 147; role with Chuck Wagon Gang, 147

Davis, Blind Willie, 9–10, 32

Davis, Esther Mae, 12

Davis, James H. "Jimmie," xi–xii, 1–2, 5, 9–10, 14, 44, 91, 93, 95, 131, 133, 143, 146, 161; and 1944 governor's race, 57–78, 87; and 1960 governor's race, 102–14; and 1971 governor's race, 144, 147–50; and Baker Bank and, 120, 140, 144, 148; band, 6, 23, 33–32, 33, 39–40, 47–50, 65–76, 79–84, 85, 87–89, 94, 96–97, 106–8, 122, 150; becomes gospel singer, 97–101, 141; Blues recordings, 6, 17, 24–28, 75–76, 154; buys "Sunshine," 6–8, 18; civil rights record, 110–14, 115–20, 124–28, 139, 142, 154, 160; early life, 20–22; early musical career, 22–29, 30–34; early political career, 24, 26, 30, 38–39; first gubernatorial term, 79–89; funeral, 159–60; hit records, 34, 39, 41–43, 45–47, 69, 81, 83–85, 100, 127, 135; legislative accomplishments, 84–85, 88, 115–19, 122–24, 127; LSU master's thesis, 20, 22, 19; motion picture appearances, 47, 48, 49, 61, 75, 77, 80, 81, 82, 85–87, 90, 97, 107, 109, 126; on if he wrote "Sunshine," 15–20; records risqué songs, 25–28, 33, 75, 77, 111–12; records "You Are My Sunshine," 40–42; recordings with Black performers, 25–27, 77, 105, 154; refusal to engage in negative campaigning, 73–76, 106, 109–10; relationship with Willie Rainach, 105, 107, 110–13, 115–17; returns to music career after first gubernatorial term, 89, 96–101; rides horse into state Capitol, 123–26, 145; scandals in second term, 120–23, 140, 148–49; second gubernatorial term, 115–28, 134–36, 138; song-buying practices, 33–37; travels as governor during first term, 80–84; uncertainty about birth year, 20; views on race, 25, 105, 119–20

Davis, Henry (brother of Davis), 122

Davis, Sam Jones (father of Davis), 20

Davis, Sarah Works (mother of Davis), 20

Dawson, Carl, 144; sponsors bill to make "Sunshine" state song, 144–45

Dead South (band), 154

Decca Records, 4, 6–7, 24, 33, 34, 38; 1942 musicians strike and, 57, 61; Davis and, 25, 28, 29, 34, 40, 46, 57, 61, 76, 81, 99, 141; "Faith Series" of, 89; other artists signed by, 4, 6, 7, 33, 46, 67, 75, 91, 99

Democratic National Convention of 1944 (Chicago), 80

Dessau Hall (Texas), 98

Dinning Sisters, 48, 90
Division of Health and Hospitals (Louisiana), 80
Dobro, 25. *See also* Hawaiian guitar; Slide guitar; Steel guitar
Dodd, Monroe E., 22
Dodd, William "Bill": and 1960 governor's race, 104, 107, 109–10; attacks on Davis by, 107, 109–10; defends Earl Long, 102; praise for Davis by, 109
Dodd College, 22, 24
Domino, Fats, 130–31
Don't Fence Me In: Songs of the Wide Open Spaces (album), 47
Dorsey, Thomas, 99
Durbin, Deanna, 47
Dyer, Jack M., 124

Ed Sullivan Show, 112
Edwards, Edwin W., 148, 152, 158, *159*
Eisenhower, Dwight D., 52, 104
Enloe, James, 22, 23
Escott, Colin, 94
Estes, Sleepy John, 38
Estopinal, Jerry, 161
Ewing, Randy, 159

"Faded Love" (song), 70
Faser, Chris, 121, 148
Faubus, Orval, 118, 127, 140
Feder, J. Lester, 137–38
Feller, Sid, 132, *134*
First National Bank of Jefferson Parish, 131. *See also* Baker Bank and Trust Company
Florida Playboys, the, 129
Foley, Red, 49, 97, 99
Fontane, Doralice, 146, 152
Fontenot, Kevin, 14, 73
Fontenot, Rufus J., 83
Ford, Andrew, 155
Foree, Mel, 36
"Forever Is a Long, Long Time" (song), 101
Foster, Mike, *159*
Franklin, Aretha, 139, 155
Frazar, Lether E., 103
Freeman, Robert "Bobby," 151
Frontier Fury (motion picture), 63

Gardner, Edward Foote, 44
Garland Encyclopedia of World Music (Kaeppler and Love), 52
"Georgia on My Mind" (song), 131, 132, 153. *See also* State songs
Gid Tanner and the Skillet Lickers, 11
Gimble, Johnny, 69–70
"Give Me Louisiana" (song), 146, 151–52
Gleason, Ralph J., 133
Goff, James R., Jr., 100
"Good Time Papa Blues" (song), 28
Goodman, Charles, 122. *See also* Plainsmen Quartet
Gospel music, 1, 9, 20, 99, 133, 137; and Davis, 15, 20, 102, 106–7, 144, 147, 150, 158; Davis's conversion to, 97, 100, 106; Decca Records "Faith Series," 99; Plainsmen Quartet and Davis, 106, 121–22, 141, 143; popular gospel groups, 99, 106, 147
Gospel Music Hall of Fame, 150
Grammy Awards, 70, 156–57
Grammy Hall of Fame, 158
Grand Ole Opry, 49, 57, 71, 77, 96, 101, 106, 108, 122, 131, 150
Great British Home Chorus, The 158
"Grievin' My Heart out for You" (song), 133
Gremillion, Jack, 116, 118
Grevemberg, Francis, 102; and 1960 governor's race, 113
Guidry, Oran "Doc," 70
Guthrie, Woody, 9

Haggard, Merle, 29
Halifax, Lady (Dorothy Wood), 81
Halifax, Lord (Edward Frederick Lindley Wood), 81
Harrison, Paul, 41
Harrison, William Henry, 58
Harry Roy and His Band, 90
Hatcher, William B., 81
Hawaiian guitar, 25, 31, 41. *See also* Dobro; Slide guitar; Steel guitar
Heino, Anni, 155
Hello World (record label), 16, 17, 23
Henderson, W. K., 17; and Hello World record label, 23; owner of KWKH, 22
Hendrix, Margie, 133

Heuer, William L., 121
Hi Records, 94
Hilburn, Wiley, 147, 160
Hillbilly Flour, 59
Hillbilly music. *See* Country music
Hofner, Adolph, 34
Hokanson, Minnie, 8
"Home Town Blues" (song), 25
Hood, Easter Mandy Nappier (wife of Oliver Hood), 11
Hood, Oliver, 12–14, 20; as author of "Sunshine," 12; early life of, 10, 164n13; musical ability of, 11; songwriting by, 11–13
Horne, Lena, 77, 105, 109, 112
Horton, Johnny, 122
Hortoneda, Luis Sans Y, 1
Howard, Shemp, 47
Huber, Patrick, 36
Hunter, Tab, 132

"I Can't Stop Loving You" (song), 131, 132, 136
"(I Heard That) Lonesome Whistle" (song), 101
"I'd Love to Call You Sweetheart" (song), 41
Ike & Tina Turner, 138
In Old Santa Fe (motion picture), 48
"I'm Beginning to Forget You" (song), 83
"I'm Going to Write Myself a Letter" (song), 82
"I'm Sorry Now" (song), 47
"Is It Too Late Now" (song), 81
"It Makes No Difference Now" (song), 33–34, 36, 39, 47, 80, 131
"It's Been Years (Since I've Seen My Mother)" (song), 28

Jack Halloran Singers, 133
"Jambalaya (On the Bayou)" (song), 71
Japan: affection for "Sunshine" in, 157
Jeansonne, Glen, 120
Jimmie Davis Souvenir Album, 84
Jimmie Davis Tabernacle, 141, 159–60
Jimmie Show, The, 22
Johnny and Jack (Anglin), 95, 101
Joint Legislative Committee (Louisiana), 104, 112, 115
Joint Legislative Committee on Un-American Activities (Louisiana), 115. *See also* Joint Legislative Committee (Louisiana)
"Jole Blon" (song), 69, 144
Jones, Sam H., 102, 143; on Davis as a candidate, 73; Davis's endorsement in 1948 governor's race, 87–89; persuades Davis to run for governor in 1943, 62–63, 74; record as governor, 61–62, 85; supports Davis for governor in 1943, 77, 80
Jonesboro, LA, 65, 67, 147
Jordon, French, 122
"Just a Closer Walk with Thee" (hymn), 99

Kane, Harnett T., 126
Kapp, David, 34
Kapp, Jack, 46–47
Katz, Allan, 147
Kennon, Robert F., 85, 87–88, 102, 113, 143, 145
King, Pee Wee, 24, 57, 150, 152
King, Wayne, 42, 45
KTBS (Shreveport radio station), 6
Kurtz, Michael L., 62
KWKH (Shreveport radio station), 5–6, 16–18, 22–24, 29, 32, 47, 101, 165n5

LaBorde, Adras, 146
LaGrange, GA, 10–12
Laird, Tracey E. W., 26, 44, 59
Landrieu, Moon, 118
Lani McIntyre's Hawaiians, 32
Lavoy, Lou, 145
Leake County Revelers, the, 59
LeBlanc, Dudley J., 65, 77
LeBlanc, Leroy "Happy Fats," 70
Leche, Richard W., 62, 64
Leo Soileau's Rhythm Band, 74–75
Letcher, Robert P., 58
Lewis, Jerry Lee, 71, 93, 154
Liberto, Carl, 149
Library of Congress National Recording Registry, 158
Liebling, A. J., 62, 111
Light Crust Dough Boys, 26, 31, 57, 70. *See also* O'Daniel, Wilbert Lee "Pappy"; Wills, Bob
Líšt'any (Czechoslovakia), 56
"Little Darling, Pal of Mine" (song), 9
Little Rock Central High School, 104
"Live and Let Live" (song), 68
Lombardo, Guy, 53

Long, Blanche, 103
Long, Earl K., 61, 62, 63, 64, 84–85, 102, 107, 140–41; and 1943 governor's race, 64–65, 73, 75, 76, 77; and 1948 governor's race, 87, 88, 89; attacks on Davis by, 73, 109, 110; and Blaze Starr, 103; and civil rights, 103, 112, 116, 131; and Davis, 62, 63, 64, 73, 88, 109–10, 114; endorses Davis for governor, 112, 113; planned campaign for consecutive term in 1960, 102–4, 142; sent to mental institution, 103
Long, Gillis, 148–50
Long, Huey P., 39, 49, 59, 61, 66, 79, 88, 140, 142, 145, 147
Long, Russell B., 88, 103
"Louie, Louie" (song), 93
Louisiana (motion picture), 48, 85–87
Louisiana College (now Louisiana Christian University), 19, 21–22
Louisiana Department of Commerce and Industry Department, 121–22
Louisiana Hayride, 5, 101
Louisiana House, 121, 124, 140, 144–45, 151–52; 1968 bill to make "Sunshine" state song, 144–46; 1972 bill to make "Sunshine" state song, 151–52; Davis sings "Sunshine" to members, 80; Earl Long and, 103–4; segregation legislation and, 104, 115, 118
"Louisiana, My Home Sweet Home" (song), 145
Louisiana Office of Civilian Defense (OCD): Davis gives band job at, 79–80
Louisiana politics: 1944 governor's race, 60–78, 87; 1948 governor's race, 84, 87–89; 1960 governor's race, 101–14; 1972 governor's race, 147–50; Huey Long's influence on, 49, 59, 61, 88, 142, 147; "reformers" vs. Long organization, 62, 77, 85, 87–88, 148
Louisiana Public Service Commission, 6, 49, 50, 59, 61, 63, 64, 73, 140, 150
"Louisiana scandals" of 1939–40, 88
Louisiana Senate: and 1968 bill making "Sunshine" state song, 144–46; and 1972 bill making "Sunshine" state song, 151–52
Louisiana State University (LSU), 62, 81, 89; Davis and, 16, 18, 20, 22, 60, 79, 80, 114, 119, 142, 143, 145, 155
Louisiana Weekly (New Orleans), 127, 135
Loyola University Field House, 131
LSU Men's Glee Club, 31
McAlister Auditorium (Tulane University), 131
McAuliffe, Leon, 31
McClain, Jesse, 144
McConnell, Raymond A., Jr., 54
McGuire, Jack, 103
McKeithen, John J.: appoints Davis to LSU Board, 143; campaigns for constitutional amendment in 1967, 146–47; as Davis adversary, 140, 143–44; on Davis scandals, 121, 140, 143; description of, 140; first term as governor, 141–42; elected to second term, 143; vetoes "Sunshine" state song bill, 145–46
McKenzie, Sammie, 145
McVoy, Carl, 93–95, 133
McWilliams, Elsie, 36
Maestri, Robert, 87
Mainord, Jack Lee, 122. *See also* Plainsmen Quartet
Malone, Bill C., 26, 44, 59
Malone, Gareth, 158. See also *Great British Home Chorus, The*
Marcels, the, 138
Mazor, Barry, 34
"Meet Me Tonight in Dreamland" (song), 29, 39
Miles, William, 58
Milton Brown and His Musical Brownies, 16, 31, 32. *See also* Brown, Milton
Mississippi Rhythm (motion picture), 97
Mitch Miller and the Gang, 95
Mitchell, Charles: as Davis band leader, 19, *23*, 31–33, 40–41, 69, 80, 88; buys "Sunshine" with Davis, 6, 8–9; death of, 150; early collaboration with Davis, 19, *23*, 31–33; given state job by Davis, 80, 88; meets Davis, 18, 31; as reputed coauthor of "Sunshine," 18, 74; runs for elected office, 150; sells his half of "Sunshine" to Davis, 19, 40; as a steel guitar player, 31–33, 41
Mitchell, Ova, 33
Mitsui, Toru, 7, 17, 157
Modern Sounds in Country and Western, Vols. I and II (albums), 131–34, 136–38
Mollere, Jules, 144
Moman, Chips, 11; on who wrote "Sunshine," 13
Monogram Pictures, 45, 85, 97
Monroe Times, 75
Montana, Patsy, 53

Montgomery Ward, 28
Morgan, Lewis, 64, 77; criticizes Davis, 75–76
Morocco, 53
Morrison, deLesseps: and 1960 governor's race, 107–8, 111–12, 113; and 1960 New Orleans desegregation crisis, 117; and 1964 governor's race, 123
Morrison, James H. "Jimmy": candidate for governor in 1940, 64; candidate for governor in 1944, 74–75; candidate for governor in 1948, 87; political attacks on Davis by, 74
Moseley, Vincent, 65
Motion pictures, 23, 38, 46, 124; country music stars in, 48–49; Davis in, 47–48, 61, 63, 75, 77, 80, 81, 82, 85–87, 90, 97, 107, 109, 126; importance to the popularity of country music, 48; "Sunshine" in, 45, 156–57
Mullican, Aubrey Wilson "Moon," 141; as cowriter of "Jambalaya," 71; in Davis's band, 69–70, 72–73, 106, 122; as *Grand Ole Opry* member, 71; given state job, 122; hit recordings, 71; influence on other artists, 94; piano-playing style, 70; relationship with Davis, 72; reputation for drinking, 72
"My Blue Bonnet Girl" (song), 32
"My Blue Heaven" (song), 16

Nashville Songwriters Hall of Fame, 150
"Nashville Sound," 97, 136
National Association for the Advancement of Colored People (NAACP), 111–12
National Barn Dance (radio show), 57, 82, 101
NBC radio network, 42, 57
Neal, Jocelyn R., 133
Nelson, Ozzie, 47
Nettles, Bill, 28–29, 36, 47
Nettles, Norman, 28–29, 36
Nettles Brothers, 29, 36
New Orleans desegregation crisis of 1960, 104, 116–19, 125–26, 154
New Orleans Jazz and Heritage Festival, 154
New Orleans Municipal Auditorium, 131
"New San Antonio Rose" (song), 36
"No Letter Today" (song), 133
"Nobody's Business" (song), 17, 24
"Nobody's Darlin' But Mine" (song), 28–29, 32, 38, 47, 75, 85, 98
Northern Mariana Islands, 52

O Brother, Where Art Thou? (motion picture), 156
"O My Loving Brother, When the World's on Fire" (song), 9
O'Daniel, Wilbert Lee "Pappy," 156; possible influence on Davis, 59
Okeh Records, 7, 30
"Old Folks at Home" (song), 137
Old Regulars (New Orleans political organization), 87, 110, 112
"Old Rugged Cross" (hymn), 109
"Old Timer" (song), 40
"Organ-Grinder Blues" (song), 27
Orleans Parish School Board, 116–18
"Out of Town Blues" (song), 17, 24, 25

Page, Patti, 29
Paich, Marty, 132
Palmer, Robert, 95
Pappas, Theodore, 11, 12, 13
Pat O'Daniel and His Hillbilly Boys, 59. *See also* O'Daniel, Wilbert Lee "Pappy"
Patton, John S., 49
"Peace in the Valley" (song), 99, 106
Pearce, Dave, 122
Pearl, Minnie (Sarah Ophelia Colley Cannon), 57, 108, 150
Pecknold, Diane, 24, 137, 138
Peer, Ralph, 35; and buying rights to songs, 34–35; his importance to early country music, 38; relationship with Davis, 17, 24–25, 35–36
Peoples, Morgan D., 62
Perez, Leander, 126; Davis and, 110–12, 117, *118;* racism of, 117
Perrin, William "Curly," 69–70
Peyton, Rupert, 62
Pfister, James H., 115
Phillips, Sam, 94–95
Pickin' on Peachtree (Daniel), 12
Pine Ridge Boys: recording of "Sunshine," 1–4, 7–8, 20, 40. *See also* Spivey, Doug; Taylor, Marvin
"Pistol Packin' Mama" (song), 47
Plainsmen Quartet, 141, 143, 144; and 1960 governor's race, 106; members take state jobs in Davis administration, 121
PT-244 (US Navy vessel), 52
Pyle, Ernie, 56

Rainach, William "Willie," 103–5, 107, 110–13, 115–17, 126
Rainbow Ramblers (Davis's band), 48
Raelettes (Ray Charles's singers), 132–33
Raley, Leo, 70
Raley, Randall "Red," 70
"Ramona" (song), 23
Rarick, John, 143, 144
Raven, Eddy (Edward Futch), 147
RCA Records, 24, 99
Reagan, Nancy, 157
Reagan, Ronald, 157
Recording industry: 1942 musicians strike and, 57, 61; early country music industry and, 24–25, 34–36, 38, 48–49; Ralph Peer and, 17, 30, 34–36; royalties for performers and songwriters, 30, 35–36, 41, 45, 135, 157
"Red Nightgown Blues" (song), 75
Republic Pictures, 45
Rice Brothers, 5–7, 10–11, 18, 30, 41, 163n5; record "Sunshine," 4–5
Rice, Hoke, 4–8, 12, 20, 146
Rice, Paul, 4, 12, 20; claim of "Sunshine" authorship, 6–8; sells "Sunshine" to Davis, 6, 8, 18–19, 40, 74, 146
Riddle, Nelson, 91
"Ridin' Down the Arizona Trail" (song), 32
"Ridin' Down the Canyon (When the Desert Sun Goes Down)" (song), 46
Riding Through Nevada (motion picture), 48, 61
Risqué songs, 77; by Davis, 26–28, 33; as issue in Davis's political campaigns, 75–76; by other artists, 28, 166n22
Ritter, Tex, 29, 49, 90; first to sing "Sunshine" in a movie, 45, 48
Rivingtons, the, 138
"Rock of Ages" (song), 9
Rodgers, Jimmie, 17, 22, 23, 24, 25, 26, 30, 35, 36, 38, 41, 161, 165n17; as a role model for Davis and other early country performers, 23, 25, 27
Roemer, Charles E. "Buddy," *159*
Rogers, Roy, 49, 124
"Roll Along, Kentucky Moon" (song), 40
Roosevelt, Franklin D., 53, 81
Rose, Fred, 36
Rose, Jessica, 14
Root, Herschel D., 56
Royal Navy (UK), 56
Rudy Sooter's Ranchmen, 34
Russell, Tony, 25, 26, 28, 34, 40, 165n

Saipan, 52
Samuel, David B., 24
San Antonio, 32, 33, 39
Sanjek, Russell, 48
Satherley, Art, 7, 163n8
Saturday Night Roundup (radio show), 5–6
"Saturday Night Stroll" (song), 26
Saunders, John, 151–52
Scates, Shelby, 105
Seeger, Pete, 52
Segregation, 26, 103–5, 110, *113*, 115–19, 129–30; 1960 New Orleans school desegregation crisis, 116–19; Davis as supporter of, 107, 110–12, 114–20, 124–28, 135–36, 138; in concerts, 130–31; Louisiana laws on, 26, 104, 131; Ray Charles defies, 130–31, 137–39
Schaffer, Ed "Dizzy Head," 25, 165n17
Shane, Jackie, 138
Sharp, Dee Dee, 138
Shelton, Bob (Bob Attlesey), 67, 69–70
Shelton, Joe (Joe Attlesey), 67, 69–70, 79
Shelton Brothers, 67, 70
"She's a Hum Dum Dinger from Dingersville" (song), 25, 27–28
Shehee, VA, 152
"Shirt Tail Blues" (song), 28
"Shotgun Wedding, The" (song), 27
Showboys, the, 70
Shreveport Home Wreckers, the, 25
Shreveport Municipal Auditorium, 5–6
Silvey, Rufus "Uncle Bud," 4
Sinatra, Frank, 57; Davis appears on his national radio show, 82
Sindler, Allan P., 84
Skyliners, the, 40
Slide guitar, 25
Smith, Bessie, 38
Smith, Kate, 90
Snow, Hank, 23, 91, 131, 161
Solomon Islands, 51–52; affection for "Sunshine" by people of, xi
"Somebody Stole My Sunshine Away" (song), 13. *See also* Hood, Oliver
"Song of Louisiana" (song), 145

Songs, Odes, Glees and Ballots (Miles), 58
Songwriting, xi, 7–8, 11–14, 30, 33, 70–72, 100, 157; Davis as songwriter, 6, 16, 18–19, 28, 34, 45, 49, 101, 119, 128, 161; Ralph Peer and, 17, 34–36; song-buying practices of Davis and others, 15–16, 18–19, 26–27, 29, 33–36, 74, 101, 139
Southern Governors' Association, 81
Spaht, Carlos, 102
Speer Family, the, 99, 147
Spivey, Doug, 1–3, 7–8
Square Dance Katy (motion picture), 97
Stables, the (nightclub), 96, 150
Stanphill, Ira, 100
Stapleton, Chris, 155
Stapleton, Morgan, 155
Starr, Blaze, 103
Stardust on the Sage (motion picture), 45
Starrett, Charles, 48, 63, 81
State songs: Georgia, 153; Louisiana, xi–xii, 81, 144–46, 150–52; Tennessee, 152
Steel guitar, 4, 31–33, 40, 69, 91, 97, 150. *See also* Dobro; Hawaiian guitar; Slide guitar
Stewart, Redd, 152
Stine J., 156
Stopher, Vashti Robertson, 145
"Story of Nobody's Darlin', The," (song), 29
Strictly in the Groove (motion picture), 47, 61
Strother, Raymond, 125; on 1971 governor's race, 148–49; on Davis fundraising, 149
Stuart, Marty, 155
Summersby, Kay, 52
Sun Records, 94
Sunshine (Davis's horse), 123–24, 139; Davis rides into Capitol on, 124–26; death of, 126
Sunshine Boys, 67. *See also* Shelton Brothers
Sunshine Bridge, 122–23, 143
"Suppertime (song), 100, 109, 114, 159–60
"Swanee River Rock (Talkin' 'bout That River)" (song), 137
Sweethearts or Strangers (album), 91
"Sweethearts or Strangers" (song), 49, 91

Take Me Back to Oklahoma (motion picture), 45
Taylor, Marvin, 1, 3, 8
"Tennessee Waltz" (song), 152
"That's What I Like about the South" (song), 72
"There's a Chill on the Hill Tonight" (song), 46, 81
"There's a New Moon over My Shoulder" (song), 46, 82, 85
"Think of Me Thinking of You" (song), 23
"This Land Is Your Land" (song), 9
Thomason, Jimmy, 69–70, 79
Thurmond, Strom, 85
Tillman, Floyd, 47; Davis buys "Makes No Difference Now" from, 33–34, 38, 131; on Davis and songwriting, 34
Tippecanoe Song Book, 58
"Tom Cat and Pussy Blues" (song), 27
Tom Dickey's Show Boys, 34
Tosches, Nick, 26, 33
Treen, David, 150, 158, *159*
Troutman, John, 31
Truman, Harry S.: Davis and, 81, 96
Tubb, Ernest, 23–24, 36, 45, 47, 48, 49, 53, 70, 97, 99, 161; Davis tries to buy "Walking the Floor over You" from, 33
Tucker, Stephen R., 29
Tumbling Tumbleweeds (motion picture), 46
"Two More Years (and I'll Be Free)" (song), 39

United Service Organizations (USO), 57
Universal Pictures, 47
Universal Studios, 47
US Copyright Office, 8, 9, 15
US Department of Justice, 117
US Fifth Circuit Court of Appeals, 116
USS *O'Brien*, 51
USS *Wasp*, 51

Vagabonds, the, 90
V-Disc (record label), 57
Verret, J. Emile, 83
Victor Records, 1, 16, 17, 24, 25, 26, 28, 38, 46, 99
Victor Young's Orchestra, 46
Vincent, Crawford, 74
von Matthiessen, Maria, 15

Wagner, Robert, 104
Walking in the Sunshine (album), 158
"Walking the Floor over You" (song), 33, 47, 48, 70
Wallace, George C., 118, 120, 138
Ward, Bryan, 36
Ward, Reggie, 6–7

Watson, Tom, 58
Weill, Gus, 119
Welborn, Howard, 122. *See also* Plainsmen Quartet
Welk, Lawrence, 44, 90
Western swing music, 31, 36, 38, 41, 70; early stars of, 16–17, 26, 31, 59, 70; influence on Davis's music, 31–34
WGST (Atlanta radio station), 2–4
"When It's Round-Up Time in Heaven" (song), 32
"When It's Roundup Time in Texas" (song), 32
"When Mother Prayed for Me," (song), 1
"Where the Old Red River Flows" (song), 1, 135; lyrics altered by Davis, 119; racist lyrics of, 119
White, Georgia, 38
Whitstable, UK, 54
Williams, Andre, 93
Williams, Hank, 71, 131, 161; royalties from Ray Charles's recordings of songs by, 135; songwriting with Davis, 101
Wills, Bob, 26, 31, 36, 49, 57, 59, 70, 161; Davis's influence on, 31. *See also* Bob Wills and His Texas Playboys
Wilson, Gerald, 132
Without a Penny in My Pocket (Centro), 53
WLS (Chicago radio station), 101
Women's Auxiliary Air Force (UK), 54
Woods, Oscar "Buddy," 25–26
Work, Cliff, 47
World War II, 40, 51, 55–56, 68, 73–74, 80, 82, 84, 88; Churchill and "Sunshine," 53–54; popularity of "Sunshine" in England, 54–56; popularity of "Sunshine" in South Pacific, xi, 51–53; and V-Disc records, 57
"Worried Mind" (song), 131
Wright, Frederick, 56
Wright, J. Skelly: and 1960 New Orleans desegregation crisis, 116–17, 125
WSM (Nashville radio station), 49, 101
Wynne, Michael, 19

"Yo Yo Mama" (song), 27
"You Are My Sunshine" (song), xi–xii, 24, 34, 49, 82–84, 98, 100, 123–25, 140, 150, 157–59, 161; 1968 effort to make it Louisiana state song, 144–46; 1976–77 effort to make it Louisiana state song, 151–53; accolades for, xii, 158; alleged composers of, 1–14; Bing Crosby and, 44–47, 57, 91, 95, 133; Carl McVoy and, 93–95, 133; Davis acknowledges buying, 19; Davis buys, 6–8, 18; Davis's claims of authorship, 15–20, 45; Davis's first recording of, 40–41; different styles of, 2, 10, 40–42, 45, 46–47, 90–96, 133–35, 138–39, 154–57; first recording of, 1–3; hit recordings of, 41–46, 85, 94, 131, 155, 158; Johnny Cash and, 101, 154–55, *156*, 157; lyrics to, 2; in motion pictures, 45, 47–48, 85, *86*, 156–57; Oliver Hood and, 11–14, 20; Pine Ridge Boys and, 1–4; Ray Charles and, xii, 132–39; reputational damage to song in the early 1960s, 126–28, 136, 139; Rice Brothers and, 3–7, 10–11, 18, 41; Richard Berry and, 92–93; similarity to other songs, 9–10; songs and poems with the same name, 8–9; uncertainty over which was most popular recording, 41–45; use in commercials, 155, 157; use in politics, 28, 64, 67, 73–74, 76–81, 84, 87, 101, 107–9, *110*, 113–14, 141, 143–44
Young, Faron, 91, 101
"Your Cheatin' Heart" (song), 133
Your Hit Parade (television show), 42, 144
"You're as Welcome as the Flowers in May" (song), 43

Zak, Albin J., 95